# The Allotment Seasonal Planner & Cookbook

# The Allotment Seasonal Planner & Cookbook

Andi Clevely

Collins

This book is dedicated to plot-holders everywhere, especially those past, who developed the way of self-reliance, and those to come, who will surely need these skills again.

First published in 2008 by Collins
an imprint of HarperCollins Publishers
77–85 Fulham Palace Road
London W6 8JB

Collins is a registered trademark of HarperCollins Publishers Ltd
**www.collins.co.uk**

12 11 10 09 08
10 9 8 7 6 5 4 3 2 1

**Created and produced by Airedale Publishing Ltd**

**For Airedale Publishing**
Publisher: Ruth Prentice
Creative Director: Ruth Prentice
Art Editor: Murdo Culver
Project Editor: Helen Ridge
Cookery Editors: Alison Bolus, Norma MacMillan
Colour: David Murphy
Index: Diana Lecore
All main photography by Sarah Cuttle, David Murphy, Mike Newton

**For HarperCollins**
Editorial Director: Jenny Heller
Assistant Editor: Ione Walder
Cover Design: Anna Martin

ISBN        978 0 00 726347 9

Colour reproduction by Colourscan
Printed in Italy by Lego

*Terms that may be unfamiliar to the novice plot-holder are italicized at their first mention, then defined in the glossary on page 218.*

# contents

# foreword

Everyone dreams of good food. But good food requires good ingredients, and since a lot of bought produce looks like heaven but tastes like hell (or nothing at all), that means growing your own.

More and more people are doing just that. After a few decades of indifference, vacant plots and creeping neglect, waiting lists for allotments have reappeared in many districts, while seed companies report an explosion in orders for vegetable seeds. Interest extends far beyond time-honoured favourites like runner beans and Brussels sprouts to heirloom varieties and staples from other cultures, which might be worth the gamble of raising for yourself – at worst, all you lose is the cost of a packet of seeds. They will often thrive happily side by side with more subsistence crops like peas, beans or beetroot, and under your own supervision they will be fresher than anything you can buy, and well able to survive in peak condition the short journey from plot to pot.

The typical allotment site now is a livelier, younger social scene that resonates with modern perceptions. Instead of the narrow, uniform attitudes formed as much by fear of being different as by ignorance of wider choices, plot-holders are likely to come from a spectrum of classes and cultures, with a whole range of motives and ambitions. Diversity is a social as well as genetic virtue.

The crops grown reflect this variety. Culture is not just about music, art and literature, but includes everyday details like the traditional herbs you add to home-made bread or the ingredients used in a favourite salad, the way you grow leeks or cook cabbage. Cultivation and cookery are as cultural as any classics, and the places where they meet and mingle are on the plots, while growing the raw ingredients, and in the club house (or the aptly named *King Edward* pub that graces one allotment site) during discussions about what to do with them or how to cope with a glut of courgettes, runner beans or tomatoes.

After the excitement or apprehension of being offered an plot, many newcomers suddenly experience a rush of elation at the realization that (provided it is legal and neighbourly) they can do almost anything they want to. The moment you start making plans and working the soil, you will begin to forge a style and participate

**Andi Clevely**

in the continuous and changing cycle of seasonal growth that is constantly evolving all around us. This book focuses on the seasonal aspect of allotment life – the patterns of sowing, growing and harvesting – and the ways your produce can be used in the kitchen at the relevant times of year.

You will not find all the step-by-step instructions for growing every individual crop here, although key tasks for each season are included for novice gardeners and as *aides-mémoires* for the more experienced. The detailed mechanics are covered in the companion volume *The Allotment Book* (Collins, 2006), which supplies answers to the fundamental question 'How?'.

This book focuses on timing, the other essential question 'When?'. Every crop has its natural season, although this can be extended and modified by shrewd choice of varieties and dexterity with delaying or forwarding techniques that help stretch its availability. All allotment produce has a time of year when quality is at its peak – harvested too soon, it might be low in flavour, sugars and minerals; too mature, and sugars could be turning to starch, while flavour, texture and vitamin content are all declining. Quality is all-important in the kitchen and on the table.

Familiarity with varieties and their growth patterns, especially the time they need to mature and the season when they are ready for use, can help you plan to harvest something every day of the year. In addition to familiar allotment crops, there are many other less common kinds that ripen at crucial times or perhaps grow fast to fill possible periods of shortage, and many of these are mentioned or profiled where appropriate in these pages.

Exploring all these choices could vary and supplement the kitchen repertoire, and seasonal recipes offer ways to serve this wide range of produce, familiar or novel, and to preserve surpluses for the store-cupboard. Growing an expanded assortment of seasonal crops will certainly help fulfil every plot-holder's creative urge while ensuring a steady supply of good home-grown food in the larder all the year round.

*Andi Clevely*

# introduction

Growing your own food is a deeply rewarding activity, which brings you into close contact with the living soil and the open-air world of plants and other creatures that share this planet with us. Tending the plot may be a satisfying, even spiritual experience for some, for others an effective way to take control of their own food supply: all need to discover the practical realities of caring for the soil and the crops that grow there.

# introduction

# growing your own

Working the land, growing fruit and vegetables, then preparing and serving up your own home-grown food is deeply satisfying, and whether you do it out of philosophical conviction or for gourmet rewards, it is an essentially creative activity. For many of us, it is possibly the only direct participation we have with nature and the changing seasons.

**Every well-planned plot is a carefully choreographed sequence of food supplies. Here, the mature peas will be followed seamlessly by summer-long pickings of runner beans and courgettes, while leeks, crinkly Tuscan cabbage and leafy broccoli plants will fatten for later harvest.**

## THE BENEFITS

Few allotment gardeners need reminding about the various joys and rewards of growing their own. Almost certainly some of these persuasive reasons will have been in your mind when you were considering taking on a plot and the responsibilities that go with it, and experience usually confirms that the benefits were not exaggerated. Although self-sufficiency might not always be cost-effective if you take your time and effort into account, home-grown produce can reduce household food expenses (especially if you eat seasonally, and becomes completely worthwhile if you include all the other rewards as well.

The key to good food is tasty and nutritious produce that's been harvested in peak condition and then freshly prepared. Growing your own allows you to choose varieties that are renowned for their flavour, even if the yields are sometimes less than standard commercial kinds. For example, most parsley available in shops is the decorative curled variety, even though flat-leaved parsley has a far superior flavour.

You may choose to grow a range of varieties for different kitchen uses, or just one esoteric favourite that's seldom found in the shops. You are also at liberty to grow your fruit and vegetables organically (*see pages 22–3*), which is a huge advantage when the price of organic produce in the shops is often artificially inflated and much of it is imported. Whether you opt for a completely *organic* approach or use organic methods for just a few crops is entirely up to you.

All kinds of people garden on allotments, from taciturn individualists to happy families. You can choose to mix with all of them or none, but you'll usually find yourself sharing the site with supportive plot-holders who can help and advise in cases of failure or disappointment, and rejoice with you when crops succeed.

Gardening is one of the best outdoor fitness routines for all ages, with benefits for the planet's health as well as your own. It may come as a surprise to learn that digging isn't compulsory (even though it is an excellent and creative work-out), but there are many other physical activities involved in the care and upkeep of a plot, most of which are carried out in the open air at a pace you can set to suit your own ability and inclination.

Remember, though, that allotment life isn't all hard work! Although poverty is not confined to developing countries, most of us are lucky enough to garden from choice rather than a need for food security, and tending an allotment is a leisure activity in the modern world. Enjoy the plants, the exercise and the company and, finally, the best of all possible produce on your plate.

**A sound, dry allotment shed is a congenial place from which to survey (and sometimes admire) your plot while planning and reflecting on progress over a mug of tea.**

## THE SERIOUS BIT

Growing food on an allotment is a step towards consumer liberation, with important benefits for the community and wider environment. Compared with buying supermarket food, gardening has a low negative impact on the environment. Energy costs are minimal when food is produced locally, carbon emissions are reduced almost to zero (in fact, organic gardening can safely lock up carbon in the soil), and land use is more efficient: an intensive allotment plot is up to 12 times more productive than large-scale agriculture.

Supermarket produce may come from hundreds or thousands of miles away, and crops that are transported long distances lose some of their nutritional value as they age.

By growing your own, you can help reduce the pollution and energy consumption involved in mechanized growing: the lavish use of water, equipment and fertilizers; the processing and treating of foods with preservatives and other additives; and the packaging.

As the world changes, there is a growing consensus that growing your own could become a vital skill. In industrialized societies, we are used to having choice, and for several generations growing our own food has not been a necessity, but progressive oil depletion could eventually put the cost of buying food beyond the easy reach of many people. Honing the essential skills to produce this food will then become a priceless legacy to hand on to our children, as well as ensuring our own food security.

An allotment is an investment, not just for the produce we hope will reward our seasonal efforts, but as a key resource to tend and develop for an uncertain future.

## PLANNING A START

Everyone starts from a different point, with varying levels of experience and understanding. If you are completely new to allotment gardening, don't think you must do everything at once: simply clear or prepare a small area, sow or plant something, and feel the surge of confidence as crops begin to grow for you. Don't leave ground bare, though, because a clear weed-free patch will only host more weeds unless you *mulch* it or plant and tend a crop there instead. Sow something: it's never too late – in a good year you could triumph, and at worst you will cover the soil and grow a compost crop. Remember that plants are programmed to grow and seeds to germinate, and all you need supply is a little opportune and creative encouragement. And spend time getting used to the feel of your soil and microclimate: you can read all about the science of growing, but the art is absorbed through the senses.

Your own motives for wanting to have an allotment could be many and varied. You might find sowing any kind of seed, pip and fruit stone irresistible, whatever the odds against success, or simply prefer to buy young plants from a garden centre to grow on for dependable crops of familiar vegetables. Perhaps you want to impress dinner party guests with unusual fruits and vegetables, explore Caribbean or Eastern cuisines and try a few of their exotic crops, or simply know where your daily food comes from, how it was grown and how far it has travelled.

These are all reasonable ambitions with a sporting chance of achievement if you first make thorough preparations and assemble as much relevant information as you can find before making any irrevocable decisions.

THE LIFETIME PLOT-HOLDER

Henry, a retired circuit judge, is a long-term allotment holder. He started out over 40 years ago and still has an allotment now. When he was working, even at his busiest, he would still visit his plot most summer evenings as well as at least one day at the weekend. Even now he is 80, the pace hasn't slackened – he puts in one to two hours a day. For Henry, growing vegetables is therapeutic, and his favourite time of day is the morning. He enjoys the hard graft like digging, but what he enjoys most is the harvesting.

He grows the basics – potatoes, onions, runner beans, leeks, broad beans, tomatoes, lettuces and cabbages – but his favourites have to be tomatoes, leeks and runner beans. He also loves that he is able to dig up his potatoes and have them cooking in the pot five minutes later – that's how close he lives to his allotment.

Henry was raised in the country. His father was a keen gardener and Henry started growing crops on his father's vegetable garden at an early age. As a child, he knew all about seasonal eating, as well as preserving and storing. Today, though, he can't contemplate life without a freezer – he couldn't keep the bucketfuls of tomato soup that he makes for the winter without one!

**p.59**   *see* Stuffed onions
**p.96**   *see* Henry's tomato soup

growing your own

15

**ask the EXPERT** See *The Allotment Book* by Andi Clevely (Collins, 2006) for a history of allotments and a detailed look at various gardening techniques.

**Good paths, a dry shed and convenient water butt are essential for a well-equipped allotment, but it's up to you whether you trench the ground, clear weeds with a sheet mulch or enjoy a cottage garden muddle on your plot.**

## GATHERING INFORMATION

First, compile a list of what you want to grow and how much of each crop, and when you would like it to be ready. Involve everyone in the family in choosing favourites. Then find out everything you can about your chosen crops. An allotment plot can grow prolific quantities but over-enthusiastic planting means that it will soon fill up. You need to know how much space each crop needs, its possible yield, and how long it will be in the ground. Make sure you can cope with possibly huge amounts, especially if you plan a holiday at a crucial harvest time.

If you are a seasoned long-term plot-holder, you will probably have evolved a successful cropping routine over the years. New gardeners, however, often find they have planted too little or too much of a crop, possibly in an unsuitable position, leading to an embarrassing glut or dearth of produce, and at an inconvenient time of year.

Decide where you would like each crop to be, as you'll imprint your personal style on the plot the moment you begin creating an allotment garden of your own. Reconnoitre the site to make sure it offers everything the crops need, in case you have the wrong type of soil (*see page 24*), climate or exposure. Inspect the plot for sunny and shady sites, exposure and shelter. Remember to gauge the amount of care the plot could need, and your ability to provide it. Talk to neighbouring plot-holders to find out when to expect last and first frosts, how the soil tends to behave, and whether you might reasonably count on their help if you are away or overwhelmed at any time.

Armed with all this knowledge, you will be in a better position to decide which crops to grow and where, when to sow and plant them, and what (if anything) is to follow afterwards should there be enough of the growing season left.

## GETTING ORGANIZED

Walk round the whole site and appraise each plot you pass. One of the great joys of an allotment community is its huge diversity of styles, designs and crops. An observant tour could suggest fresh ideas for your initial plans, as well as reassuring you that nothing should be ruled out until you have tried it.

Some plots will be rigorously clean and disciplined, others an apparent riot of undergrowth in which crops seem nonetheless to thrive. There might be virtual *monocultures* of potatoes or brassicas next to complex patchworks of numerous, possibly unfamiliar crops; small beds and blocks separated by a network of narrow paths contrasting with other plots divided into long, widely spaced rows of evenly graded plants. They reveal the tastes and temperaments of their tenants, and all work in their own ways. How you set about managing your own plot will depend on a number of factors.

### SOURCES OF INFORMATION

Arm yourself with as much information as possible about allotment gardening and the crops that are likely to grow well on your site.

▶ Start by consulting the Resource section (*see pages 219–20*), which offers a selection of useful addresses, books, websites and organizations. Browse classic books like *Dig for Victory* or *The Vegetable Grower's Handbook*, written before allotment gardening was a leisure activity.

▶ Listen to elderly people who might have had a plot when growing food was a national necessity and when skill ensured simply having something to eat.

▶ Talk to neighbouring plot-holders about crop varieties and methods of growing.

▶ Search the internet: online encyclopedias offer masses of information, while blogs and forums often discuss the very questions you might be asking.

▶ Explore the websites of seed companies, collections and exchanges for guidance on growing and even saving your own seeds.

▶ If you can't find a satisfactory answer, experiment and keep a record of methods and results.

**THE RETIRED PLOT-HOLDER**

Raj was a sound engineer with the BBC for ten years before he took early retirement. His allotment then turned from an evening and weekend hobby to a full-time job. Raj always wanted to grow the vegetables that he remembered from his years growing up in India, and he was able to source some of his seed locally, although a lot was sent to him from India. He grows chillis, okra, bitter gourds, coriander, as well as the usual allotment fare, such as spinach, leeks and runner beans. Alongside his runner beans, he grows padne beans, which are smaller but with a similar taste.

Raj has two plots, one for growing Indian vegetables, the other herbs and flowers – he particularly likes to grow dahlias for the allotment show. His young grandson also likes to visit the allotment and Raj is trying to teach him how to grow crops. At the moment, though, the boy really just likes watching his grandpa and the other plot-holders at work. Raj's allotment neighbours come from all over the world: Jay, who has the plot next door, is also Indian, and he grows much the same as Raj, while the Chinese couple on the other side grow nothing but Chinese vegetables for stir-fries.

**p.138**   *see* Squash & green bean coconut curry
**p.171**   *see* Bitter gourd curry

growing your own

Only you know how much time you can or are willing to devote to your plot's upkeep. New tenants often visit daily in their excitement and hurry to do everything at once, sometimes losing enthusiasm when weeds return and seeds take weeks to emerge. Discovering a realistic pace comes with experience, but plans and personality are important influences. Some tenants spend long, frequent sessions tidying, weeding and fine-tuning their crops. At the other extreme is the fashionable 'half-hour allotment' that assumes a single short daily or weekly visit, very meticulous organization, perfect weather and well-behaved plants. The realistic minimum is somewhere in between, depending on the variety of crops you grow, their cultural demands, and how they are arranged for easy management.

Gardeners who favour order and efficiency may prefer to spend time hoeing long rows of plants, while others are happy to hand-weed *broadcast* patches. Plan your plot accordingly, perhaps quartering it to create four equal-sized areas for digging and organizing a classic rotation of vegetables (*see page 20*) in widely spaced rows for easy access. Or you might prefer to divide the ground into long, narrow *no-dig* beds filled with short transverse rows and blocks of closely spaced equidistant plants for access without treading on the cultivated soil.

By growing staples like carrots, onions and cabbages, or a large area of a single crop such as potatoes, it is possible to confine most of your work to a few concentrated sessions. On the other hand, growing a rich mixture or a little of everything can increase demands for routine jobs such as *thinning*, *successional sowing*, tying up, watering, grooming or pruning, and frequent regular picking.

If you enjoy all the business of growing, you could welcome diversity and complexity; if you simply want plain and productive results, streamline your plans and limit crops to single dependable varieties, perhaps for mass harvesting to fill the freezer or to preserve in some other way.

**The soil recognizes no cultural or national boundaries, and allotments are often cosmopolitan communities where food traditions from around the world meet on equal terms.**

## CHOOSING VEGETABLES

A cursory glance at a few seed or plant catalogues might suggest a daunting infinity of choices, but some basic criteria can quickly narrow the field.

▶ Concentrate (at least initially) on vegetables you and your family like, and plan for quantities that reflect your main aim, whether this is for mass harvests to freeze and store, or small regular amounts for year-round consumption.

▶ Explore varieties. Those mentioned on the following pages are only some of the best, and you will discover more, either from catalogue descriptions or by trial and error, eventually building up a tested repertoire of favourite kinds.

▶ Avoid *F1 hybrids* if you want to save your own seeds, but select varieties that have pronounced pest or disease resistance if you intend managing your plot organically.

▶ Make the most of your growing space by choosing a range of long-stay crops like parsnips or Brussels sprouts, plus several 'sprinters' – fast vegetables such as rocket and oriental greens to grow and clear as *catch crops* in the intervening spaces.

▶ Remember to include a few *green manure* crops like clover and grazing rye (*see pages 88–90*) to grow wherever ground is vacant for two to three months or more, to cover and protect the surface and improve the soil when turned in. Add *companion plants* (*see page 29*) such as tagetes for 'alternative' pest control, and any flowers for cutting – tables need decorating as well as victualling.

## PLACES FOR FRUIT

Although sometimes thought to be too demanding and difficult to include in an allotment, many fruits can be pruned or trained to fit between, around or over other crops without much competition.

Top fruits such as apples, pears, peaches and cherries grow naturally as trees with single stems or trunks, and on their own roots they can make large shady specimens. But when *grafted* on *dwarfing rootstocks*,

introduction

**You are never alone on the plot with a scarecrow, a traditional and appealing way to dissuade marauding pigeons from reducing your brassicas to shreds.**

which predetermine size and vigour, their height and spread are better suited to the confines of a plot, and are easier to net against birds. Growing them in restricted forms like *cordons* and *espaliers* also helps to limit their size.

Soft fruit such as gooseberries and redcurrants grow on their own roots. They can be trained as bushes (which occupy the most space) or in smaller versions of top fruit forms like cordons, *fans* and espaliers that need a strip of soil no more than 30cm (12in) wide. They also make excellent dwarf standards, growing no more than 90–120cm (3–4ft) high, with their canopy of fruiting branches held high above growing space for strawberries, herbs or compact vegetables.

## CROP ROTATION

Moving vegetables to a new part of the plot each year is intended to prevent any build-up of specific soil pests and diseases. It also helps stop the possible depletion of minerals and nutrients that might occur if a particular type of vegetable is grown constantly in the same position.

Elaborate and sometimes confusing rules have evolved that separate related (and therefore equally susceptible) crops, sometimes for many years before they return once more to their original planting sites. The most familiar and basic rotation scheme groups vegetables into brassicas (the cabbage family, *see also pages 190–3*), legumes (peas and beans, *see also pages 186–9*) and root crops (*see also pages 182–5*). A bed or section of the plot is allocated to each group, which moves on the following year to the next bed in the sequence, until it finally returns to its first bed.

There are advantages with this method of planting. Each crop group shares a preference for a particular kind of soil preparation and fertility level, as well as being affected by similar ailments. Devoting a bed to each group makes it easy to cater for their tastes and to remember where individual crops should go each year.

The disadvantages are that many popular vegetables, such as tomatoes, sweetcorn and onions, are not related to any of the main groups and must be fitted in wherever there is space. Rotation groups do not all occupy the same amount of ground, and some of their member crops remain in place from one year to the next, causing an awkward overlap.

Many gardeners find that the simplest and most flexible strategy is to make sure that no crop is planted where it (or a relative) was growing the year before. Just moving it a few paces to one side can be enough to avoid the problems of replanting in the same soil. Some vegetables, like onions and runner beans, can even stay safely in the same place for many years unless ailments or declining yields indicate that a move is advisable.

Although this simplified version works most of the time on most soils, it can encourage a blasé indifference to the underlying purpose of rotation, which is to avoid unnecessary pest and disease risks, a key strategy of the organic approach. Dismissing rotation as altogether unimportant can lead to problems, especially with a changing climate creating more congenial habitats for hitherto uncommon disorders.

For example, torrential summer cloudbursts in recent seasons have resulted in the appearance of rust on runner beans. This is a novel ailment in some parts of the country and one that is likely to persist if successive crops of beans are grown in the same place because the spores can overwinter in the soil. Caution is always better than regret.

Another important benefit of rotation is resting the soil, the allotment equivalent of the farmer's fallow, or break, crop. Growing a green manure for a whole year restores the soil's condition and fertility, and helps break the carry-over of pests and diseases. Alternatively, spread layers of newspaper or cardboard topped with compost, weeds and cut grass for a season, then plant through the mulch the next spring.

Raspberries are usually lined in rows like slim hedges, supported on wires, and will fit neatly down the centre of a bed or along one side, but they can also be grouped around a central supporting stake, making slender upright clumps.

Brambles like blackberries are flexible cane fruits that need a fence or freestanding run of wires for support, and these also make fruitful divisions between rotation beds or plot boundaries.

Strawberries can be grown and rotated with vegetables, and they crop well planted under taller trained fruit or along the foot of a row of raspberries.

## CHOOSING A METHOD

There are hidden aspects of growing food that you can choose to ignore if the basic routine of raising and consuming produce is your chief concern, or to explore if you are aware of its wider implications.

For some people, allotment gardening makes a political statement by taking control over how and where crops are grown, challenging a system that accepts denatured food produced by energy-intensive methods and using a limited range of varieties approved for qualities other than flavour and nutritional value. For others, growing fruit and vegetables is a small but vital lifestyle decision to help repair the environment by rejecting the 'consumer culture' and its ecological costs in favour of more appropriate methods that emphasize sustainability and working with rather than against nature. Organic gardening is the most popular and familiar example of this approach (*see pages 22–3*).

**Always a key allotment structure for protecting early sowings and tender summer vegetables, a greenhouse could have a vital role in a warmer world for housing exotic crops such as okra, lima beans, citrus and watermelons. Careful shading and ventilation will be crucial as temperatures rise, however.**

# the organic approach

Wanting a plentiful, affordable and high-quality supply of organic vegetables and fruit is often the main motivation for taking on an allotment. By growing organically, you know that your food is free from chemical residues and that it has been produced by methods that respect the soil and the wider environment. In addition, this often leads to an improvement in the taste and quality of the food on your table: organic root crops like carrots and parsnips, for example, or cucumbers and early potatoes have remarkably enhanced flavour, while all crops from organically managed soils tend to accumulate greater amounts of essential minerals.

A wild area, complete with a natural pond and a variety of native flowers, is a key feature of many allotment sites, attracting a range of natural predators as allies to help control vegetable pests by non-chemical means.

## WHY GO ORGANIC?

Organic gardeners justify their approach with a number of arguments. It is less expensive both practically and in more indirect ways. For example, feeding plants with compost makes use of recycled waste, and using barriers, deterrents and crop companions to reduce pests, weeds and diseases avoids the expense of buying chemical fertilizers, herbicides and pesticides.

Organic gardening also causes little pollution, whereas conventional methods incur hidden costs of removing nitrates and pesticides from water courses, and can harm wildlife. The organic emphasis on feeding the soil rather than the plant, encouraging natural predators to control pests, favouring local knowledge and traditional expertise, and protecting endangered crops and varieties can help ensure a healthier world for future generations.

If you follow organic arguments to their logical conclusion, you will probably find that growing your own food on an allotment plot introduces much wider issues such as energy consumption, nature conservation and environmental ethics. *Forest gardening*, *biodynamic gardening* and *permaculture* (*see The Allotment Book*) are all alternative approaches to gardening that adhere to organic principles.

## THE DECISION IS YOURS

The immediate reward of growing organically could be an improvement in your quality of life as well as a contribution to a healthier planet. It might also stimulate further reflection, perhaps about the lower yields of organic plots compared with their benefits, or the fact that no-dig methods are considered the most environmentally friendly way to tend your allotment. You might even evolve your own hybrid mix of methods and principles.

In the end, your choice of approach depends on what feels right for you, and that is just one of the special privileges of having an allotment.

**THE ORGANIC PLOT-HOLDERS**

Jon and James are not your typical plot-holders: both hold high-powered jobs in the media industry and they have a hectic social life. However, nothing stops them from visiting their allotment. Most mornings before work and every weekend during summer, Jon and James can be found working on their plot – even in their formal business attire! They are extremely commited to their allotment and have won best plot in their borough for three consecutive years.

Their plot was derelict until they took it on a few years ago, but now it is immaculate, with perfect raised beds and crops growing in the straightest of straight lines. Above all, their allotment is totally organic – this summer all their neighbours' tomatoes were struck down by blight but because Jon and James had grown a blight-resistant variety, and also sprayed judiciously with *copper sulphate* (which is organic), they were able to save their crop.

Keen and talented cooks, they grow an enormous variety of vegetables but their favourites are broad beans, asparagus and green romanesco cauliflower, which is particularly pleasing to the eye. Due to the abundance of the crops they grow, anything left over they give to the people whose houses back onto the allotment in exchange for a regular cup of welcomed coffee.

**p.45**  *see* Broccoli & cauliflower with toasted garlic
**p.96**  *see* Cool tomato jellies

*growing your own*

23

Mains water is usually very cold and liable to chill plants if applied direct. Instead, fill a tank or water butt from the site tap and allow to stand at least overnight before dispensing the water at something closer to the ambient daytime temperature.

Soil in good heart, with a friable structure for strong roots and plenty of fertility for vigorous growth, results in healthy plants, luxuriant foliage and heavy crops at harvest time.

## UNDERSTANDING SOIL

Soil is everything on an allotment. Don't make the mistake of assuming it is a passive, inert medium to fill with plants that are then dosed with water and fertilizers to make them grow. It is a living resource, at best seething with organisms and vital processes that will help your crops prosper. Getting soil care right is the first step towards growing good food.

Types of soil vary dramatically, both in physical makeup and state of health. Yours might be naturally acid or chalky (use a test kit to measure and, if necessary, correct an imbalance), so fine that its grains run through your fingers or as sticky and pliable as dough. If full of humus and life-giving organic matter, it could be dark and softly friable; on a rocky hillside it might feel like a fistful of flints and shards. In good arable areas, the *topsoil* may be deeper than you need to dig, but just a thin veneer over bedrock on chalk downs or in mountainous country.

None is beyond repair and improvement, but you need to discover the type you have early on so as to decide whether you can plant straight away or need to work the ground into a reasonable condition first. In most cases, it will be manageable, the result of cultivation and improvement by previous tenants, but even the best soil needs regular attention to maintain its good status, especially since cropping makes heavy demands on fertility.

## WATERING STRATEGIES

There is nothing you can do to alter the amount and frequency of rain that falls on your plot. Plants, however, need adequate supplies of water during their growth, whatever the weather. Most sites have some kind of water supply, but this could be interrupted or rationed in times of shortage.

### CREATING A HEALTHY SOIL

▶ Improve depth and drainage on shallow or wet ground by loosening the subsoil. *Double-dig* the area if possible, or break up solid rocky layers with a mattock; even deeply working a fork back and forth can give good results. Sometimes an easier option is to build raised beds, filled with compost and topsoil from paths.

▶ Avoid digging when the ground is wet or frozen, and wherever possible use an alternative method that does not disturb the soil structure and processes unnecessarily.

▶ Check acidity levels with a *soil testing kit* or *soil pH meter*, which will advise how to adjust the pH to between 6.5 and 7.2, the preferred range for most vegetables, or 6.0–6.5 for most fruits. Very acid or alkaline soils can lock up various nutrients out of roots' reach and cause deficiency symptoms.

▶ Annually replenish the fertility and organic content of all soils with at least a bucketful of rotted manure or garden compost per square metre, worked into the top spade-depth or spread on the surface as a mulch.

The answer is to capture and store rainwater as a reservoir for times of need. Install a water butt (enquire whether your local council sells these at a discount) and direct rainwater running off your shed or greenhouse into this. Add more butts to take the overflow from the first one – you could even direct any surplus water through a trough of watercress plants into a pond.

A length of guttering fixed to a fence makes a good water collector, as does a corrugated tin sheet supported in the shape of a scoop and directed towards a large container. Stand empty bins, buckets and drums out in the rain, and empty their contents into the butts, a large tank or old bath, keeping these covered to prevent losses in windy or sunny weather.

Ration the amount of water you need by topping up the organic soil content to help absorb rainfall, mulch lavishly to decrease losses through evaporation, and target the water you have at the neediest plants: seedlings, transplants, leafy vegetables and any crop bearing flowers or fruit.

## CLEARING A PLOT

Reclaiming an overgrown allotment is best spread out in easy stages over a couple of seasons if necessary. Much depends on when you take on the plot. In autumn, there is plenty of time ahead to clear sufficient ground for spring sowing and planting. If you're starting in spring, clearing a nursery bed might be a high priority to get some early crops under way while you prepare more ground.

First, choose the spot for a compost heap, and start building it with a base layer of crop residues like old sprout or sweet corn stems, plus fibrous material from tall grasses and woody herbs. Cut down softer *topgrowth* with shears or a sickle, and add this on top and between the woody stems.

Keep trimming weed growth for the heap while you prepare the first patch of clean soil. Forking out all the weeds for composting is a thorough method if you are not in a hurry; digging them in is faster, but you will need to control regrowth of *perennial* weeds. Sheet

Sarah is one of the new breed of allotment holders: young, female, with a successful career and a desire to grow her own. As she has only ever bought organic produce, taking on an allotment plot, which conveniently backed onto her house, was a logical step.

Sarah has a gardening pedigree – not only does her dad write gardening books but she has been brought up on vegetables grown on her dad's smallholding.

There was one problem, though, for someone itching to start: the plot she was allocated was totally overgrown. On the phone to her dad, she was advised to start with a proper compost bin so that all the weeds and brambles she was about to clear off could go to good use. She was also told to plant potatoes as her first crop because they are brilliant ground cleansers.

Many evenings and weekends later, the plot was cleared and the first crop planted. Then Sarah had to go away for a short period of time. When she returned, she found that the weeds had come back and the clearing had to start all over again. The lesson she learned then was that having an allotment was a commitment but she also learned very quickly that with good organization nothing was impossible. Her allotment is now flourishing.

**p.74**    *see* Summer salad soup

**p.160**    *see* Beetroot fairy cakes

growing your own

mulching with layers of cardboard topped with a thick mulch of manure or garden compost is a simple and non-invasive method, or you could cover the weeds with black geo-textile matting perforated with planting holes. Grow potatoes or brassicas as the first pioneer crops.

Lush weed growth suggests adequate fertility levels for most vegetables. Where growth is sparse, try undemanding vegetables that thrive on meagre rations, such as carrots, all types of beans, onions and tomatoes. Feed these with a complete fertilizer as they grow, and mulch if possible with any available organic materials, even grass clippings that you have trimmed from paths.

## PREVENTING WEEDS

No matter how thoroughly the ground is cleared, more weeds will almost certainly appear from overlooked root fragments, dormant seeds in the soil, and ripe seeds brought in by birds or on the wind. Although many weeds are harmless, even pretty, they compete with your crops for nutrients, water and space, and may even host transmissible pests and diseases. Prevent them by mulching, hoeing bare soil before they get beyond seedling stage, and pulling or forking up larger specimens for composting. Weedy patches after crops are cleared could be *rotavated* if there are not too many invasive perennials (these multiply when tilled in).

## PESTS & DISEASES

Whole encyclopedias have been written about plant ailments, but the problems you meet on the plot are likely to be common in most gardens. Take sensible precautions: choose robust and resistant varieties, grow them well, inspect them regularly and act promptly if you see trouble. Make sure you identify the symptoms accurately, and then choose the most eco-friendly remedy, such as a forceful blast of water for aphids and a barrier of spent coffee grounds or crushed eggshells to deter slugs. Avoidance, deterrence and protection are often more effective than treatment.

# THE BAD GUYS

## DISEASES & PESTS

**Tomato and potato blight** spoils foliage and fruit, especially in wet summers. Grow resistant kinds, keep tomatoes well away from maincrop potatoes, remove infected leaves and mulch to control spore transmission.

**Leek rust** also affects other members of the onion family, stunting growth and depressing yields. Improve drainage and soil fertility. Rotate onion relatives, allowing at least 3–4 years before replanting infected soil.

**Powdery mildew** is a common problem on many crops in a warm, dry year, especially late in the season as nights cool down. Water regularly and mulch plants, avoid overfeeding, prune affected leaves and grow resistant kinds.

**Blossom end rot** appears on tomatoes and sometimes peppers suffering from a lack of of calcium. This may be caused by acid soil, but is most commonly the result of insufficient or irregular watering in a hot, dry season.

**Potato eelworm, wireworms and slugs** can all tunnel into tubers, making them hard to prepare, even inedible. Choose resistant varieties on infected ground, carefully harvest all tubers, and always rotate potato crops annually.

**Carrot fly grubs** can tunnel widely and destructively through the roots. Prevent by growing under a covering of fleece or inside a fleece fence at least 50cm (20in) high. Early summer sowings can dodge fly generations.

**Slugs** are everywhere that plants grow, especially in a wet season. Protect vulnerable crops with resistant varieties, barriers such as copper or crushed eggshells, *nematode* solutions and beer traps, or collect them by hand.

**Rosemary beetles** are recent arrivals in the UK and spreading northwards. Both adults and larvae feed voraciously on the leaves of rosemary, lavender, thyme and sage. Hand-pick beetles, and spray grubs with an organic pesticide.

**Blackflies** are one of several kinds of aphid that multiply fast into sap-feeding colonies on a range of plants, and also help transmit virus diseases. Blast them with a water jet, encourage bluetits with food or spray with an organic pesticide.

**Caterpillars** spend their whole brief lives feeding and can strip foliage from plants like brassicas, nasturtiums and gooseberries. Watch for adult moths and butterflies, crush egg clusters on leaves and hand-pick caterpillars.

**Mice** regard seeds, bulbs and stored crops as convenient food caches, and soon find any that are accessible, particularly in winter. Store crops and seeds safely and check regularly. Cover pea and bean sowings with prickly leaves.

**Pigeons** are common and insatiable robbers of juicy foliage, especially on young peas and green brassicas. Netting crops is advisable and efficient if it is sturdy, while old CDs, glittery streamers and scarecrows deter them.

## TRY THIS
### KEEPING SLUGS AT BAY

Growing vegetables above ground level is one way to defeat slugs, whether in a hanging basket or a raised bed encircled with a strip of copper tape; copper rings around individual plants are also effective. At ground level, mulch plants with grit, fresh soot or crushed dried eggshells. Beer traps are irresistible but must be kept topped up. Rhubarb leaves or halves of grapefruit skins are hiding places where they will gather for you to collect each morning.

**Protective cloches and copper tape.**

**Growing salads in a hanging basket.**

# MORE BAD GUYS

## WEEDS

**Horsetail** resolutely colonizes damp ground. This prehistoric weed is reputed to be ineradicable but its rhizomes and accompanying small tubers may be smothered out of existence with thick carpet or a dense planting of nasturtiums.

**Ragwort** is a very common weed with conspicuous yellow blooms. Pull up the dormant basal rosettes in winter before they can flower and seed. It is poisonous to grazing animals, so discard carefully.

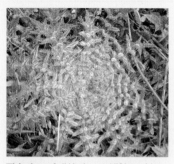

**Thistles** of all kinds need lifting with a spade or fork because most have thick, fleshy taproots that can go down deep. Handle with gloves and clear them before they flower because the wind-blown seeds spread far and wide.

**Couch grass** is a villain once established, its tufts of dull green leaves sprouting at intervals from underground rhizomes that wind for yards in the soil, even through potato tubers. Fork up the roots patiently.

**Stinging nettles** are ugly but valuable weeds that spread into dense patches. Fork or pull up (wear gloves!) all the roots and soak plants in water to make liquid fertilizer before discarding. Leave some to feed moths and butterflies.

**Bindweed** is a vigorous smotherer and strangler, with deep wandering roots that regenerate from overlooked fragments. Fork them out patiently or mulch infested ground with carpet or geotextiles for 1–2 years.

# THE GOOD GUYS

## BENEFICIAL INSECTS & PLANTS

**Hoverflies** are efficient allies, with green, slug-like larvae that feed hungrily on aphids. Encourage adults with flowers like eschscholzia and sweet alyssum, provide winter hiding places and avoid using insecticides.

**Ladybirds** are popular gardeners' friends, the adults conspicuous and colourful beetles that efficiently graze on colonies of aphids. They can be bought as biological agents to control pests and then hibernate in your shed.

**Common blue butterflies** are beautiful, often browsing open flowers on the plot while their larvae feed harmlessly on green manure crops of vetch. But remember that attracting butterflies encourages friend and foe alike.

**Ladybird larvae** are as welcome as the familiar beetles, but less often noticed as they settle down amid their favourite feast of green- or blackfly. Inspect aphid colonies carefully and avoid chemical sprays.

*Limnanthes douglasii*, the poached egg plant, is a beneficial hardy annual that seeds freely to produce mats of feathery leaves almost smothered in full sun by the colourful blooms that attract hosts of bees. It comes quickly from seed sown in spring, while the self-sown seedlings are easily moved if in the way.

**Bees** are essential pollinators, both the wild and hive kinds. Many bumble bees are decreasing in numbers, so encourage them by gardening organically and growing favourite flowers such as bergamot and clover.

**Companion plants** like garlic and tagetes support healthy growth by attracting beneficial insects like predators and pollinators, deterring pests that avoid them or protecting vulnerable crops with their own confusing scents.

# seasonal growing guide

This basic guide to sowing, planting and harvesting the commonest outdoor allotment vegetables is an *aide-mémoire* that could simplify planning what to grow and when. It is a chart of average times only: seasonal weather, your locality, the choice of variety and any extra protection you can provide could vary timings by a few days or weeks, with sowing and planting taking place earlier or later, and harvesting perhaps delayed or even considerably extended. Crops that need to be sown under glass are indicated by ∩.

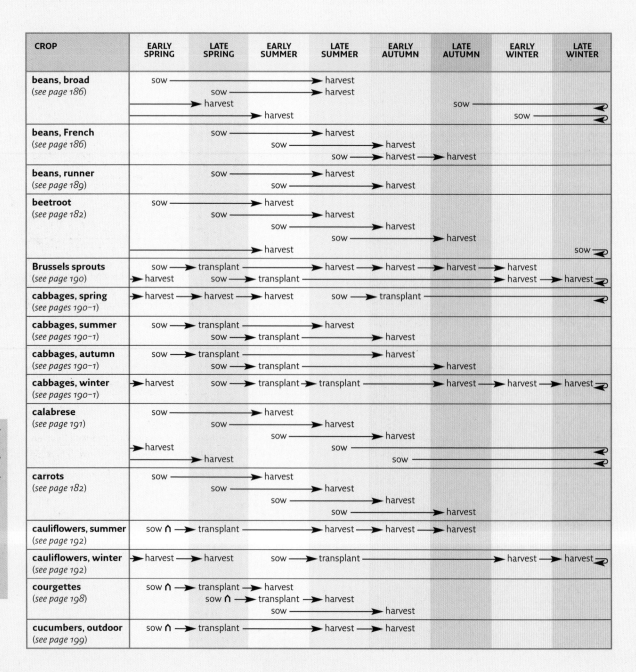

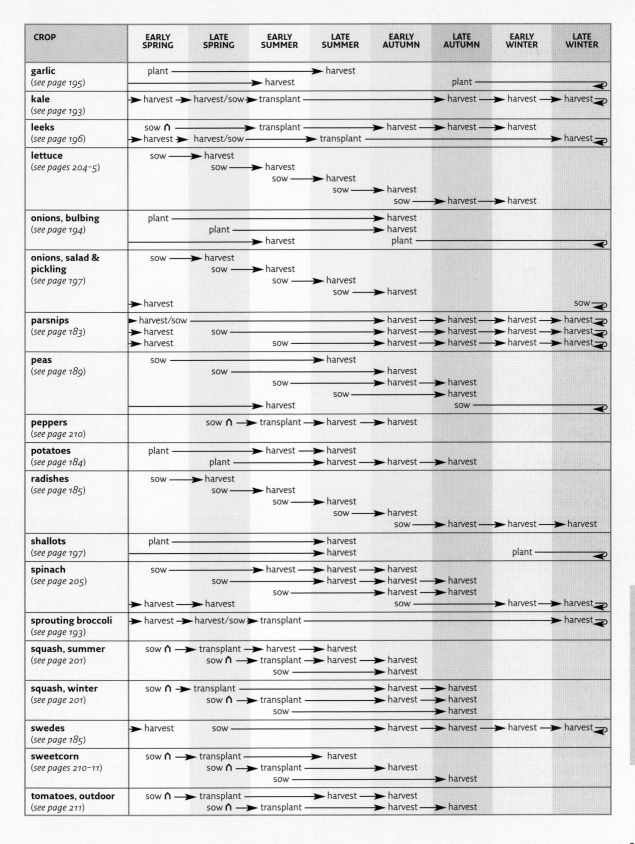

| CROP | EARLY SPRING | LATE SPRING | EARLY SUMMER | LATE SUMMER | EARLY AUTUMN | LATE AUTUMN | EARLY WINTER | LATE WINTER |
|---|---|---|---|---|---|---|---|---|
| **garlic** (see page 195) | plant | | | harvest | | | | |
| | | harvest | | | | | | |
| | | | | | | plant | | → |
| **kale** (see page 193) | harvest | harvest/sow | transplant | | | harvest | harvest | harvest → |
| **leeks** (see page 196) | sow ∩ | | transplant | | harvest | harvest | harvest | |
| | harvest | harvest/sow | | transplant | | | | harvest → |
| **lettuce** (see pages 204–5) | sow | harvest | | | | | | |
| | | sow | harvest | | | | | |
| | | | sow | harvest | | | | |
| | | | | sow | harvest | | | |
| | | | | | sow | harvest | harvest | |
| **onions, bulbing** (see page 194) | plant | | | | harvest | | | |
| | | plant | | | harvest | | | |
| | | | harvest | | plant | | | → |
| **onions, salad & pickling** (see page 197) | sow | harvest | | | | | | |
| | | sow | harvest | | | | | |
| | | | sow | harvest | | | | |
| | | | | sow | harvest | | | |
| | harvest | | | | | | | sow → |
| **parsnips** (see page 183) | harvest/sow | | | | harvest | harvest | harvest | harvest → |
| | harvest | sow | | | harvest | harvest | harvest | harvest → |
| | harvest | | sow | | harvest | harvest | harvest | harvest → |
| **peas** (see page 189) | sow | | | harvest | | | | |
| | | sow | | | harvest | | | |
| | | | sow | | harvest | harvest | | |
| | | | | sow | | harvest | | |
| | | | harvest | | | sow | | → |
| **peppers** (see page 210) | | sow ∩ | transplant | harvest | harvest | | | |
| **potatoes** (see page 184) | plant | | harvest | harvest | | | | |
| | | plant | | harvest | harvest | harvest | | |
| **radishes** (see page 185) | sow | harvest | | | | | | |
| | | sow | harvest | | | | | |
| | | | sow | harvest | | | | |
| | | | | sow | harvest | | | |
| | | | | | sow | harvest | harvest | harvest |
| **shallots** (see page 197) | plant | | | harvest | | | | |
| | | | | harvest | | | plant | → |
| **spinach** (see page 205) | sow | | harvest | harvest | harvest | | | |
| | | sow | | harvest | harvest | harvest | | |
| | | | sow | | harvest | harvest | | |
| | harvest | harvest | | | sow | | harvest | harvest → |
| **sprouting broccoli** (see page 193) | harvest | harvest/sow | transplant | | | | | harvest → |
| **squash, summer** (see page 201) | sow ∩ | transplant | harvest | harvest | | | | |
| | | sow ∩ | transplant | harvest | harvest | | | |
| | | | sow | harvest | | | | |
| **squash, winter** (see page 201) | sow ∩ | transplant | | | harvest | harvest | | |
| | | sow ∩ | transplant | | harvest | harvest | | |
| | | | sow | | | harvest | | |
| **swedes** (see page 185) | harvest | sow | | | harvest | harvest | harvest | harvest → |
| **sweetcorn** (see pages 210–11) | sow ∩ | transplant | | harvest | | | | |
| | | sow ∩ | transplant | | harvest | | | |
| | | | sow | | | harvest | | |
| **tomatoes, outdoor** (see page 211) | sow ∩ | transplant | | harvest | harvest | | | |
| | | sow ∩ | transplant | | harvest | harvest | | |

growing your own

33

# seasonal planner

Forward planning on an allotment is vital if produce is to be ready for picking and eating at its best and just when you want it – there is an optimum time for many gardening tasks, and every crop takes a minimum number of days or weeks to reach maturity and be ready for the table. To help you make realistic plans, this chapter is divided into approximate seasons, each featuring seasonal tasks, harvest highlights and recipes appropriate to that particular time of year. Remember to be flexible, though. Every year is different, and gardening strictly according to the calendar isn't always possible, so keep a detailed diary of activities and outcomes on your own plot to help refine the guide for your personal use in years to come.

# early spring
## setting the scene

A capricious time of year: lengthening days beckon irresistibly and then catch you out with sudden cold snaps and chilly nights. However, the increasing influence of global warming has advanced the arrival of spring by three to four weeks in some places compared with a few decades ago, and it is usually worth gambling on some early sowings if you take sensible precautions. Press on under glass, where conditions are more predictable: delays in sowing and planting indoors might jeopardize your head start and result in a bottleneck later if work is held up. Plunder remaining winter crops now, as they will soon bolt or deteriorate.

Overwintered crops and early sowings make rapid growth in the early spring sunshine.

**IN SEASON NOW**
Brussels sprouts (+ tops), cabbages (spring/winter), cauliflowers (winter), celeriac, chicory (forced), good king henry, kale, land cress, leeks, lettuces, parsnips, perpetual spinach, radishes, rhubarb (forced), salad onions, salsify, scorzonera, seakale (forced), sorrel, spinach (winter), sprouting broccoli, swedes, turnip tops, winter purslane

**SOW NOW**
**indoors/cold frame** aubergines, calabrese, cauliflowers (summer), celeriac, celery, French beans, parsley, peppers, tomatoes (greenhouse/outdoor)
**nursery bed** Brussels sprouts, cabbages (summer), globe artichokes, leeks, lettuces
**outdoors** beetroot, broad beans, carrots, chard, kohlrabi, land cress, onions (bulbing), parsnips, peas, perpetual spinach, radishes, rocket, salad onions, salsify, scorzonera, spinach (summer), turnips

**PLANT NOW**
**indoors/cold frame** salad crops (early), tomatoes
**outdoors** asparagus, cabbages (spring/summer), cauliflowers (summer), garlic, globe artichokes, horseradish, Jerusalem artichokes, mint, onions (bulbing), potatoes, shallots, strawberries

# SEASONAL TASKS

**PREPARING A SEEDBED** Seeds are programmed to grow – watch any itinerant weed seed for evidence of its ability to germinate unaided the moment its surroundings are suitable. The key stimulants that seeds require are adequate warmth, moisture and air. The first depends on ambient soil temperature, which, in turn, is affected by the time of year and any steps you might take to improve conditions. Making sure there is also sufficient moisture and air is the reason for preparing a congenial seedbed to supply just the right balance for rapid and even germination.

Whether you sow seeds where the plants are to remain growing or in a nursery bed for transplanting later, you should loosen at least the top 8–10cm (3–4in) of topsoil,

**Shield seedlings from the cold with jam jars.**

where most early root growth takes place, and remove all weeds, large stones and hard lumps of soil (tamping clods with a rake held vertically can crush them into smaller fragments).

Choose a time when the soil is moist but not so wet that it clings to your tools (especially on clay), and rake the surface to a level crumbly *tilth*. There is no need to sieve out all the stones and bigger fragments for sowing large seeds like peas, beans and sweetcorn, but small seeds need fine soil to ensure contact all round: save some old potting compost to add to the line of the drill or to use for covering seeds after sowing.

If you can't sow immediately, cover the prepared bed with clear polythene to prevent the top 8mm (¼in) from crusting over after heavy rain. If you can leave the bed for 3–4 weeks, many weed seeds may have germinated and can be pulled out to leave a clean site for sowing.

**ADVANCING SOWINGS** Seed germination is often more temperature-sensitive than plant growth – when sowing indoors, for example, temperatures can usually be reduced once seedlings emerge. Most outdoor sowings germinate best above 5–7°C (41–45°F); tender crops need at least 10°C (50°F), which doesn't occur until late spring or even early summer in colder districts. In a cold spring, seedlings may take as long as 4–6 weeks to appear unless you artificially raise the temperature (or sow indoors). There are several options:

▸ Sow seeds on a fine day when the sun has warmed the soil. Cover sowings with 2–3 layers of fleece to trap this heat (fleece can stay in place over growing seedlings).
▸ Cover the soil for 2–3 weeks beforehand with black or clear polythene, and replace this after sowing for 2–3 days, but check daily to see if any seedlings have emerged.
▸ Cover the ground before and after sowing with *cloches* or a low plastic tunnel, which can then be left over the growing plants to advance the time of maturity.
▸ Cover sowings at spaced stations with inverted jam jars to warm the ground locally.
▸ Sow indoors in pots or modules those vegetables that will later tolerate transplanting. When moving them outside, plant out through a clear plastic mulch laid to warm the soil (this is an excellent way to recycle plastic carrier bags).
▸ If timing is not critical, wait a few weeks before sowing: seeds sown later often germinate fast and catch up earlier batches.

If you have overgrown ground to clear, use potatoes as a *pioneer crop*: they will give a yield of some kind (even when planted as late as midsummer), their cultivation and harvest will help break up the ground, and their roots will start adding fibrous material to impoverished soil.

► Cut all grass and weeds down as short as possible.
► Cover with overlapping sheets of cardboard or thick piles of newspapers.
► Water thoroughly.

► Spread a layer of manure, garden compost or straw over the top.
► Cover with a sheet of black geo-textile matting and make slits approximately 8cm (3in) long and 38cm (15in) apart each way.
► Insert seed potatoes through the slits (*see below left*).
► Harvest by lifting the matting to reveal the crop just underneath (*see below*).
► Clear and then dig in all the organic materials.

**p.174**  *see* Potato recipes
**p.184**  *see* Crop focus: potatoes

**PLANTING POTATOES** There are many ways to grow potatoes (even peelings with dormant eyes will grow happily in a compost bin). All will produce a crop of some kind, but for maximum yields adequate growing space is important, as well as careful choice and management of seed potatoes at *chitting* time.

Yield depends as much on the density of stems – each tuber develops several – as the planting distances between tubers. Every sprouted eye develops into a stem, which behaves like an individual plant, producing its own crop of tubers at the end of the season. Too many shoots on a fast-growing early variety can lead to overcrowding,

with numerous potatoes clumping together and often lying close to or above the surface, where they turn green. Maincrop varieties, on the other hand, take longer to grow, so their tubers are planted further apart, and the more shoots they have, the heavier the yield over a greater area.

Ideal tubers for planting have shoots about 2–2.5cm (¾–1in) long, 2–3 on early varieties (rub off any surplus

**Always block the ends of cloches and tunnels to trap the maximum amount of heat and avoid creating a cold wind tunnel.**

## EXTENDING YOUR
## LETTUCE HARVEST

Although loose-leaf lettuces like 'Oakleaf' and 'Mascara' give the longest harvest, repeat-sowing is essential for heading lettuces. The frequency of sowing depends on the growth rate of the plants.

Sink a 10cm (4in) plastic pot at the end of a bed, fill with seed compost and sow the first batch of seed thinly and evenly under a shallow covering of compost. Transplant seedlings from the pot into the bed when they are large enough to handle without causing damage, and resow the pot immediately with the same variety. To extend the season still further, transplant the last sowings to a greenhouse or cold frame.

or control chitting carefully) and as many as possible on maincrops. Recommended spacing is 30–38cm (12–15in) apart in rows 38–50cm (15–20in) apart for earlies (even closer for an extra-early variety, such as 'Rocket' or 'Swift'). For maincrop potatoes, this should be every 25–40cm (10–16in) in rows 75cm (30in) apart, spacing very small tubers at the closest distances and large at the maximum. The aim is to have about 30–40 shoots emerge per square metre (3–4/sq ft).

On light soils, you can save yourself time and effort by leaving digging or forking the ground until planting time:

**ask the EXPERT** Potatoes that are growing from tubers left in the ground from the previous year (these are known as 'volunteers') may be unwanted where another crop is to be grown. Rescue them while they are still small by carefully forking up each plant, complete with its tuber, and transplanting elsewhere.

bury early tubers about 10cm (4in) deep as you go, and grow them on the flat without any earthing up. Start planting early potatoes now (followed by late varieties in late spring) and be prepared to protect emerging shoots in case of frost by covering them with cloches or earthing them up to their tips.

**CONTINUITY OF SUPPLY** No one, however expert, can guarantee a continuous supply of produce without occasional gluts and shortages, because weather is a constantly unpredictable influence. A rise of 10°C (about 18°F), for example, can double growth rates, while drought, strong winds or excessively high temperatures may curtail cropping. Various strategies, however, can help avoid shortages (a glut is more easily solved by storing, sharing or even composting the surplus).

Distinguish between crops that do not deteriorate with time, such as carrots and parsnips, and others that have a limited harvest period, like lettuce, peas and spinach.

Sow these short-life crops repeatedly for a succession of pickings, about 3–4 weeks apart early in the year when growth is slower, down to every two weeks in high summer. Harvest while young, and clear each batch as soon as the next comes on stream.

Successional sowings are usually made with the same fast or early variety. Alternatively, sow a range of early, mid-season and late varieties at the same time, and transfer picking from one to the next as each matures. Sow the early variety again as the mid-season batch ripens, to supply a final end-of-season crop.

Experiment with modifying the growing environment. Simultaneous sowings in a warm sunny place and a cooler shaded spot will often mature 1–2 weeks apart. Sow several rows, cloche some in order to advance picking, and leave the others to mature at their normal rate. Closer spacing can hasten maturity, but also produces small plants.

Try altering your growing method. Pinching out the tips of pea or runner bean plants will stimulate sideshoots that flower later than unstopped plants; staggered planting from a nursery bed sowing (*see pages 66–7*) will space out maturing times; cutting off the tops of broad beans as soon as they are in full flower speeds up ripening and stimulates the production of more sideshoots.

## STARTING ONIONS IN GOOD TIME

Unless you are prepared to sow seeds early and transplant or thin the seedlings, the best way to grow onions is by planting sets, which already represent several weeks' growth, suffer less from ailments and perform better on poor soils.

Plant as soon as soil conditions are fit, as early as late winter if you can: the ultimate number of leaves determines onion size (each leaf produces another layer in the bulb), and no more leaves form after midsummer. Do not plant heat-treated (and usually bolt-resistant) sets until the soil warms up in late spring, however.

Choose medium-size sets – large ones are more inclined to bolt, while tiny ones make smaller onions (so plant closer together) – and plant so their tips are just covered by soil to deter inquisitive birds. Use a trowel to plant them and never push them into the ground, which can damage the basal rooting area.

## TRY THIS...

Multi-crop large, deep containers by planting them about halfway down in autumn with a liberal range of spring-flowering bulbs to cut for the house. Then, in spring, sow or transplant a selection of salad leaves among the dying bulb foliage to harvest as cut-and-come-again crops, or sow fast carrots to grow at a safe height from low-flying carrot root flies.

## IT'S NOT TOO LATE TO...

Plant new strawberries (*see left*), particularly if you buy special cold-stored runners that will crop fully this summer. Ordinary runners are best encouraged to make strong growth for next year, so nip off flower trusses as they form this season. However, you could relent and allow a few plants to fruit, which will simply delay maximum yields for a season. Divide and replant alpine strawberries now for new, more vigorous plants.

## IF YOU HAVE TIME...

Move the last parsnips and leeks out of the way of new cultivations: lift them carefully with a fork and then bury in groups up to their old growing depth in a spare piece of ground, where they will stay good for a few more weeks.

# HARVEST HIGHLIGHTS

**JERUSALEM ARTICHOKES** Depending on how it is grown, the Jerusalem artichoke is either a weedy and ineradicable perennial windbreak growing to about 3m (10ft) or a prolific and nutritious crop of large crisp tubers. For best results, dig up all the tubers now and choose the smoothest specimens, about the size of a hen's egg, for replanting 45–60cm (18–24in) apart in fresh rich ground. Keep the rest cool and dark, and use them roasted, deep-fried as chips or in soup. They are sweetish and delicately flavoured (but cause flatulence in quantity unless cooked with savory, the 'bean herb') and contain the carbohydrate inulin, a form of sugar tolerated by diabetics. For heavy yields of smooth long tubers, choose the variety 'Fuseau'; 'Dwarf Sunray' has shorter stems and simple 'sunflowers' in late summer to early autumn. (*See also page 208.*)

**RHUBARB** If you started *forcing* crowns in good time (*see page 133*), tender sticks of rhubarb will be ready for pulling now to supply the first fresh 'fruit' of the season. Check under pots and boxes every few days, pull sticks away cleanly with a sideways twist, and always leave a

> ### BRUSSELS SPROUTS
>
> Start clearing the latest varieties of Brussels sprouts, packed full of flavour but soon to 'blow' as each solid button expands into a loose miniature cabbage and flower shoot. Harvest them before this happens, and try smaller sprouts blanched and then stir-fried in hot oil, served with crispy bacon. The leafy tops, larger in some varieties than others, are a delicious vegetable in their own right, similar to spring greens but with a richer flavour. Cut them off for use as you pull up exhausted stems (complete with roots). These stems are woody and difficult to compost intact, so crush them first with a hammer or by running them over with a laden wheelbarrow, and slice with loppers into short segments. (*See also page 190.*)

few of the smallest to sustain the plant. Continue forcing until exposed crops are ready, then uncover them and allow to grow undisturbed for the rest of the season. Don't force the same plants next year.

Unlike rhubarb in the open air, these forced sticks will be mild, sweet and very tender, needing the briefest cooking. Use them for special desserts, and relieve any sourness by adding sweet cicely or a teaspoonful of

Jerusalem artichoke 'sunflowers'.

Harvesting Jerusalem artichokes.

redcurrant jelly during cooking; add plenty of raisins in rhubarb pies and crumbles (or use a flapjack topping for the perfect balance of tartness and sweetness). Bottle or freeze any surplus. The more robust (in every sense) open-air sticks are the ones to use for wine and preserves, such as rhubarb and ginger jam. (*See also page 208.*)

**SWEDES & TURNIPS** Some other crops coming to the end of their lives often produce new growth now as they come up to flower. Swedes and turnips are both biennials, and surplus roots left in over winter will be growing masses of young leaves that can be harvested as 'greens' when little else is available – in southern Italy they are traditionally served with pasta, such as cavatelli or orecchiette. Either leave the tops to appear naturally (gather them as you pull up the ageing root and slice thinly for boiling like spring cabbage) or blanch them to force more tender growth. Earth up roots under a mound or ridge of soil 15cm (6in) high, and when growth emerges at the top, scrape back the soil to reveal the blanched tops. Sow a stubble turnip variety, such as 'Typhon', in late summer for the heaviest yield of tops. (*See also page 185.*)

**Turnip 'Primera'**

### TRY THIS
#### WINTER PURSLANE
Also known as claytonia, miner's lettuce and spring beauty, this hardy annual can be available all year round if it is sown twice – in late spring for summer picking, and in late summer for the more valuable winter crop. Cover with cloches in late winter for a lush harvest now of cool succulent leaves and stems (oddly fused together) to add to salads. Leave some plants to self-sow, and transplant groups of seedlings to fresh soil.

Do not confuse winter purslane with the ordinary type, a half-hardy wild flower with selected green or golden cultivated forms. Its leaves and young shoots are crisp and peppery, perhaps too strong on their own but a popular ingredient of salads, pickles, soups and Middle Eastern fattoush. Sow from late spring to late summer for picking 2 months later.

### PROTECTING YOUR CROPS
The earliest sowings of the year are a lottery – seeds may sulk in cold soil and young plants succumb to sudden chill – unless you take every precaution to encourage their steady growth. Covering crops to modify the environment in which they are growing shields them from various weather hazards, especially at this unpredictable time of year. If covers are left in place as plants develop, their maturity can also be advanced by up to 2–3 weeks.

▶ Choose a favoured site for your seedbed, sheltered from cold winds and early morning sunshine, and avoid low-lying or enclosed frost hollows.
▶ Cover the seedbed with black mulching paper or clear or black polythene for 2–3 weeks to warm the soil.
▶ Cover sowings with cloches or clear polythene tunnels, or 2–3 thicknesses of fleece.
▶ Keep newspapers handy as emergency covers for seeds and seedlings if frost threatens.
▶ Use a first early variety of a crop or one that is recommended for its hardiness.
▶ Keep back some of the seeds to resow just in case you lose the first batch.

**Swede 'Brora'**

# EAT NOW

With winters perceptibly warming as the climate changes, it's hard to be sure whether balmy days are a brief and deceptive respite or a triumphant signal of spring's arrival. Winter can't last forever, though, nor winter's staple crops, and a change of emphasis creeps into the kitchen as well as allotment sheds everywhere. Maincrop roots like swedes and parsnips – concentrated reserves of food and flavour – can be used up in the last hearty stews and casseroles. Leafy crops such as savoys, sprouts and leeks can be cleared in advance of the first spring greens, turnip tops and young pickings from leaf beet and good king henry. To follow: the first blush of forced rhubarb to greet spring with traditional pies and crumbles. (*See* In season now, *page 36*.)

## RECIPES

seasonal planner

## SALAD ONION SOUP

**SERVES 6**

This fresh-tasting soup uses the first
of your spring crops and the remains
of last summer's shallots, garlic and
overwintered leeks – and some of the
fresh herbs you potted up last winter.

> 45g (1½oz) unsalted butter
>
> 2 leeks, including green parts, halved
> lengthways and chopped
>
> 2 large salad onions, including green parts,
> trimmed and chopped
>
> 4 large shallots, peeled and chopped
>
> 1 crisp green apple, peeled and chopped
>
> 3 garlic cloves, chopped
>
> salt and freshly ground pepper, to taste
>
> 1 tsp plain flour
>
> 1 tsp wine vinegar
>
> 1 tsp chopped mixed fresh thyme and sage
>
> 1.3 litres (2¼ pints) hot vegetable stock

- Heat the butter in a large pan over
  a medium-low heat. Put in the leeks,
  salad onions, shallots, apple, garlic,
  a pinch of salt and a grind of pepper.
  Cook on a low heat, being careful not
  to brown, for about 30 minutes or
  until very soft.
- When the onion mixture is ready,
  sprinkle with the flour and stir to
  coat well. Add the vinegar and herbs.
  Pour in the stock and bring to the
  boil. Reduce to a simmer and cook
  for 30 minutes.
- Set aside 75g (2½oz) of the onion
  mixture in a small bowl. Purée the
  remaining onion mixture in a food
  processor or (in batches) in a blender
  until creamy. Transfer to a clean pan
  and add more salt and pepper to
  taste. Reheat until piping hot.
- Serve immediately, topped with the
  reserved onion mixture.

## DEEP-FRIED BROCCOLI WITH GARLIC & MINT DRESSING

**SERVES 4–6 AS A STARTER**

This simple dish transforms broccoli into
a total treat. A lemon, mint and garlic
dressing really lifts it. You could also use
cauliflower or courgettes instead. Serve
as a starter or side dish.

> 1 head broccoli, broken into small florets
>
> sunflower or vegetable oil, for deep-frying
>
> salt

### Dressing

> 1 large garlic clove, chopped
>
> 30g (1oz) fresh mint leaves
>
> juice of 1 lemon
>
> 150ml (5fl oz) extra virgin olive oil
>
> salt and freshly ground pepper, to taste

- First make the dressing. Put the
  garlic, mint and lemon juice in a
  blender. With the machine running,
  trickle in the olive oil. Season with
  salt and pepper. Set aside.
- Steam the broccoli until almost
  cooked but still slightly al dente.
  Tip on to a tea towel or kitchen paper
  and leave to dry.
- In a deep saucepan heat some
  sunflower or vegetable oil to
  180°C/350°F for deep-frying. Test
  that it has reached the right
  temperature by dropping in a piece
  of bread – the oil should sizzle and
  bubble around it.
- Fry the broccoli, in several small
  batches, for just a minute or two
  until crisp. Lift out and drain on
  kitchen paper. Season with salt.
  Drizzle the dressing over the top.

## BROCCOLI & CAULIFLOWER WITH TOASTED GARLIC

**SERVES 6**

Very few people are indifferent about
broccoli and cauliflower – they either love
them or hate them – but most will be sure
to like them cooked this way. Caramelizing
the vegetables in a hot pan brings out
their true deliciousness. Both of these
vegetables are extremely nutritious.

> 1 large head cauliflower, cored
>
> 2 large heads broccoli, stalks attached
>
> 2 tbsp sunflower or light olive oil
>
> salt and freshly ground pepper, to taste
>
> 2–3 garlic cloves, thinly sliced
>
> 1 tbsp extra virgin olive oil

- Heat a large cast-iron pan over a
  medium heat. While it's heating,
  slice the cauliflower and broccoli
  from top to bottom into 2.5cm (1in)
  thick slices. Brush both sides of every
  slice with some of the sunflower oil
  and season with salt and pepper.
  Place the slices in the hot pan and
  press them down with a fish slice.
  Cook until nicely browned. Turn and
  cook on the other side until browned
  and tender. Transfer the slices to a
  warmed plate.
- Add the remaining sunflower oil
  (about 2 teaspoons) to the hot pan.
  Add the garlic slices and sauté,
  stirring constantly, until lightly
  browned. Transfer to a plate lined
  with kitchen paper and sprinkle with
  salt and pepper.
- Sprinkle the toasted garlic slices over
  the broccoli and cauliflower, drizzle
  with the olive oil and serve.

## SPINACH TARTLETS

**SERVES 8**

These little tarts make a very fresh starter, or a light lunch with a mixed salad of overwintered salad leaves.

225g (8oz) shortcrust pastry
450g (1lb) baby leaf spinach, washed
225g (8oz) cottage cheese or ricotta
1 egg, plus 2 egg yolks
100ml (3½fl oz) crème fraîche
15g (½oz) freshly grated Parmesan cheese
1 onion, finely diced
2 tbsp olive oil
salt and freshly ground pepper, to taste

- Preheat oven to 200°C/400°F/gas 6. Roll out the pastry and line eight 9cm (3½in) diameter tartlet tins. Prick the base of each pastry case, then chill for 30 minutes.
- Bake the empty tartlet cases for 15 minutes or until lightly browned. Remove from the oven and reduce the temperature to 190°C/375°F/gas 5.
- Cook the spinach in a minimal amount of water until wilted. Drain and cool immediately under cold running water, then squeeze as much water from the leaves as possible.
- Put the cottage cheese or ricotta, the spinach, egg, egg yolks and crème fraîche in a food processor and process until the spinach is finely chopped. Tip into a bowl and add the Parmesan.
- Fry the onion in the oil until soft. Stir into the spinach mixture and season with salt and pepper. Spoon into the cooked pastry cases and return to the oven. Bake for 20 minutes until the filling is flecked brown and lightly set. Serve hot or warm.

## SPANISH OMELETTE

**SERVES 3**

A delicious version of a traditional potato omelette with onion and spinach, which can be served warm or cold as tapas or for lunch or supper with a salad. Other ingredients that Spaniards sometimes add to their omelettes include ham or chorizo, cheese, mushrooms and artichokes – anything goes.

about 250ml (8fl oz) olive oil
2 onions, thinly sliced
500g (1lb 2oz) potatoes, peeled and thinly sliced
800g (1¾lb) baby leaf spinach
4 eggs
salt and freshly ground pepper, to taste

- Heat half the oil in a frying pan, add the onions and fry, stirring occasionally, until they are golden. Remove from the pan and put on kitchen paper to drain off some of the oil. Add the potatoes to the pan, and fry until golden. Drain on kitchen paper.
- Cook the spinach in a minimal amount of water until wilted. Drain and cool immediately under cold running water, then squeeze as much water from the leaves as possible and chop finely.
- Beat the eggs well with some salt and pepper. Add the potatoes, onions and spinach and mix thoroughly.
- Preheat the grill to high. Put enough olive oil in the frying pan to cover the bottom in a thin layer. When the oil is hot, add the egg mixture. Shake the pan gently over the hob as you move the mixture to prevent it from sticking. Once the omelette is nearly cooked, put the pan under the grill until the omelette is perfectly cooked through and golden.

## WARM SALAD OF GRILLED LEEKS, CHICORY & SCALLOPS

**SERVES 6**

Young leeks are available for pulling now as you thin the rows. Forced chicory is also in season.

2 tbsp lemon juice
6 tbsp extra virgin olive oil
salt and freshly ground pepper, to taste
350g (¾lb) baby leeks, washed and trimmed
3 heads red chicory, trimmed
6 large scallops, cleaned
Chinese chilli sauce

- Whisk together the lemon juice, 3 tablespoons of the olive oil, salt and pepper to make a vinaigrette.
- Drop the leeks into a pan of boiling water and cook until just tender. Drain and cool under cold running water. Pat dry and set aside.
- Preheat a ridged griddle pan. Cut the chicory in half lengthways. Slice each scallop horizontally into two discs, leaving the coral on. Season the leeks, chicory and scallops and brush with the remaining olive oil.
- Cook the leeks lightly on each side on the griddle pan and set aside. Griddle the chicory until slightly wilted and add to the leeks. Dress both with the vinaigrette.
- Place the scallops on the hot griddle pan. As soon as the first side is seared with light grill marks, turn the scallops over. Depending on their thickness, it will take 1–2 minutes to cook each side.
- Arrange the leeks and chicory on warmed plates. Add the scallops. Drizzle chilli sauce round the edge of the plates and serve.

## GLUT BUSTER
### RHUBARB

Rhubarb is not strictly a fruit (*see page 209*), but makes a welcome change in early spring when there is not much else growing. Forced rhubarb will give you something sweet for puddings and jams. It has a strong affinity with ginger and orange. If you just want something simple, roasting it is the best way to cook it. It also makes a sharp sauce that is perfect with oily fish.

## BAKED MACKEREL WITH RHUBARB SAUCE
### SERVES 8

Rhubarb makes a classic tart sauce for mackerel or herrings. Another sharp fruit such as gooseberries can be substituted.

8 mackerel, cleaned and filleted
8 bay leaves
handful of whole black peppercorns
salt
6 tbsp cider
15g (½oz) butter

**Sauce**
450g (1lb) rhubarb, trimmed and chopped
120ml (4fl oz) cider
squeeze of lemon juice
4 tbsp brown sugar
½ tsp grated nutmeg or ground mace

- Preheat oven to 190°C/375°F/gas 5.
- Open out the fish, skin side down, and on each lay a bay leaf, some peppercorns and a pinch of salt. Roll them up and place side by side in an ovenproof dish. Pour over the cider and dot with butter. Cover with foil and bake for about 30 minutes or until the flesh flakes easily.
- Meanwhile, combine all the sauce ingredients in a pan and cook gently until soft. Serve the sauce hot with the mackerel.

## RHUBARB FINGERS
### SERVES 6

This recipe uses whole sticks of rhubarb and encases them in sweet pastry. You can either eat the fingers whole or cut them up and serve as a dessert with double cream.

175g (6oz) plain flour
pinch of salt
85g (3oz) chilled butter, diced
30g (1oz) caster sugar
1 egg, separated
cold water, to mix
6 stalks young rhubarb, trimmed and cut into 30cm (12in) lengths
icing sugar, to sprinkle and dust
egg white, to glaze

- Preheat oven to 190°C/375°F/gas 5.
- Sift the flour and salt into a bowl. Add the butter and rub it in with your fingertips until the mixture resembles fine breadcrumbs. Stir in the caster sugar. Mix in the egg yolk and enough cold water to form a firm dough. Knead gently on a lightly floured surface. Wrap in clingfilm and chill for 1 hour.
- Roll out the pastry thinly to a rectangle 45 x 33cm (18 x 13in). Cut into six equal lengths, 33cm (13in) long. Place a stalk of rhubarb on each strip and sprinkle with some icing sugar.
- Brush the edges of the pastry with a little of the egg white and fold over to enclose the rhubarb, pressing the edges together with the back of a knife to seal. Repeat with the remaining rhubarb and transfer to a baking sheet. Brush with more of the egg white and bake for 25 minutes until golden.
- Cut each stick into three pieces, if wanted. Dust with icing sugar and serve warm or cold .

## RHUBARB STEAMED PUDDING
### SERVES 8

A very healthy but totally warming pudding. Made with a mixture of white and wholemeal flour, it is surprisingly light. The addition of orange is delicious.

115g (4oz) unsalted butter, softened
115g (4oz) soft light brown sugar
2 eggs, beaten
60g (2oz) self-raising flour
60g (2oz) wholemeal self-raising flour
½ tsp baking powder
60g (2oz) fresh breadcrumbs
175g (6oz) rhubarb, trimmed and finely chopped
grated zest of 1 orange

- Cream together the butter and sugar until light and fluffy, then beat in the eggs, one at a time. Fold in the flours and baking powder with the breadcrumbs, then gently mix in the rhubarb and grated orange zest.
- Turn the mixture into a greased 900ml (1½ pint) pudding basin. Cover with a double thickness of greased greaseproof paper or foil (this will stop it sticking to the pudding as it rises), twisting and folding under the rim to secure. Place in the top part of a steamer and steam for 1 hour.
- Turn out on to a warmed serving plate and serve hot.

## RHUBARB FLAPJACK

**SERVES 4**

A crumble with a difference, with the fruit enveloped in a delicious syrupy, crunchy flapjack mixture that contrasts perfectly with the tart fruit.

  900g (2lb) rhubarb, trimmed and sliced
  75g (2½oz) sugar
  140g (5oz) butter
  4 tbsp golden syrup
  225g (8oz) rolled oats
  ¼ tsp salt
  1 tsp ground ginger
  icing sugar, to dredge

- Preheat oven to 190°C/375°F/gas 5. Grease a shallow 20cm (8in) pie dish.
- Simmer the rhubarb gently with 40g (1½oz) of the sugar in a covered pan until soft.
- Warm the remaining sugar with the butter and syrup until dissolved. Stir in the oats, salt and ground ginger.
- Use three-quarters of the oat mixture to line the bottom and sides of the dish almost to the top. Pour the rhubarb into the centre and cover with the remaining oat mixture, pressing down lightly.
- Bake for 30–35 minutes until crisp and golden. Dredge with icing sugar, and serve with custard.

## ROASTED RHUBARB

**SERVES 4**

Rhubarb roasts wonderfully. It really brings out the flavour and you will be surprised at the intensity of taste. Later in the season try roasting strawberries with rhubarb for a great marriage of flavours and a true surprise that cooked strawberries can taste quite so good.

  750g (1lb 10oz) rhubarb, trimmed and cut into 15cm (6in) lengths
  1 orange
  45g (1½oz) caster sugar
  4 tbsp water

- Preheat oven to 200°C/400°F/gas 6.
- Peel the orange and cut roughly into pieces. Cut the peel into thin strips.
- Put the rhubarb into a shallow baking dish with the pieces of orange, strips of peel, sugar and water. Roast for 40 minutes or until tender.
- Serve hot, with custard or cream.

## RHUBARB & GINGER CREAM LAYERS

**SERVES 8**

This is a kind of rough cheesecake. Ginger is a great companion to rhubarb.

  60g (2oz) unsalted butter
  250g (9oz) ginger biscuits, crushed
  250g (9oz) mascarpone cheese
  300ml (½ pint) double cream, whipped into soft peaks
  75g (2½oz) icing sugar
  500g (1lb 2oz) cooked rhubarb

- Melt the butter in a pan. Add the crushed biscuits and stir them in well. Put aside.
- Fold together the mascarpone, cream and sugar.
- Put alternate layers of biscuit crumbs, cream and rhubarb in eight small dishes or glasses.
- Chill for at least 1 hour.

## RHUBARB & GINGER PRESERVE

**MAKES 3 JARS**

Another recipe marrying rhubarb with ginger for a classic preserve.

  1.1kg (2½lb) rhubarb, trimmed and cut into short lengths
  1.1kg (2½lb) sugar
  30g (1oz) fresh root ginger, bruised
  115g (4oz) crystallized ginger

- Layer the rhubarb and sugar in a bowl. Leave overnight.
- Transfer to a pan and add the root ginger tied in a muslin bag. Bring to the boil and boil hard for 15 minutes.
- Cut the crystallized ginger into small pieces and add to the pan. Continue to boil until the mixture reaches setting point (*see page 80*).
- Remove the bag of root ginger. Pour the preserve into hot jars and cover (*see page 80*).

# late spring
## setting the scene

This is the pivotal season on the plot, an enchanting time of year, with new growth and blossom and the first early produce all to celebrate. Keeping up a steady momentum now can help to lay a sound foundation for the rest of the year, but what should be an exhilarating bustle can be frustrated by fickle weather. Don't drop your guard for a moment – all things are possible in the late spring climate: frost or fire or flood. Soils are becoming ever more receptive as warmth and day length increases, and many crops can or must start now, but keep an eye on them until they are safe, even if this means a week or two of daily trips to the plot.

**Yields of tree fruit depend on favourable weather and active pollinating insects at blossom time.**

**IN SEASON NOW**
asparagus, broad beans, cabbages (spring), carrots, cauliflowers (winter), chard, good king henry, gooseberries, kale, land cress, perpetual spinach, leeks, lettuce, parsley, radishes, rhubarb, salad onions, seakale, spinach (winter), sprouting broccoli, turnips (+ tops)

**SOW NOW**
**indoors/cold frame** aubergines, courgettes + other squashes, cucumbers (outdoor), French beans, melons, runner beans, sweetcorn, tomatoes (outdoor)
**nursery bed** Brussels sprouts, cabbages (winter), cauliflowers (autumn/winter), kale, leeks, sprouting broccoli
**outdoors** beetroot, broad beans, cabbages (summer/autumn), calabrese, carrots, chard, chicory (heading/forcing), endive, herbs (annual), kohlrabi, land cress, lettuce, parsley, parsnips, peas, perpetual spinach, radishes, rocket, salad onions, salsify, scorzonera, spinach (summer), swedes, sweet fennel, turnips

**PLANT NOW**
**indoors/cold frame**
aubergines, cucumbers, French beans, melons, peppers, squashes
**outdoors** artichokes (all kinds), asparagus, cabbages (summer), cardoons, cauliflowers (summer), onions, potatoes
**outdoors with protection**
celeriac, celery, French beans, peppers, runner beans, sweetcorn, tomatoes

# SEASONAL TASKS

**SOWING OUTDOORS** In districts subject to fairly predictable late spring frosts, time your sowings so that seedlings emerge just after this average date. Although this isn't crucial for relatively hardy crops such as peas, a late frost can be lethal to tender vegetables like French beans and courgettes. Allow 2–3 weeks for seedlings to emerge into the open air; when starting crops indoors, add another 3–4 weeks for their seedlings to develop into young plants that have been hardened off and are ready for planting. Always keep a supply of cloches, fleece or newspapers handy in case of the unexpected.

Far-sight now can help ensure food throughout the winter. As you cut the first asparagus, sow brassicas such as hardy cauliflowers, Savoy cabbages and Brussels sprouts for your Christmas dinner, some calabrese and Italian sprouting broccoli for late summer and autumn, and plenty of curly kale and purple sprouting broccoli to fill next spring's hungry gap.

If possible, sow them all in a nursery bed, thinning seedlings to 5–8cm (2–3in) apart and transplanting the surplus to adjacent rows. Alternatively, sow and then prick out in cell trays indoors or into a frame. This does, though, involve a lot more work and needs careful management to stop seedlings becoming soft, drawn and leggy. Transplant in 4–6 weeks' time when they have made 2–3 true leaves (*see pages 66–7*), at full spacings, and then sow catch crops in between.

**DIFFERENT WAYS TO SOW** Although sowing fundamentally means burying seeds in conditions that favour growth, there are various ways to do this, all valid for certain crops or circumstances.

**Narrow drill** This is a single, straight row of seeds used for vegetables like lettuces; seedlings can be thinned (with thinnings discarded or transplanted). The resulting row of plants is easy to support, weed and harvest.

**Wide drill** Several rows or a scattering of seeds in a shallow 'trench' dug out with a spade can economize on space with crops like peas, which can be supported en masse, or carrots, thinned out and picked in large regular quantities. Weeding is a little more time-consuming.

**Station sowing** Vegetables that have large seeds or need a wide space are often sown a measured distance apart, with 2–3 seeds or a small pinch of smaller ones

Narrow drill

Wide drill

Station sowing

at each place. This saves seed and a lot of thinning (seedlings just need singling to leave the strongest), and other faster vegetables can be sown in intervening spaces down the row at the same time.

**Broadcast sowing**

Difficult to accomplish evenly, but this is an easy method of growing crops like cut-and-come-again lettuces in patches, a whole cold frame full of

Broadcast sowing

carrots or a band of green manure plants. Seeds are scattered as if sowing a lawn and then gently raked into the soil or covered with a sifting of fine soil (old potting compost is ideal). Seedlings are thinned only where seriously congested. Weeding is a very delicate job.

## ADAPTING PLANTS TO LIFE OUTDOORS

When calculating indoor sowing times for tender crops like outdoor tomatoes, courgettes and French beans, allow at least an extra week, ideally two, for acclimatizing plants to the world outside. Sudden change does no plant any good, especially those raised in artificial warmth.

Standard methods of acclimatizing plants are to move them to a cold frame and then progressively adjust the lid to admit more fresh air for longer periods, or simply to stand plants outdoors on mild days for increasing lengths of time. Don't assume they are then immune to cold weather, however.

Warming the soil beforehand by covering with plastic film and then planting out under cloches is the most reliable way to guarantee an easy transfer from cosseted surroundings. Alternatively, you can keep crop covers handy for emergency protection in the event of frost. Remember, chilly wind can scorch or lacerate tender leaf tissues, so protect against this with crop covers or some kind of screen or shelter. Newspapers held down with bricks have often saved the day.

## PLANTING GREENHOUSE CROPS

Overcrowding is common under glass at this time of year: seeds, seedlings and overwintered exotics occupy all the available space, while greenhouse crops wait to be planted in their final positions.

### COMMON CAUSES OF POOR GERMINATION

Indoor sowings in almost ideal conditions can produce impressive germination rates close to statutory minima for various vegetables, but seeds outdoors are exposed to all kinds of hazards, and 50 per cent emergence is a more reasonable expectation. Possible explanations of poor germination include:

**Dry soil** To prevent, flood open drills with water and leave to drain before sowing.

**Lack of air** Counter capping by rain on fine soils after sowing by covering seeds with potting compost, and water gently with a rose to keep the cover moist.

**Rich soil** Don't add a full dressing of any fertilizer until seedlings are growing strongly.

**Wrong depth** Sowing too deep exhausts seedlings before they can reach the light and generate more energy.

**Uneven depth** Patchy germination can result from some seeds being too deep, with others drying out near the surface.

**Too cold** Sow temperature-sensitive crops after the soil has warmed up naturally or with the aid of cloches.

**Too hot** Some seeds, notably lettuce, go dormant or scorch in very hot weather. Help prevent this by sowing in the late afternoon and covering with damp paper for 1–2 days.

Relieve the congestion with a cold frame, or even just a makeshift corral of boxes roofed with plastic, or straw bales topped with a recycled car windscreen, for example. This way you can combine easing pressure with starting to harden off plants before they are finally planted outside. Consider adapting greenhouse staging so that it can be moved outdoors to a sunny sheltered spot, where plants can be covered with fleece or plastic on cold days and exposed to fresh air during milder spells.

These measures to reduce overcrowding could release enough space for planting tomatoes, cucumbers, melons, peppers, aubergines and any other heat-loving crop that is to grow permanently under glass. Decide how to accommodate the plants: they might fit best in large containers of potting compost, in growing bags or in the soil of a permanent greenhouse bed, an option that

**Sow runner beans about 8 weeks before the last frosts under a low, clear plastic tunnel. Once seedlings emerge, insert canes through the plastic and tie as wigwams. When leaves reach the top of the tunnel, slit the plastic from end to end to liberate plants.**

ask the EXPERT

## GREENHOUSE TOMATOES

These are adaptable plants that are easily grown in a number of different ways.

▶ Use double-decker growing bags, cutting holes in the base of the top one to match those below and allow the roots full run of the extra compost.

▶ Train plants up string, tying one end to the greenhouse roof and tucking the other under the rootball. Twist the string around the growing stem for support.

▶ Grow a tall variety as cordons with a bushy kind at their feet. If they are sown and planted at the same time, the bushes will usually crop earlier.

▶ Remove the first sideshoots on a cordon when they are about 10cm (4in) long and root them as cuttings in water or pots of cuttings compost to make extra plants.

▶ Leave the lowest sideshoots to develop and train the plant as a fan or multiple cordon for increased yields from the same ground space.

▶ Stop a cordon after the first *truss* or two to hasten ripening; allow a sideshoot to form and train this on to continue the plant's upward growth.

▶ Use tomato grow pots to give greater root depth and make watering easier. Simply cut holes in the growing bags, insert the bottomless pots and plant onto them. Stake as normal (*see left*).

**TRY THIS...**
For light relief and simple utilitarian charm, root cuttings of rosemary, myrtle, bay, santolina, lavender, scented pelargoniums or lemon verbena, grow them on in 15cm (6in) pots with cane supports, and clip into standard, mophead, conical, spiral or pompon topiary.

**IT'S NOT TOO LATE TO...**
Check blackcurrants for evidence of *big bud*. Affected buds will be distended and unopened, whereas healthy ones should be sporting young leaves now. Pick off and burn affected buds, and then spray bushes with an organic pesticide once or twice in late spring as the gall mites migrate to new sites.

**IF YOU HAVE TIME...**
Bring forward the strawberry harvest by 2–3 weeks by covering a few plants or a complete row with cloches or a low plastic tunnel, but ventilate in warm weather to admit pollinating insects. Keep jam jars handy and tuck open-air trusses inside them to hasten ripening and deter slugs and birds (*see left*).

offers more latitude with watering and ample room for unchecked root development.

Arrange permanent plants in the greenhouse according to their preferences. Climbers such as trailing squash varieties and yard-long beans can supply dappled shading for vulnerable leafy salads and herbs growing below, as well as leaving ground space for compact bush forms of the same crop. Cold-sensitive vegetables that enjoy humidity, like cucumbers, should be furthest from the door and vents, where more resilient tomatoes can be grown to screen draughts. Don't compromise good air circulation, though, which can prevent moulds forming on peppers. Melons don't have to be trained upwards: arrange them as groundcover on a bed of straw, perhaps under a vine or trained top fruit, to make full use of space and reduce the need for watering. Remember to adjust watering and ventilation for these permanent plants, which usually need higher temperatures and humidity than the plants they are replacing in the greenhouse.

## UNDERSTANDING FRUIT FERTILITY

Although many fruits yield well, even exuberantly, with little or no encouragement, crop failures do occur and can be a huge disappointment, resulting in store-cupboard gaps for a whole year. A poor crop is often the consequence of cold or windy weather at flowering time, and there's little you can do about it. Other causes can be remedied, however.

**Unsuitability** A variety can be locally unsuitable. Where summers are short, for example, late-ripening kinds are unlikely to succeed. Similarly, early-flowering varieties can be regularly injured where spring frosts linger late. As climate change raises temperatures, crops like blackcurrants and gooseberries that need winter chilling will give progressively lower yields in mild areas.

**Disease** Many soft fruits are affected eventually by viral diseases, which can depress yields without any other visible symptoms, and most varieties need replacing with fresh disease-free plants after a few years. Even woody, long-lived fruits like blackcurrants should be renewed after 7–8 years. Don't take cuttings from old plants unless you are certain of their good health.

**Infertility** The flowers of some fruits must be fertilized with pollen from a different but compatible variety. Even nominally self-fertile kinds such as 'Stella' cherries and 'Conference' pears crop more heavily with the aid of a partner that blooms at the same time. This may not be a problem where nearby plots grow a range of fruits, but it could explain why an isolated tree bears meagre crops.

**Try the effective old ruse of introducing fertile pollen to fruit trees by suspending a few sprays of open blossom from a compatible variety in jam jars of water among the branches of your trees, and then leaving bees to do the rest.**

ask the EXPERT

# HARVEST HIGHLIGHTS

**ASPARAGUS** The start of the short asparagus season is a key event in every gourmet's calendar, marked in many districts by parties, formal dinners and even auctions of the first 'round of grass'. This is a long-lived perennial, cropping for 30 years or more, so plant tenderly in well-prepared ground, feed in midsummer after cutting ceases with a 10cm (4in) mulch of garden compost, and keep plants clear of weeds and inferior seedlings from the female red berries. Watch out for the destructive yellow/black asparagus beetles: discourage them by cutting every spear and spray adults and grubs with derris or insecticidal soap. Stop cutting at midsummer and leave the fern to grow, although stealing some for flower arrangements will not harm the plants. (*See also page 206.*)

**BUNCHING CARROTS** Sow a very fast variety like 'Amsterdam Forcing' or 'Nantes Express' in a cold frame in late winter, and you could be pulling the first young juicy carrots just 8 weeks afterwards. Although more slender than maincrop varieties, they need wider spacing apart (about 10cm/4in) for rapid growth and bulk. Harvest them greedily to crunch raw or gently steam on their own – they are too sweet and tender to lose in the mêlée of a stew or casserole. Firm or water the soil after pulling because the female carrot root fly is on the wing from now until midsummer and will certainly not miss the penetrating scent of freshly disturbed roots. (*See also pages 182–3.*)

**Harvesting bunching carrots.**

## TRY THIS
### GOOD KING HENRY

An ancient and easily grown vegetable introduced to Britain by the Romans, this is a cousin of weeds like fat hen (also edible), as well as such major crops as spinach, beetroot and the staple cereal quinoa. It is a sturdy and productive perennial, giving several pickings in spring of tender leaves, to treat like spinach, and an even earlier harvest of young shoots that can be forced under pots as a substitute for asparagus. Sow seeds in spring and plant about 40cm (16in) apart in rich soil in a lightly shaded position; cut off flowers before they set seed to avoid intrusive offspring all over the plot.

Red gooseberry 'Whinham's Industry' is a tasty and prolific choice for shade and heavy soils.

Lettuce 'Lollo Rosso', a non-hearting kind, to harvest for weeks on end, a few leaves at a time.

**CABBAGES** These spring 'greens' have a rich and invigorating flavour – you can almost taste the goodness. For maximum yields, plant a heading variety, like 'Durham Early', 10–15cm (4–6in) apart, and pull alternate plants as early greens, leaving the others to heart up – when cutting these, leave a 2.5–5cm (1–2in) stump to sprout extra loose leafy shoots later. In small gardens, grow 'Pixie' 15cm (6in) apart; for a continuous supply, sow 'Duncan' every month from late winter (under glass) to early autumn, and keep some of the last sowing back to plant in early spring. Use as a main green vegetable (for sheer self-indulgence, douse it in mint sauce as a robust partner for roast lamb) or cut into thin shreds and stir-fry. (*See also pages 190–1.*)

**GOOSEBERRIES** Training or pruning gooseberries to an open framework of branches eases access at picking time, a benefit quickly appreciated when heavy crops are thinned now to promote larger berries ripening in summer. Simply remove alternate fruits and thin clusters to single berries. The firm, immature thinnings are best for freezing or bottling, and for turning into traditional gooseberry tarts, crumbles and fools. Adding a head or two of elderflowers to the acid berries makes a classic partnership. Wait until fruit is fully ripe before using it raw or in jams and wines: most varieties, including the mundane 'Careless' and red 'Whinham's Industry', taste very similar at the thinning stage, whereas a host of seductive qualities will develop later as different heritage kinds like 'Crown Bob', 'London' or 'White Lion' ripen in the sun. (*See also page 215.*)

**LETTUCES** Two kinds of lettuce could be ready for gathering now: non-hearting and loose-leaf varieties, such as 'Lollo Rosso' and 'Salad Bowl', sown about 6 weeks ago in a frame or reused growing bag in the greenhouse, and hardy cos varieties, like 'Rouge d'Hiver' and 'Winter Density', sown in late summer and early autumn. Winter kinds grown outdoors are less prone to fungal diseases than cold-tolerant varieties in a greenhouse or polytunnel. Hearting lettuces maturing now need clearing fast in warm weather – try using up cos hearts in lettuce and yoghurt soup. For best results, sow fresh lettuce seed each year, mixing all your left-overs from last season with surplus chicory, endive, cress, spinach and oriental greens to blend a home-made *saladisi*, or *mesclun*, for growing as a seedling crop and cutting when 10–15cm (4–6in) high. (*See also pages 204–5.*)

# EAT NOW

This is a joyous time of year, with young leaves everywhere, vegetable beds seething with new life and a growing bill of gastronomic fare. Forget cautionary predictions of a 'hungry gap': with a little forward planning, there need be no shortage of good food on the allotment as increasing supplies of young produce make those earlier devotions worthwhile. The list of available produce lengthens with the days, from plebeian broad beans and fast turnips to more aristocratic asparagus, seakale and jubilant dishes of forced strawberries. Fresh salads are firmly on stream, with sweet bunching carrots, mild early radishes and all kinds of crisp juicy leaves resolutely maturing. (*See* In season now, *page 50*.)

## RECIPES

seasonal planner

## ONION SOUP

**SERVES 4**

This simple soup will take you to France instantly. A restorative, it will use up those onions just finishing from your stores. Do use a good stock.

350g (12oz) butter

8 onions, thinly sliced

1.8 litres (3 pints) beef, chicken or vegetable stock

4 large slices baguette

60g (2oz) Gruyère or Emmental cheese, grated

salt and freshly ground pepper, to taste

1 shot of dry sherry (optional)

- Melt the butter in a large pan, add the onions and cook, covered, for 30 minutes, stirring occasionally. Preheat the grill to high.
- When the onions are translucent and caramelized, add the stock. Cook, covered, for a further 15 minutes.
- Place the bread on a baking tray and toast under the grill. Cover with the cheese and grill until the cheese melts and bubbles.
- Add the sherry to the soup, if using, and stir, then ladle the soup into bowls. Put a toast on top of each bowl and serve immediately.

## STUFFED ONIONS

**SERVES 4**

A simple, light supper dish made with two varieties of onions. Serve with fresh green vegetables on the side.

2 tbsp olive oil

1 onion, finely chopped

2 garlic cloves, crushed

450g (1lb) lean minced steak

1 carrot, finely chopped

1 celery stick, finely chopped

300ml (10fl oz) white wine

4 large red onions, unpeeled

4 large regular onions, unpeeled

2 tbsp freshly grated Parmesan cheese

1 egg

4 tbsp milk

2 tbsp double cream

salt and freshly ground pepper, to taste

1 tbsp chopped fresh parsley

- Heat 1 tbsp olive oil in a pan. Add the onion and garlic and soften for 2–3 minutes without browning. Add the minced steak, carrot, celery and wine. Simmer gently for 1½ hours.
- Meanwhile, bring a large pan of water to the boil and cook the onions in their skins for 10 minutes. Remove from the pan, cool, then peel off the loose outer skins. Cut off the tops and scoop out most of the inside, leaving about 1cm (½in) of outer rings. Preheat oven to 190°C/375°F/gas 5.
- Mix the meat with the Parmesan, egg, milk, cream, parsley and remaining olive oil. Season well with salt and pepper. Evenly fill the onions with the stuffing, place in an ovenproof dish, then bake them for 20 minutes or until the stuffing looks crisp and brown. Serve hot or warm, garnished with parsley.

## ONION MARMALADE

**MAKES 2 JARS**

Particularly popular in France, onion marmalade is a cross between a jam and a chutney, but it doesn't contain enough sugar and vinegar to keep for much longer than a couple of months in the fridge. It is a useful accompaniment to a robust terrine such as rabbit or duck, as well as bread and cheese.

15g (½oz) butter

6 tbsp olive oil

6 onions, finely sliced

1 tbsp whole black peppercorns

1 bay leaf

2 tsp sugar

½ tsp salt

1 tsp freshly ground pepper

2 tbsp red wine vinegar

1 tbsp sherry

- Heat the butter and olive oil in a pan and add the onions, peppercorns and bay leaf. Season with the sugar, salt and pepper. Simmer gently over a medium-low heat for 45 minutes .
- Add the vinegar and sherry and cook for a further 15 minutes. Allow to cool, put in a small bowl or a couple of jars, then cover and chill.

## ROASTED ASPARAGUS

**SERVES 4**

Although most people grow asparagus for its fresh, clean taste, and will only steam it and serve it with a simple dresssing, sometimes another recipe is called for – particularly if you have a glut. If you don't like anchovies, or are vegetarian, leave them out, although you won't taste them: they are used to impart a flavour rather than a fishy taste.

- 450g (1lb) thin asparagus, 1cm (½in) trimmed from ends
- 3 tbsp olive oil, plus more for drizzling
- 4 tbsp lemon juice, freshly squeezed
- 4 anchovy fillets, chopped
- 2 tbsp capers
- Parmesan cheese, freshly grated
- salt and freshly ground pepper, to taste

- Preheat oven to 220°C/425°F/gas 7.
- Put the olive oil in a medium bowl. Add the lemon juice and chopped anchovies and whisk the mixture together. Place the asparagus in a shallow baking dish. Add the capers and pour the oil mixture over the asparagus. Make sure that all the spears are coated.
- Place in the oven and roast for 8 minutes. Turn the asparagus over with a spoon and roast for a further 4 minutes.
- Spoon the juices in the baking dish over the asparagus. Sprinkle with the Parmesan, drizzle over some olive oil, season with salt and pepper and serve hot.

## ASPARAGUS FRITTATA

**SERVES 4**

A frittata is a cross between a tortilla and an omelette. Like a tortilla, it is finished off under the grill to give a slightly puffy top.

- 2 tbsp extra virgin olive oil
- 115g (4oz) sliced onion
- 1 large garlic clove, sliced
- 350g (12 oz) asparagus, cut into 2.5cm (1 in) pieces
- 6 eggs
- 1 tsp grated lemon zest
- 1 tsp finely chopped fresh oregano
- ½ tsp finely chopped fresh rosemary
- salt and freshly ground pepper, to taste
- 30g (1oz) butter
- 200g (7oz) mozzarella, thinly sliced

- Heat the oil in a large, heavy frying pan and sauté the onion and garlic until the onion is golden and translucent. Preheat the grill.
- Meanwhile, cook the asparagus in boiling water until tender. Drain and refresh under cold running water.
- Beat the eggs. Add the asparagus, lemon zest, onion mixture, herbs and a seasoning of salt and pepper.
- Heat the butter in the frying pan. Pour in the egg mixture and spread it evenly in the pan. Cook over a medium heat until the frittata is set and the base is golden brown.
- Lay the cheese slices over the top and place under the hot grill. Cook until golden. Cut in wedges and serve immediately.

## ASPARAGUS RISOTTO

**SERVES 4**

This is a very Italian way to use asparagus. The secret is two-fold: when cooked, the rice should be creamy but with a bit of bite, and only add the asparagus tips at the end so they don't lose their flavour.

- 1 onion, finely chopped
- 2 garlic clove, finely chopped
- 4 tbsp olive oil
- 30g (1oz) butter
- 350g (12oz) arborio (or risotto) rice
- 450g (1lb) asparagus, chopped into 2.5cm (1 in) pieces and tips kept separate
- 1 glass white wine
- 600ml (1 pint) vegetable or chicken stock, heated
- salt and freshly ground pepper, to taste
- 60g (2oz) Parmesan cheese, freshly grated, plus extra for sprinkling

- Sauté the onion and garlic in the oil and butter until soft. Add the rice and stir until coated with the buttery oil. Add the asparagus stalks and continue to stir. Add the wine and bubble until it is absorbed.
- Slowly add the stock, a ladleful at a time, stirring as you go. Wait until each addition is absorbed before adding the next and always stirring. The total cooking time is about 20 minutes. Just before the risotto is done, season with salt and pepper.
- While the risotto is cooking, steam the asparagus tips, but keep them slightly crunchy.
- Right at the end, stir in the cheese and add the asparagus tips.
- Sprinkle the extra cheese over the top.

## BROAD BEAN SOUP

**SERVES 4**

Try this smooth, creamy soup for using up the larger broad beans whose skins can be a little chewy. The mixture is sieved after puréeing, so you get all the flavour without the fibres.

115g (4oz) onion, chopped

2 garlic cloves, chopped

60g (2oz) butter

350g (12oz) broad beans, podded

3 clean bean pods

900ml (1½ pints) water or vegetable stock

2 tbsp chopped fresh parsley

salt and freshly ground pepper, to taste

6 tbsp double cream

croûtons, to serve

- Cook the onion and garlic gently in the butter in a frying pan for about 3 minutes until soft, but don't let them brown.
- Add the podded beans and pods, the water or stock and parsley. Bring just to the boil, then simmer for about 10 minutes or until the beans are very tender.
- Take out the pods and discard them. Purée the soup in a blender or food processor, then press through a sieve. (Alternatively, use a food mill for puréeing.) Pour into a clean pan.
- Season the soup with salt and pepper. Reheat, then stir in the cream. Serve with croûtons.

## BROAD BEAN DIP

**SERVES 4**

This is a Turkish dip used as a mezze. It is best made with the smaller broad beans that are not too mealy.

100ml (3½fl oz) extra virgin olive oil, plus extra for drizzling

1 tsp ground cumin

¼ tsp hot chilli powder

300g (10oz) broad beans, podded

1 fat garlic clove, chopped

200ml (7fl oz) water

2 sprigs fresh oregano, leaves only

salt and freshly ground pepper, to taste

juice of 1 lemon

6 slices bread, toasted and halved

- Heat 2 teaspoons of oil in a frying pan, add the cumin and chilli powder and cook for 1 minute. Add the beans, garlic and water. Simmer for 5 minutes.
- Using a slotted spoon, transfer the beans to a blender, reserving the cooking liquid. Blend the beans with the oregano until roughly chopped, then, with the motor running, gradually add almost all of the remaining olive oil. Thin the mixture down with 90–120ml (3–4fl oz) of the cooking liquid to give it a dipping consistency.
- Season with salt and pepper and add lemon juice to taste. Drizzle over the remaining olive oil, and serve with toast or pitta chips.

## BROAD BEAN, LIME & CORIANDER DIP

**SERVES 6-8**

Here's another dip with different spices and herbs added. Like the previous dip, it is very easy to make. Try them both.

500g (1lb 2oz) broad beans, podded

grated zest and juice of 2 limes

2 tsp sea salt

freshly ground black pepper, to taste

2 tsp freshly ground coriander

100ml (3½fl oz) olive oil

handful of fresh basil, chopped

handful of fresh parsley, chopped

2 salad onions, chopped

extra virgin olive oil, for drizzling

2 tsp black onion seeds

2 handfuls of chopped mixed fresh parsley, basil and salad onion

- Cook the beans in boiling water for 5 minutes. Drain, reserving the cooking liquid.
- Put the beans and the rest of the dip ingredients into a food processor and process until smooth. Add enough of the reserved cooking liquid to make a dipping consistency. Taste and adjust the seasoning.
- Drizzle with olive oil and sprinkle with the onion seeds and mixed herbs and salad onion. Serve with toast or pitta chips.

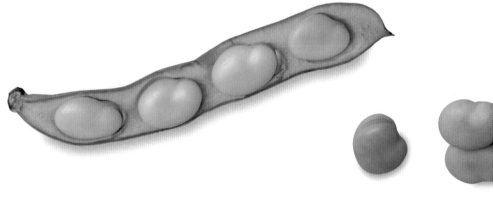

## POTATO WEDGES WITH GREMOLATA

**SERVES 8**

This a great way to use parsley, preferably the flat-leaf variety. Simple baked potato wedges are tossed in a parsley, lemon and garlic mixture to give you an entirely different accompaniment to your Sunday roast, or a good party snack. The parsley mix is also a wonderful topping for fish or meat. It will keep in the fridge for a couple of days or you can freeze it.

> 4 large potatoes, unpeeled, cut into wedges
>
> 2 tbsp olive oil
>
> salt
>
> handful of flat-leaf parsley with stalks, very finely chopped
>
> pared zest of 2 lemons, very finely chopped
>
> 3 garlic cloves, very finely chopped
>
> 1 tsp black peppercorns, very finely crushed

- Preheat oven to 180°C/350°F/gas 4.
- Place the potato wedges in a baking tray, pour over the oil and sprinkle with a little salt. Toss to coat. Bake for 1 hour or until tender and crisp.
- Meanwhile, make the gremolata by combining all the remaining ingredients with ¼ teaspoon of salt and mixing together well. (Alternatively, put all the ingredients unchopped into a food processor and process until finely chopped and combined. This will make a finer topping.)
- Take the potatoes out of the oven, add the gremolata and toss well. Serve immediately.

## WHITE FISH WITH PARSLEY & WINE

**SERVES 4**

A delicious fish dish using masses of fresh parsley. Parsley overwinters extremely well and you should always have a row handy as it is high in vitamin C and a very welcome addition to the stored vegetables you are using up. The fish is layered with onions, leeks, potatoes and parsley with the wine poured over. This is a dish to serve as a one-pot quick lunch.

> 5 tbsp olive oil
>
> 1 onion, chopped
>
> 1 leek, white part only, chopped
>
> 3 garlic cloves, finely chopped
>
> 4 tbsp chopped fresh parsley
>
> 5 large potatoes, peeled and thinly sliced
>
> salt and freshly ground pepper, to taste
>
> 100ml (3½fl oz) water
>
> 1kg (2¼lb) hake, cod or any other firm white fish fillet or steak, cut into large pieces
>
> plain flour, to coat
>
> 150ml (5fl oz) dry white wine

- Heat the olive oil in a flameproof casserole or sauté pan. Add the onion and leek and fry on a low heat until they are golden brown and translucent.
- Add the garlic, parsley, sliced potatoes and a seasoning of salt and pepper. Pour in the water. Simmer until the potatoes are nearly cooked – this takes about 20 minutes, depending on the thickness of the potato slices.
- Coat the fish pieces in flour and add them to the casserole. Shake the casserole once the fish has been added, to prevent sticking.
- Pour the white wine over the fish and simmer over a low heat for about 10 minutes until the fish is cooked. Serve immediately.

## GOOSEBERRY JOY

**SERVES 4**

This dessert can be made in late spring with unripe gooseberry thinnings and again later in summer when the fruit is ripe – the flavour and colour of the end result will be quite different.

> 675g (1½lb) gooseberries, topped and tailed
>
> 85–115g (3–4oz) caster sugar
>
> 60g (2oz) unsalted butter
>
> 85g (3oz) breadcrumbs
>
> 2 eggs, lightly beaten

- Preheat oven to 180°C/350°F/gas 4.
- Cook the gooseberries in a saucepan with the sugar and a little water until soft. Remove from the heat. Stir the butter into the hot fruit, then leave to cool.
- Add the breadcrumbs and eggs to the gooseberries and mix well. Transfer to a pie dish or baking dish and bake for 35–40 minutes. Lovely served hot or cold.

# early summer
## setting the scene

As the longest day approaches, plant behaviour subtly changes. Crops respond to lengthening or shortening days in various ways – some, like onions, switch perceptibly from leaf development to storage mode as they begin laying down food in their bulbs to fuel winter dormancy and next year's growth. Midsummer also heralds the season of plenty, with many early crops maturing in quantity. Celebrate with a festive platter of every different kind of young vegetable, followed by a salad of fresh soft fruits sweetened with elderflowers or sweet cicely and decorated with borage flowers and calendula petals. They are all there now for picking.

**Low-maintenance beds and wide paths help when tending the plot at busy times of year.**

### IN SEASON NOW
asparagus, berries (hybrid), broad beans, cabbages (spring/summer), calabrese, carrots, cauliflowers (summer), chard, cherries, endive, gooseberries, kohlrabi, lamb's lettuce, land cress, lettuces, onions (bulbing), peas, perpetual spinach, potatoes, radishes, raspberries, rhubarb, salad onions, spinach (summer), strawberries, turnips

### SOW NOW
**nursery bed** perennial herbs, winter brassicas
**outdoors** beetroot, carrots, chard, chicory (forcing/heading), endive, French beans, herbs (annual), kale, kohlrabi, land cress, lettuces, oriental greens, parsley, peas, perpetual spinach, radishes, runner beans, salad onions, squashes, swedes, sweetcorn, sweet fennel, turnips, winter radishes

### PLANT NOW
**indoors/cold frame** celery (self-blanching), melons, sweet potatoes, tomatoes
**outdoors** brassicas (autumn/winter), Brussels sprouts, celeriac, celery, cucumbers, globe artichokes, leeks, lettuces, melons, peppers, sprouting broccoli, squashes, strawberries, sweetcorn, tomatoes

# SEASONAL TASKS

**GETTING READY TO WATER** Throughout the UK, rainfall has become more variable and unpredictable during the past 20 years, and further surprises are likely with climate change taking effect. It would be sensible to review the way we water plants, adopting rainfall capture and water conservation as a habit rather than an occasional drought measure. However, a lot depends on where you live: for example, less than 10 per cent of rainfall in western Scotland is lost by evaporation, compared with 70 per cent in southeast England.

The first priority must be to maximize the soil's water storage capacity to help it absorb rainfall and then retain it for as long as possible. When watering becomes essential, this should be targeted where it is used most efficiently. There are several beneficial ways to use and conserve water wisely.

**MAKING A RAIN POND**

A pond of any kind, even a bowl sunk in the ground, is an allotment asset, encouraging carnivorous allies, like toads and newts, to help reduce pest levels. A rain pond combines these virtues with capturing rainfall and increasing irrigation supplies. Trap rain initially in water butts, duct the overflow to extra adjacent containers and, finally, lead surplus water from these to a pond made with a pre-formed unit or flexible liner. Plant at least half the edge with a few native marginal flowers to attract wildlife, and make sure one end of the pond is left clear and deep enough to dip in an occasional watering can in emergencies.

- Add plenty of organic matter, dug in or as a mulch, to soak up rainfall and help it infiltrate the soil.
- Increase cultivated soil depth with raised beds or imported topsoil.
- Dig heavier ground deeply every few years to admit more water to the subsoil.
- Reduce soil disturbance and conserve soil moisture by minimal cultivation: mulch bare soil or sow cover crops, such as green manure or prostrate vegetables.
- Time major cultivation for when soil moisture levels are high but the surface dry.
- Cover prepared beds with polythene in hot weather, and leafy crops with fleece to reduce transpiration (loss of water through the leaves).
- Transplant through sheet mulches of damp newspapers, cardboard or landscape fabric.
- Study individual crop needs: some require moist soil throughout, others only at critical growth stages.
- Fit guttering to sheds, greenhouses and fences to duct rainwater into tanks and butts, and capture the overflow in a pond (*see box, left*).

**Reduce soil disturbance in summer by sowing as many crops as possible in situ, then thinning the seedlings rather than transplanting them from elsewhere.**

**TRANSPLANTING TECHNIQUES** Crops like late leeks or winter- and spring-maturing brassicas need transplanting if they have been grown in trays or a nursery bed. Moving them to their final growing positions by the longest day means that they will make maximum growth before light and warmth levels start to decline. Although transplanting bare-root plants damages the root system, you can encourage rapid recovery by moving them at an earlier rather than late stage: 5–6-week-old brassica seedlings settle in faster than those 8–12 weeks old, for example.

Help transplants settle in effortlessly by tucking them up in congenial surroundings so that they don't have to work hard: research shows that struggling roots send hormone signals to the shoots, retarding and even suppressing their development to maintain a growth equilibrium. Make sure the ground has been loosened to a fork's depth a few weeks previously; use a fork or trowel rather than a dibber (which can firm and polish the sides of the planting holes). Clear their intended sites of weeds and crop residues, fork or rake in a dressing of balanced organic fertilizer (not too much nitrogen), and water the ground first if it is dry – transplanting into dusty soil is tedious and frustrating. Water plants thoroughly beforehand and then transfer them to final spacings, ideally during a showery spell or in the evening to reduce transplant shock. Water them in when you finish with a dilute liquid feed and then mulch all round to trap the moisture. In hot, dry weather, 'puddle' transplants in by flooding them in their holes with water just before refilling with soil, and cover leafy transplants with upturned pots during the day for 2–3 days to help them establish quickly.

**Don't waste surplus seedlings.** *Dibble in* **extra leeks close together to use as flavouring or soup ingredients when they're the size of salad onions. Most spare brassicas will make leafy greens if lined out 5–8cm (2–3in) apart or transplanted in small bundles.**

ask the EXPERT

Intercropping makes the most of temporarily empty space.

**ENSURING CONTINUITY** It is important to keep future supplies in sight. Enjoy present successes, but make sure it continues that way. As each batch of a crop that needs repeated sowing (lettuces, radishes, peas, spinach, for example) emerges above ground, make plans to sow the next lot within the week. For vegetables with a longer season (potatoes, runner beans, courgettes), remember which crop you intended should follow in that piece of ground and sow in good time so that plants are ready to take the place of the exhausted crop as it is cleared. For example, early potatoes can be lifted soon and, depending on your rotation plan, could be followed immediately with young leeks, autumn cabbages or Italian sprouting broccoli, all sown about 6 weeks ago.

Maximize your use of space by intercropping (filling the gaps between rows) with fast-growing compact vegetables, like radishes, turnips, kohlrabi, salad onions and cutting lettuce: they take up little room and may be sown between rows of slower-growing maincrops while these are still small. Young plants, like Brussels sprouts or purple sprouting broccoli, can be transplanted between rows of a crop that has nearly finished picking – spring cabbage or first early peas, for example.

Another option is undercropping, using prostrate vegetables like asparagus peas, New Zealand spinach and trailing squashes tucked as groundcover under vegetables that do not cast heavy shade – sweetcorn or leeks, for example. By shrouding the exposed soil, these crops help reduce hoeing, weeding and watering, while enhancing the total productivity of a limited space. Avoid teaming poor companions, such as onions and beans, though (*see box, below*).

**THINNING & PRUNING FRUIT** A favourable spring often leads to a heavy set of fruit that can overburden a tree or bush, resulting in masses of inferior fruit or, at worst, broken branches. The way to avoid problems is to pick off some of the crop while it is still small. Gooseberries are the only soft fruit that might need thinning. Plums often set lavishly and branches break easily, so thin to leave perfect fruits about 8cm (3in) apart. Reduce peaches and nectarines to single fruits 15cm (6in) apart, apples and pears to

**INCOMPATIBLE PARTNERS** Plants can actively alter their immediate environment so that some combinations of plants do not seem to work very well, perhaps because the cultivation or growth habit of one interferes with the other's or because of a chemical antipathy. Notable mismatches include beetroot and carrots or leeks; garlic with beans, peas or brassicas; onions and brassicas or peas; sweetcorn and beetroot or celery; tomatoes next to squashes, peas or turnips.

Keeping upright plants vertical is an essential part of their care routine, especially where crops are grown closely together or if hot, moist weather has encouraged soft, weak growth. Always provide support before it is needed: salvaging a collapsed row of peas, for example, can be long and heartbreaking, and recovery is rarely total. Enclose blocks of tall plants, like maincrop broad beans, with stakes and string, and prop up weak-stemmed crops, such as French beans, with twiggy sticks. Support climbers like runner beans, Japanese cucumbers and tall peas with strong canes or poles installed at planting time. Plants may need a little guidance so help them out with string, plastic twists or sweet pea rings before they are self-sufficient.

10–15cm (4–6in) after removing the largest fruitlet in clusters, plus any misshapes.

This is also the time to summer-prune trained forms of tree and bush fruits (cordons, fans, espaliers and similar restricted shapes) to fine-tune their performance, encourage more flower buds next season and control unwanted extension growth. As a basic routine, cut back all new sideshoots to about 5–6 leaves to check growth, and then shorten these further to just 1–2 buds in winter. Start around the longest day with gooseberries and red- and whitecurrants, move on to plums and cherries, and finish 3–4 weeks later with apples and pears.

**HARVESTING & PRUNING HERBS** Most annual and perennial herbs can be heavily cut 2–3 times during the season for immediate use, and this helps stimulate further and bushier growth, but when drying or freezing for winter supplies, the best time to harvest is just before flowering, when flavour is at its peak. Choose a dry morning for this, and start towards the end of spring with thyme and sage as their flower buds start to open.

Gardeners often chop off bundles from the topgrowth and then festoon them around the kitchen, which is ornamental but less than ideal for long-term quality: aromatic oils evaporate, distinctive scents dissipate or intermingle, and leaves become dusty, mouldy in the humidity or absorb off-flavours from cooking steam. A spare bedroom away from direct sunlight or an airy loft are preferable drying places. Alternatively, you can spread the herbs on perforated sheets of paper in a cool oven with the door ajar.

When they are fully dried – crisp and easily broken, but not crumbling to dust – pack them gently into dark airtight jars, and label with the variety and date harvested. Use until next year's crop is ready and then discard.

Herbs that dry well include apple-, pepper- and pineapple-mint, bay, bergamot, chamomile, clary sage, cotton lavender, curry plant, germander, helichrysum, horehound, hyssop, lavender, oregano, rosemary, tansy, thyme and winter savory. Chives, dill, fennel, parsley and tarragon are best frozen, as they retain better colour and nutritional value. Freeze in bunches in plastic bags or chopped in ice-cube trays topped with water.

Instead of harvesting herbs now for drying, you can prune them. Fresh herbs are almost always the best kind, but some deteriorate after flowering unless they're cut back to promote new growth. Chives and all the mints benefit from this mid-season trim, as does lemon balm,

Drying herbs on a low heat (*above*) or freezing them in ice-cube trays (*right*) keeps a year's supply to hand.

a favourite for infusing as a herb tea, which tastes best when made with fresh young leaves and shoot tips. Simply trim some or most plants to about 10cm (4in) high, and water well if the ground is dry. Rejuvenated mint plants will be ready by early autumn to harvest for a winter supply of mint jelly; cut back again afterwards and lift a few roots to force in boxes indoors.

**When discarding old dried herbs, crumble the leaves and mix them all together into a dressing. Sprinkle over freshly sown seeds or alongside thinned seedlings to confuse pests.**

ask the
EXPERT

### TRY THIS...

Always give vegetables the chance to crop again after their main harvest: cutting broad beans down to 8–10cm (3–4in) as they finish about now could stimulate flowering sideshoots; removing flowering shoots from overwintered crops like kale and broccoli encourages more growth; and leaving a 5cm (2in) cabbage stump etched with a deep cross will result in several new leafy heads.

### IT'S NOT TOO LATE TO...

Sow perpetual spinach to crop from mid-autumn right through until spring. Sow at stations between broad beans as these are finishing, cut down the bean haulm (stem) and leave the roots to rot and feed the spinach.

### IF YOU HAVE TIME...

*Propagate* and renew older perennial herbs by taking soft cuttings from lush shoot ends and rooting them in pots in a propagator or inside plastic bags (*see left*). Alternatively, wait until after midsummer and take semi-hardwood cuttings from firmer shoot tips and root in a cool greenhouse or cold frame.

## PADRON PEPPERS

The Spanish can't get enough of these pretty peppers. They grow them in vast quantities, and serve them simply grilled with olive oil and salt as tapas. They are very easy to grow, but in our climate must be started off under glass. Plant out when they are growing strongly and the ground has warmed up. Crop fruits when they are around 5cm (2in) long, but beware: most are very mild but every so often a fierce one creeps in that might blow your head off – a Spanish version of 'Russian Roulette'!

# HARVEST HIGHLIGHTS

**COURGETTES** If early sowing indoors and vigilance against frost and slugs result in the safe production of the first precocious courgettes, treat them as treasure: lightly steam them in halves or quarters, or stir-fry in butter or dripping so they retain a little crunchiness (these make excellent croutons to float in soups). When well fed and watered, plants are so prolific that their non-stop supply can become an embarrassment later. Should profusion lead to boredom, try the flowers deep-fried in batter, stuffed or added to risottos, or collect several fruits for making courgette cake or bulking up jams in place of apples – you may need to add pectin. (*See also page 198.*)

**GLOBE ARTICHOKES** Young plants will head up in a couple of months, but established clumps start ripening their fat heads very soon, the biggest in the centre surrounded by smaller satellites. For large heads, thin to leave 3–4 top branches. Cut the smaller heads when 4–5cm (1½–2in) across, leaving the terminal artichoke to expand further – cut this while still soft and just starting to open. Mulch the harvested plants with a good layer of compost or manure, and you could be blessed with a second (lighter) crop in early autumn. (*See also page 208.*)

**PARSLEY** Restricting parsley to the feeble role of garnish or chopped greenery in sauces ignores the wider value of its distinctive flavour. You could sow a modest potful in late winter and another in midsummer for meagre pickings all year, or grow the stuff with a flourish: sow a lavish hedge in a vegetable bed, thin the emergent seedlings to 10–15cm (4–6in) apart to produce armfuls to harvest for fritters, soups or wine – 450g (1lb) of parsley makes a gallon of light table wine. Explore varieties for their individual flavours rather than appearance. If you can do without crisp curls, flat-leaf continental (French/Italian) kinds are often more aromatic or pungent, although this depends as much on local climate as type. (*See also page 213.*)

**PEAS** The first pods of the season could be ready for picking a month before the longest day from a late winter sowing under cloches or (in mild districts) an overwintered crop sown in mid-autumn. The round-seeded varieties commonly used, such as 'Feltham First', 'Meteor' and 'Pilot' are not the sweetest, but they are productive and still taste wonderful after a long winter. Try hardy 'Douce

**Courgette 'Green Tricolour'**

**Flat-leaf parsley**

## VERSATILE BROAD BEANS

This essential crop has a number of varied uses:

► Pinch off shoot tips when the first flowers show, and cook as a green vegetable.

► Pick the earliest pods before the seeds show and cook whole or sliced like French beans.

► Shell larger pods, freeze smaller seeds and cook the others to eat hot or cold.

► Cook and blend very large seeds to use in hearty soups.

► Fry very large seeds to split the skins, then salt them to make a crunchy snack.

► Save ripe seeds to sow as green manure or the next season's crop.

## BEWARE THE HEAT!

The strong sun, allied with drying winds and lack of rain, can quickly evaporate the soil's store of water and transform prepared beds into barren dust-baths in no time at all. Under glass, the dangers from hot, bright sunshine are enhanced, and plants can suffer seriously unless you take steps to moderate the heat and increase humidity. Although nights may still be chilly and many days genial, toiling in the midday sun can be reckless. Save exertion for early morning or evening, and relax through a hot siesta-time by gently picking or summer pruning fruit. And wear a hat and sunscreen!

**Pea 'Ezethas Krombek Blauwschok'**

Provence' for extra flavour and sweetness, or pick the first crop while very young for best quality, and look forward to the stars of the main midsummer crop with their tender, sweet wrinkled seeds to eat raw in salads or lightly cook with rice and shreds of good ham. (*See also page 189.*)

**POTATOES** As soon as you see the first flowers on early potato plants, carefully explore the soil under a few plants to test the size of tubers. Sometimes only one or two are large enough to use, but you could collect enough for a boiling from the row, firming the soil back in place afterwards to leave the rest to fatten. Once a plant is in full bloom, it is usually ready to lift – use a fork inserted well away from the centre of the plant to avoid spearing the best tubers, and lever the whole clump of stems out of the ground. Then tease through the spot to retrieve any still lurking below. Ideally, leave the tubers for a day so their skins dry and firm up to avoid disintegration in the pot. (*See also page 184.*)

**RASPBERRIES & STRAWBERRIES** These soft fruits always taste finer when fully ripe and still warm from the sun. Modern varieties are bred to travel well and linger on shelves, at the expense of flavour and texture, whereas growing your own allows classic kinds such as 'Royal Sovereign' or 'Aromel' strawberries and 'Malling Jewel' or 'Golden Everest' raspberries to hold their own as gourmet crops. Protect from birds and squirrels, check daily in hot weather, and garner freely. Surplus can be frozen, bottled, jammed or turned into desserts. (*See also page 217.*)

# EAT NOW

A landmark season leading up to the longest day, the cue for plants to fill out and bear fruit and for gardeners to celebrate a time of plenty: it is hard to go hungry in summer. Beans and peas are fattening in their pods, shallots – most exclusive of all the onions – start to turn colour as they ripen, and the first new potatoes should be ready, buried treasure that deserves to be enjoyed by the reverent plateful, unadulterated but for fresh mint and melting butter. Above all, it is the start of the soft fruit season as strawberries, raspberries and gooseberries colour in the sun, and soon, most luscious of all, gleaming red- and whitecurrants. Feast on them fresh and jealously preserve the rest to brighten the dark days of winter. Weeds are growing, too, and deserve exploring as wild foods while they are still young, whether for eating raw in salads or cooked in that classic peasant dish, lettuce and weed soup. (*See* In season now, *page 64.*)

## RECIPES

seasonal planner

## FOUR SALAD DRESSINGS FOR LETTUCE

### SERVES 4

Lettuce is an easy, easy salad to grow. By all means grow cut-and-come-again varieties, but don't forget that a simple salad of cos lettuce has a really cleansing feel on the palate – when freshly picked there is nothing quite like it. A cos salad makes a good starter with cured meats or to have after your main course.

Here are four different dressings for a simple green salad. The lettuce base is the same: a crisp cos (remove the outer, tougher leaves, then wash, dry and tear – not cut – into shreds).

### Dressing 1

This simple dressing is for a salad with the addition of chives. These give a subtle onion flavour.

  4 tbsp extra virgin olive oil
  2 tbsp white wine vinegar
  salt and freshly ground pepper, to taste
  1 tbsp snipped fresh chives

- Mix the oil, vinegar and seasoning until emulsified. Toss with the lettuce and sprinkle the chives on top.

### Dressing 2

The second dressing is for a salad with the addition of nasturtium flowers (*see page 98*). They give a peppery taste and a pretty contrast to the green of the leaves.

  4 tbsp extra virgin olive oil
  2 tbsp tarragon vinegar
  2 tsp capers, finely chopped
  pinch of caster sugar
  salt and freshly ground pepper, to taste
  12 nasturtium flowers

- Mix together all the ingredients, except the flowers, until emulsified. Pour over the lettuce and toss. Add the flowers and serve.

### Dressing 3

This favourite Italian dressing includes hard-boiled eggs and uses white balsamic vinegar. (You could substitute white wine vinegar but don't be tempted to use black balsamic, as it will muddy the dressing.)

  4 tbsp extra virgin olive oil
  2 hard-boiled eggs, finely chopped
  1 tsp Dijon mustard
  2 tbsp white balsamic vinegar
  salt and freshly ground pepper, to taste

- Beat 1 tablespoon of oil with the hard-boiled eggs. Add the remaining ingredients and mix well. Toss with the lettuce.

### Dressing 4

This Greek-style dressing uses lemon juice instead of vinegar, and is for a salad made up of lettuce, rocket, sorrel and salad onions.

  3 tbsp extra virgin olive oil
  pinch of caster sugar
  2 tbsp lemon juice
  salt and freshly ground pepper, to taste
  handful of rocket leaves, shredded
  handful of sorrel leaves, shredded
  2 salad onions, finely chopped

- Mix the oil, sugar, lemon juice and seasoning until well emulsified. Combine the lettuce, rocket, sorrel and salad onions, pour over the dressing and toss together.

It's important to use extra virgin olive oil for these dressings. Don't stint on this – a salad dressing is not the place for cheap oils. If you find extra virgin olive oil too strong in flavour, you can mix it with some sunflower oil, but do try to avoid this.

## LETTUCE SPRING ROLLS

### SERVES 8

This uses not only the herbs and early lettuces you have grown but also a selection of seed sprouts (*see page 172*), which will give you an enormous vitamin boost. Pea sprouts work very well here and add a delicious crunchiness. Alternatively, beetroot sprouts add colour and an earthiness to the mixture.

  1 tbsp rice vinegar or white wine vinegar
  1 tsp caster sugar
  1 salad onion, both white and green parts, shredded
  1 large carrot, grated
  1 small cucumber, peeled and grated
  225g (8oz) fresh pea, bean or beetroot sprouts
  60g (2oz) fresh basil, chopped
  60g (2oz) fresh coriander, chopped
  2 tbsp chopped fresh mint
  16 large crisp lettuce leaves (Webb's or similar)

- Mix the vinegar and sugar in a small bowl, stirring to dissolve the sugar.
- Mix together all other ingredients, except the lettuce leaves, in a large bowl. Stir in the vinegar mixture.
- Place a lettuce leaf flat on the work surface and make a pile of the salad mixture in the middle. Fold in the sides, top and bottom of the leaf to enclose the filling. Carefully roll up and secure with a cocktail stick. Repeat with the remaining lettuce leaves and the rest of the filling.
- Serve with a spicy salsa or a peanut satay sauce.

early summer: eat now

73

# FRESH PEA SOUP

**SERVES 6**

Freshly picked peas make the most mouthwatering soup. There is nothing quite like this brilliant green soup to make you realize summer is really here.

120ml (4fl oz) vegetable oil

250g (9oz) onions, finely chopped

3 garlic cloves, finely chopped

175g (6oz) young carrots, finely chopped

225g (8oz) potatoes, finely chopped

115g (4oz) young fennel, finely chopped

1.5 litres (2¾ pints) vegetable or chicken stock

550g (1¼lb) fresh peas, podded

2 tbsp chopped fresh flat-leaf parsley

salt and freshly ground pepper, to taste

- Heat the oil in a large saucepan. Add the onions and garlic and cook until soft and translucent. Add the carrots, potatoes and fennel and cook for 15 minutes or until tender.
- In another saucepan, bring the stock to the boil. Add half the peas and cook for 4 minutes. Lift out the peas with a sieve and put them in a food processor or blender. Process until smooth. Add the puréed peas and 180ml (6fl oz) of the cooking liquid to the pan of vegetables. Stir well.
- Cook for another 15 minutes. Add the remaining peas and the parsley, season and serve immediately.

# LETTUCE & WEED SOUP

**SERVES 4**

A slightly offbeat but delicious early summer soup, this uses up lettuce even when it's bolting and is fortified with a selection of the choicer weeds.

1 large lettuce or the equivalent in loose leaves

225g (8oz) mixed leaves from young nettles, sorrel, groundsel and chickweed

30g (1oz) butter

225g (8oz) onions, sliced

1 garlic clove, chopped

450ml (15fl oz) water

½ tsp yeast extract

freshly ground black pepper, to taste

2 tbsp chopped fresh parsley

- Shred or chop the lettuce and weeds into small pieces.
- Melt the butter in a saucepan and cook the onions and garlic gently until soft and translucent.
- Press the lettuce and mixed weeds into the onions. Cover and cook gently for 10 minutes.
- Add the water and yeast extract and stir to mix. Bring to the boil. Season with pepper, then simmer for about 30 minutes, stirring occasionally.
- Stir in the parsley just before serving.

# SUMMER SALAD SOUP

**SERVES 6**

This is a very surprising soup. Although cooking lettuce and cucumber sounds odd, both crops keep their bite, and the soup looks very fresh and pretty.

1 medium potato, peeled and diced

1 medium onion, sliced

1 litre (1¾ pints) vegetable or chicken stock

340g (12oz) fresh peas, podded

1 lettuce, shredded

300ml (10fl oz) single cream

juice of ½ lemon

salt and white pepper, to taste

1 small cucumber, peeled, deseeded and diced

- In a saucepan combine the potato, onion and half the stock. Bring slowly to the boil, then cover and simmer for 15 minutes until the vegetables are soft. Add the peas and cook for a further 3–4 minutes, then add half the lettuce.
- Purée in a blender or food mill and return to the pan with the remaining stock. Simmer for a few minutes, then remove from the heat. Add the cream and lemon juice and season with salt and finely ground white pepper. Fold in the cucumber and the remaining lettuce. Serve chilled.

## GLUT BUSTER
### COURGETTES

Courgettes have a habit of coming all at once no matter how you try to stage them. They can also grow from very small to very large practically overnight – and suddenly you have marrows. Here are some recipes to show the versatility of the courgette, from a simple salad to a rich and moist courgette chocolate cake, with some classics thrown in for good measure.

## COURGETTE & MINT SALAD

**SERVES 4**

Use small courgettes and a vegetable peeler with a swivel blade to get wafer thin slices. Using them raw is not so strange – they keep their crispness and taste delicious.

450g (1lb) courgettes
3 tbsp olive oil
2 tbsp white balsamic vinegar
handful of fresh mint leaves, chopped
salt and freshly ground pepper, to taste

● Trim the courgettes but don't peel and, using a vegetable peeler, shave off long, translucent strips.
● Spread out the strips on kitchen paper to drain off some of the excess liquid, then transfer to a shallow dish. Add the oil, vinegar, mint and seasoning. Leave to marinate in the fridge for a few hours before serving.

## COURGETTE BALLS

**SERVES 6**

These make an excellent supper dish served hot and crisp with a tomato salad. Or serve with a fresh yoghurt dip for a snack, which is very popular with children.

450g (1lb) courgettes, sliced
1 slice stale bread, about 2.5cm (1 in) thick
3 large floury, potatoes, boiled
2 onions, grated
½ tsp chopped fresh mint
2 tsp chopped fresh parsley
salt and freshly ground pepper, to taste
110g (4oz) Parmesan or Kefalotiri cheese, grated
1 egg, lightly beaten
olive oil, for frying

● Steam the courgettes over boiling water until tender. Drain in a colander for about an hour, mashing them to remove excess liquid.
● Cut the crust from the bread, then soak in a little water and squeeze dry. Purée with the remaining ingredients, except the cheese and egg, until the consistency is fine.
● Mix in the cheese and egg. Taking a spoonful of the mixture at a time, form into little flat cakes using your floured hands. Fry in hot olive oil until golden. Drain on kitchen paper.
● Serve with Moroccan tomato salad (*see page 98*).

## COURGETTE SOUFFLÉ

**SERVES 6**

This is a Mediterranean recipe that uses larger courgettes. Although it is called a soufflé, it doesn't have the usual butter, flour and milk base. This makes it light and delicious and also very easy to make. Just don't expect it to be as risen as a normal soufflé. Can be used as a starter or light lunch with a salad.

900g (2lb) courgettes, scraped and sliced
110g (4oz) butter
3 eggs, separated
170g (6oz) Kefalotiri, Pecorino or Parmesan cheese, grated
grated nutmeg
salt and freshly ground pepper, to taste

● Steam the courgettes until tender. Mash them in a colander and leave to drain for about an hour.
● Preheat oven to 200°C/400°F/gas 6. Butter six individual soufflé dishes or ramekins.
● Transfer the courgettes to a bowl and mix in the butter, egg yolks and 150g (5oz) of the grated cheese. Season with a grating of nutmeg, salt and pepper.
● In another bowl, whisk the egg whites until stiff. Fold into the courgette mixture. Pour into the dishes and sprinkle the top of each with the remaining grated cheese. Cook for 30 minutes until the soufflés are set, slightly risen and lightly browned. Serve hot.

## SAUTÉED COURGETTES WITH MINT

**SERVES 4-6**

If you can, mix the colours of your courgettes – they come in shades of green, orange and yellow. The taste will be the same, but it will look very pretty. When sautéing, don't crowd the courgettes and they will brown faster.

  3 tbsp olive oil

  1 garlic clove, chopped

  1 onion, thinly sliced

  4 medium courgettes, cut into 1cm (½in) pieces

  ¼ tsp finely chopped, deseeded chilli

  1 tbsp freshly squeezed lemon juice

  salt and freshly ground pepper, to taste

  7g (¼oz) fresh mint leaves, cut into thin strips

- Heat half the olive oil in a large frying pan over a medium-low heat. Add the garlic and onion and cook for about 2 minutes or until translucent, but still a bit crunchy.
- Raise the heat a bit and add the remaining olive oil along with the courgettes and chilli. Sauté until the courgettes and onion are tender and golden brown, stirring occasionally.
- Remove from the heat, stir in the lemon juice and season with salt and pepper. Transfer to a warmed dish, sprinkle over the mint and serve.

## COURGETTE CASSEROLE

**SERVES 6-8**

If your courgettes become a bit oversized, grating them and making them into a casserole, as the Greeks do, makes them very palatable, especially if you drain away some, but not all, of the liquid produced. This makes an ideal light lunch or a vegetable side dish with steaks or chops. The inclusion of breadcrumbs means that another carbohydrate will be unnecessary.

  900g (2lb) courgettes, coarsely grated

  1 garlic clove, chopped

  2 small onions, chopped

  115g (4oz) butter

  115g (4oz) breadcrumbs

  225g (8oz) fresh parsley, chopped

  3 eggs, lightly beaten

  salt and freshly ground pepper, to taste

  110g (4oz) Parmesan cheese, freshly grated

- Preheat oven to 180°C/350°F/gas 4. Butter a 20cm (8in) square baking dish, with about 1.5 litre (2¾ pint) capacity. Set aside.
- Put the courgettes in a colander and leave to drain.
- Meanwhile, sauté the garlic and onions in the butter until soft.
- Add the grated, drained courgettes, breadcrumbs, parsley and eggs to the onion. Mix together well. Season with salt and pepper.
- Pour into the buttered dish and cover the top with the Parmesan. Bake for about 45 minutes until the top is brown and crisp. Serve immediately.

## COURGETTE CHOCOLATE CAKE

**MAKES ONE 25CM (10IN) SQUARE CAKE**

This recipe comes from Halcyon (*see page 219*) who runs a brilliant organic vegetable business. Courgettes make the cake very moist, but not vegetabley. There seem to be a lot of ingredients, but it ends up as a lovely gooey chocolate cake that can be eaten hot or cold with custard, cream or ice cream. Who's counting the calories?

  125g (4½oz) soft unsalted butter

  115g (4oz) soft light brown sugar

  2 small eggs

  310g (11oz) plain flour

  1 tsp pure vanilla extract

  110ml (4fl oz) plain yoghurt

  2 tsp bicarbonate of soda

  ½ tsp mixed spice

  30g (1oz) cocoa powder

  1 tsp ground cinnamon

  ½ tsp salt

  340g (12oz) courgettes, grated

  225g (8oz) bar of plain chocolate, broken into small pieces

- Preheat oven to 170°C/325°F/gas 3. Prepare a 25cm (10in) square tin by greasing it and lining it with two crossways strips of baking parchment.
- Beat the butter with the sugar until light and creamy. Add the eggs, one at a time, with a spoonful of the flour to prevent the mixture from curdling. Add the vanilla extract and yoghurt and mix well.
- Sift the remaining flour with the other dry ingredients. Stir into the mixture with the grated courgettes. Turn into the tin. Sprinkle the surface with the chocolate.
- Bake for 45 minutes or until the centre of the cake is firm and an inserted skewer comes out clean.

## ARTICHOKES IN OLIVE OIL

### SERVES 4

This dish makes a perfect light lunch, or can be a starter for six. It should be eaten cold but not chilled.

12 globe artichokes

6 lemons, halved (for preparation)

12 shallots, peeled

600ml (1 pint) water

300ml (10fl oz) olive oil

salt and freshly ground pepper, to taste

12 small new potatoes, peeled

12 young carrots, scraped

2 tbsp chopped fresh dill or fennel

2 tsp cornflour

- Prepare the artichokes as for the Artichokes with broad beans (*see right*).
- Put the shallots in a large saucepan with the water and bring to the boil. Add the olive oil and season with salt and pepper. Put in the potatoes, then the carrots and, lastly, the artichokes, placing them with their heads down. If necessary, add a little more water so the artichokes are just covered.
- Cut a round of greaseproof paper to fit the pan, make a hole in the middle to let the steam escape and place over the artichokes before putting on the lid. (This will help them keep their colour.) Cook gently for 10 minutes.
- Sprinkle in the dill. Cover again and cook until the artichokes are tender – this should take about an hour. Remove the artichokes with care using a slotted spoon or tongs and arrange them on a serving dish with the shallots, potatoes and carrots.
- To thicken the cooking liquid into a sauce, mix the cornflour with a little water, then add to the pan. Cook for about 5 minutes, stirring well. Pour the sauce over the artichokes and leave to cool before serving.

## SUMMER VEGETABLE RAGOUT

### SERVES 4

You will only need the artichoke hearts for this, but don't waste the leaves – eat them separately with a dressing. This recipe uses the first of your cucumbers and lettuces. You will be eating them for rest of the summer.

4 globe artichokes

1 tbsp lemon juice

3 tbsp olive oil

2 green garlic cloves, chopped

1 bunch salad onions, trimmed and cut into chunks

225g (8oz) podded young broad beans

4 tbsp water

40g (1½oz) butter

2 mini cucumbers, peeled, deseeded and sliced

3 Little Gem lettuce hearts, quartered

salt and freshly ground pepper, to taste

pinch of fresh summer savory, finely chopped

1 tbsp finely chopped fresh chervil

- Put the artichokes in a pan of boiling salted water with the lemon juice. Cook for 40 minutes or until a leaf comes away easily. Drain and allow to cool. Once cold, strip the artichokes of their leaves. Scoop out their hairy chokes in the middle. Trim the hearts and cut into quarters.
- Heat the oil in a stainless steel pan. Add the garlic and onions and fry gently for 2–3 minutes. Add the beans, water and butter. Cover and simmer gently for 5 minutes.
- Mix in the cucumbers, lettuce and artichoke hearts. Season lightly. Increase the heat slightly, cover and cook for 3–4 minutes until tender. Stir in the chopped herbs, check the seasoning and serve.

## ARTICHOKES WITH BROAD BEANS

### SERVES 4

For this dish you must use the small variety of artichoke, which has a more delicate flavour and a smaller choke than the larger kind. Large artichokes are better served with a vinaigrette. This dish is equally good if garden peas are used instead of broad beans, in which case add 1 teaspoon of sugar.

12 small globe artichokes

6 lemons, halved, plus 1 tbsp lemon juice

700g (1½lb) podded broad beans

1 large bunch salad onions, chopped

2–3 tbsp chopped fresh dill

1 tsp chopped fresh mint

225ml (8fl oz) olive oil

salt and freshly ground pepper, to taste

- Remove all the tough outer leaves from each artichoke and slice off the pointed top of the inner leaves. Trim with a sharp knife, leaving about 2.5cm (1in) of stalk. As each artichoke is prepared, rub it all over with a lemon half and quickly throw into a bowl of salted water with the squeezed lemon half. This will help prevent discoloration.
- Put the beans, onions and herbs into a wide, shallow pan with the olive oil. Sauté gently for about 10 minutes. Put the artichokes, heads down, on top, season with salt and pepper and add the 1 tablespoon of lemon juice. Barely cover with water. Cut a round of greaseproof paper to fit the pan, place on the artichokes and press down gently with a heatproof plate being careful not to crush the up-turned stalks. Simmer very gently for about 1 hour. Remove from the heat and leave to stand for at least 30 minutes before serving.

## GLUT BUSTER
### SUMMER FRUIT

A fruit cage is an essential allotment accessory. In it you can grow the most fabulous raspberries, gooseberries, red- and whitecurrants and strawberries. You need to keep the fruit in a cage, because the birds will be as keen to eat the fruit as you are. Come early summer you will be feasting on the jewel-like fruits. Eat them simply with cream, or make sorbets and ice creams, jams and jellies, mousses, fools and crumbles. However, the time will come when you have had enough – you've made the puddings, frozen the excess, made those preserves and relishes. So now open the cage and let the birds in. After all, they deserve a treat, too – they have been eating those pesky bugs for you all year.

## JAMS & PRESERVES
### DOS AND DON'TS

- Before you start to make jam, wash the jars and sterilize in a low oven. Keep them hot until you are ready to bottle. If you sterilize the jars properly, jam will keep for at least a year.
- Always use good-quality fruit. Jams and preserves are not the place to use up bad-quality fruit.
- To test if the jam has reached setting point, place a teaspoonful on a chilled saucer and leave for 30 seconds. If it wrinkles when pushed with your finger, the jam is ready to be bottled. If not, continue to cook, testing every 3–4 minutes.
- After bottling and sealing in the hot, dry jars, wait until completely cold before labelling.

## BLACKCURRANT JAM

**MAKES ABOUT 6 JARS**

You can use black- or redcurrants for this jam. Both are high in pectin so it's easy to achieve a jellied set without boiling for a long time (boil too long and you'll lose the fresh taste of the berries). Aim for a loose consistency, which will happen as it cools. The jam can be used a day after making and it will keep for more than a year if stored properly (*see below left*).

2kg (4½lb) black- or redcurrants

1 litre (1¾ pints) water

2.25kg (5lb) granulated sugar, warmed in a bowl in a low oven

- Put the fruit in a preserving pan and cover with the cold water. Bring to the boil, then lower the heat and simmer gently until the fruit is just soft but still holding its shape.
- Add the warmed sugar. When it dissolves, increase the heat, give one stir and leave the jam to boil rapidly for about 10 minutes.
- Test for setting point (*see left*).
- Pour the jam into hot, dry sterilized jars and seal. Leave until completely cold before labelling.

## STRAWBERRY & ROSE PETAL JAM

**MAKES ABOUT 4 JARS**

Two gorgeous things emerge in early summer: strawberries and roses. What better use of both than putting them together to make a fragrant jam? (*See also page 98.*)

6 unsprayed, scented red or pink roses

1.25 kg (2¾lb) small strawberries

800g (1¾lb) preserving sugar, warmed in a bowl in a low oven

500ml (17fl oz) water

juice of 1 lemon

2 tbsp rose water (optional)

- Remove the petals from the roses and wash in cold water. Leave to dry. Cut off the bitter-tasting white base from each petal and discard, then set the rest aside.
- Hull the strawberries and put in a preserving pan with the sugar. Let the sugar dissolve slowly and stir frequently so that the granules do not catch on the bottom of the pan.
- Once the sugar has completely dissolved, add the water and increase the heat to bring the jam to the boil. Remove any scum that forms on the top using a large spoon. Boil quite fast over a medium heat for about 20 minutes, stirring, until the mixture begins to thicken.
- Test for setting point (*see left*).
- Once the jam has reached setting point, add the lemon juice, rose water (if using) and rose petals, then cook for a further 2–3 minutes. Remove from the heat and rest for 2 minutes (this will prevent the fruit from rising to the top of the jars once bottled).
- Pour the jam into hot, dry sterilized jars and seal. Leave until completely cold before labelling.

## STRAWBERRY MOUSSE

**SERVES 6**

This is one of the simplest but best ways to serve soft fruit – a mousse made from crushed, sweetened strawberries and whipped cream, with the addition of almond-tasting amaretti biscuits and Amaretto liqueur. There are endless possibilities here to use other fruit – raspberries would be ideal, but you could try peaches or any of the currants, as well as cooked gooseberries and rhubarb.

225ml (8fl oz) double or whipping cream

400g (14oz) strawberries, hulled and sliced, plus 3 strawberries, halved, to garnish

115g (4oz) caster sugar

55ml (2fl oz) Amaretto (optional)

6 amaretti biscuits, crushed

- Whip the cream until thick, then refrigerate.
- In a pan over a low heat, toss the strawberries with the sugar until it dissolves and the berries are lightly crushed. Remove from the heat and stir in the Amaretto (if using). Leave to cool to room temperature, then fold in the whipped cream.
- Serve in glass dishes with the crushed biscuits sprinkled on top and half a strawberry to garnish.

## RASPBERRY SORBET

**SERVES 6**

Raspberries make a delicious sorbet but this recipe could serve for any soft fruit, such as strawberries or redcurrants. The sugar syrup will be enough to make several other sorbets later.

500g (1lb 2oz) caster sugar

500ml (17fl oz) water

500g (1lb 2oz) raspberries

- To make the syrup, heat the sugar and water together gently until the sugar dissolves. Boil for 4 minutes, then cool. The syrup can be kept in a screw topped jar for up to 4 days.
- Purée the raspberries by pressing them through a nylon sieve (or blitz in a blender or food processor before sieving). Mix together the purée and 185ml (6½fl oz) of the sugar syrup. Freeze in an ice cream machine. Alternatively, freeze in a shallow dish; when the mixture crystallizes, break it up with a fork, electric mixer or food processor. Repeat this once or twice during freezing.
- Remove the sorbet from the freezer about 30 minutes before serving so it softens a little.

## PICKLED REDCURRANTS

**MAKES 1 JAR**

Instead of redcurrant jelly, try this pickled fruit. The tartness goes very well with pâté and with lamb.

300g (10oz) redcurrants

350ml (12fl oz) red wine vinegar

1 tbsp caster sugar

1 allspice berry

2 cloves

- Using a fork, strip the redcurrants from their sprigs into a bowl.
- Bring the vinegar to the boil in a small pan with the sugar, allspice berry and cloves. Simmer for 5 minutes, then remove from the heat and cool.
- Pack the redcurrants into one or more sterilized jars (*see opposite*) and pour over the cooled spiced vinegar. Seal and leave in a cool, dark place for about 4 weeks before serving.

## REDCURRANT RELISH

**SERVES 4**

Another alternative to redcurrant jelly, this relish is very quick to make. It will keep for a week or two in the fridge.

175g (6oz) redcurrants

2 tbsp caster sugar

2 tsp balsamic vinegar (white if possible)

grated zest and juice of 1 lime

1 tbsp finely chopped fresh parsley

- Strip the currants from their sprigs, but leave 3–4 strands intact for a garnish. Add the sugar, vinegar, lime zest (reserve a little for garnish) and lime juice to the currants. Mash lightly with a fork, then stir in the parsley. Serve garnished with lime zest and strands of redcurrants.

## CHERRY FRITTERS

### SERVES 4

Cherries have such a short season that you might think it is a sacrilege to cook them, but these hot little bundles will give you a complete surprise when you bite into them. Be warned: they are very moreish!

2 eggs

60g (2oz) plain flour

1 tbsp icing sugar

pinch of salt

1 tbsp dark rum

115g (4oz) butter

110ml (4fl oz) light vegetable oil

450g (1lb) fresh cherries with the stalks

extra icing sugar, for sprinkling

- Place the eggs, flour, icing sugar, salt and rum in a large mixing bowl and beat until smooth. Set aside to rest for 1 hour.
- Heat the butter and oil in a frying pan until hot.
- Holding the cherries by their stalks, dip them into the batter, then stand them up in the hot butter and oil. Reduce the heat to medium and fry the fritters, turning carefully by the stalks to make sure they become golden brown and crisp on all sides.
- Transfer the fritters to kitchen paper that has been sprinkled with icing sugar.
- Pile the fritters on a plate and sprinkle with more icing sugar. Serve immediately.

## RASPBERRY ROBBER

### SERVES 6

A light, rich celebration of favourite early summer fruits. Cooking raspberries seems to intensify their flavour.

450g (1lb) ripe raspberries

225ml (8fl oz) double or whipping cream

2 eggs

1 tbsp plain flour

1 tbsp caster sugar

- Preheat oven to 180°C/350°F/gas 4.
- Spread the raspberries in a baking dish and place in the oven to warm for about 10 minutes or until the juices begin to run.
- Meanwhile, put all the other ingredients in a bowl and whisk them together.
- Cover the raspberries with the mixture and return to the oven. Bake for about 20 minutes until the top is lightly browned. Serve warm.

## SUMMER FRUIT & NUT CRUMBLE

### SERVES 6-8

Adding nuts to a classic crumble mixture gives a delicious crunchy contrast to the sweet fruit filling. If you don't have a food processor, you can use ready-ground nuts, – add them with the sugar after the butter has been worked into the flour.

200g (7oz) cherries, stoned

400g (14oz) strawberries, hulled and halved

250g (9oz) raspberries

250g (9oz) blueberries

115g (4oz) caster sugar

**Crumble topping**

175g (6oz) plain flour

60g (2oz) whole unblanched hazelnuts or almonds

115g (4oz) very cold butter, diced

60g (2oz) caster sugar

- Preheat oven to 200°C/400°F/gas 6.
- Mix all of the fruit with the sugar and place in a 1.5 litre (2¾ pint) baking dish or eight small individual dishes.
- Put the flour and nuts into a food processor and blitz until the nuts are coarsely ground. Add the butter and pulse until the mixture looks like fine breadcrumbs. Mix in the sugar. Sprinkle evenly over the fruit and press down lightly.
- Bake for 25 minutes. After about 10 minutes, or as soon as the fruit filling starts to bubble, lower the temperature to 190°C/375°F/gas 5 and continue to bake until the crumble topping is golden (individual crumbles will need less time). Serve hot or warm with cream.

# setting the scene

This is transition time. Summer may be very much in evidence, with high humidity and sultry days making plants and gardeners visibly wilt, but ripening top fruit and the rich colours of the first autumn flowers insist that change is imminent. There are fewer sowings to do now, although some are crucial for later supplies – the emphasis is firmly on harvesting and storing the surplus. Make arrangements to cover any holidays – watering and picking may need frequent attention – and keep patrolling regularly for signs of pests and diseases, all of which will be having a final fling, especially in dry or torrid conditions.

**Dense late summer crop cover defends the soil against evaporation and discourages annual weeds.**

**IN SEASON NOW**

apples, aubergines, beetroot, berries (hybrid), blackberries, blueberries, broad beans, cabbages (summer), calabrese, carrots, cauliflowers (summer), celery, chard, cherries, cucumbers, currants (black, red, white), endive, French beans, garlic, globe artichokes, gooseberries, kohlrabi, lamb's lettuce, land cress, leeks, lettuce, melons, onions (bulbing), perpetual spinach, plums, potatoes, radishes, raspberries, runner beans, salad onions, shallots, spinach (summer), squashes, strawberries, sweetcorn, tomatoes, turnips, winter purslane

**SOW NOW**

**indoors** French beans (in pots)
**cold frame/nursery bed** cabbages (spring/red), kale
**outdoors** carrots, chard, chicory, endive, kohlrabi, lamb's lettuce, land cress, lettuces, onions (bulbing), oriental greens, perpetual spinach, radishes (summer/winter), sweet fennel, turnips, winter purslane

**PLANT NOW**

**indoors** autumn salads, potatoes (in pots)
**outdoors** cabbages (winter/spring), cauliflowers (winter/spring), kale, leeks, sprouting broccoli

# SEASONAL TASKS

**HARVESTING FRUIT FOR STORING** There is a certain amount of inevitability about fruit growing: a cold spring can result in a sparse or non-existent crop, whereas an ideal flowering season often leads to a glut. There is nothing we can do about shortages, while excess means finding ways to use up the surplus.

Fruits that keep well – mid-season apples and pears (plus quinces) last for 2–3 months, and later kinds for up to 8 months – are simply stored in boxes or trays in a cool, airy room no warmer than about 7°C (45°F), or on shelves in a dry, cool shed. They will also keep in clear plastic bags with the bottom two corners snipped off, up to about 2kg (4–5lb) per bag.

Almost all fruits can be frozen successfully, although strawberries and pears suffer in quality. Either freeze raw soon after picking, or prepare and cook them first for instant use later. Bottling is traditional, and visually satisfying as pantry shelves fill with the various types – the process cooks the fruit and changes its flavour, however.

**Gently lift ripe apples to test if they come away easily.**

---

**LIQUID GOLD**

In western cultures, urine, with its high nitrogen content and valuable amounts of other nutrients like potassium and phosphates, is a wasted resource. Tests show that European adults produce enough urine-based fertilizer to grow at least half their food, while NASA trials have successfully grown tomatoes and beans *hydroponically* in a solution of 0.5 per cent urine and water.

If you can (and are inclined to) save urine, keep it in a sealed container to prevent nutrient loss in the form of ammonia. Use as a feed for fruit, leafy crops that will be cooked, and compost plants like comfrey – mix 1 part urine to 3 parts water – or neat as a compost activator to speed up the decay of carbon-based materials like paper, cardboard, tree leaves and sawdust.

---

**STRAWBERRY MAINTENANCE** The end of the maincrop strawberry season is time to overhaul existing beds and establish new ones.

Plants are normally kept for 3 years, after which quality declines, although you might choose to wait an extra season: 4-year-old plants give huge crops of small berries, which are perfect for jam-making. After this, plants are scrapped, and a new row or bed planted up with fresh bought-in stock or your own runners, provided they are completely healthy and vigorous.

Cut back younger plants after fruiting, removing all their foliage, runners (unless needed) and mulching materials like straw or reusable mats. Compost plant debris and clean mats for storing. Give the shorn crowns a balanced feed to build them up for next season. Perpetual (everbearing) varieties will normally crop again this year, so do not cut these back.

When using your own runners to stock a new bed or row, select the strongest plantlets, usually the first to form on a runner and the nearest to the parent plant. Discard the others where there is plenty of choice. If you need every plantlet, even unrooted tips will form plants if cut off and pressed into pots or trays of compost in a greenhouse or cold frame.

A few large spare plantlets can be potted up now (or transferred to a nursery bed for potting later) to force for early pickings if brought into the greenhouse in late autumn. After they finish fruiting in early spring, you can plant them out to make a new row (where they will sometimes fruit again in autumn) and produce strong plants for the following year.

**THE VALUE OF GREEN MANURES** As crops mature and finish from this time of the year onwards, it is becoming common practice to fill the vacant ground with a green manure crop (although there is still time to sow a number of vegetables – *see page 90*). This is a domestic version of an agricultural ley, or break, crop, resting the ground from production while protecting its surface with vegetation that is eventually turned in to improve the soil's texture with organic matter, or 'humus'.

This is still the real value of a green manure, which adds relatively small amounts of nutrients compared with fertilizer, animal manure or garden compost. The most beneficial use of green manures is as winter cover for ground that would otherwise be left empty and exposed to extreme weather and leaching of nutrients. Between now and late autumn, if you have a patch of

Treat your best keeping apples as individuals, wrapping each perfect
fruit in newspaper to preserve its good quality and appearance.

## HOLIDAY WATERING

If you go away for a week or two at this time of year and you're unable to find anyone to do the watering during your absence, there are a number of things you can do to help reduce water loss and keep vulnerable plants well supplied.

▶ Water all plants at the last minute and then apply, loosen or top up mulches.
▶ Cover leafy crops with a single layer of fleece to provide light shade and shelter from wind.
▶ Pick all produce, even if slightly immature, to avoid it spoiling over a hot or dry week.
▶ Make sure all glass is shaded and vents left open.
▶ Move seedlings and young plants out of the greenhouse to a cool, shady and sheltered spot.
▶ Stir water-holding gel granules into containers and then water well; stand containers in shade and shelter.
▶ Install automatic watering under glass, using individual water reservoirs (*see left*) or a system of interconnected drip or trickle pipes attached to a large filled tank.
▶ Arrange trays of greenhouse plants on capillary matting linked to a water reservoir supply.
▶ Stand a full bucket beside an outdoor container, and link them with a rope or material wick to siphon water as needed.

ground that will not bear a crop again until next year, broadcast sow a hardy variety like field beans, grazing rye or winter tares to dig in during early spring, about 3–4 weeks before you want to use the ground. As an alternative to digging, cut the green manure as short as possible, mulch heavily with compost and plant through the surface layer.

**MID-TERM REVIEW** As you enjoy the summer fruits of your labours, pause and reflect on the season's progress so far. If this is your first year, you will probably be surprised at how much you have harvested already and, with good planning, there should be more to come. Walk round other plots for inspiration and reassurance, for ideas – ways to fit in fruit or use recycled materials, for example – and to compare growth: are your plants pale, a sign of nutrient deficiency, perhaps, or are they backward (ask others when they sowed theirs, and which variety)? Be prepared to change your plans if necessary: buy extra seeds or young plants to squeeze in another crop, for example, resow where a batch has failed or been fast and successful, even reconsider your layout of beds

perhaps. Above all, do not give up: a poor summer of drought or cold wet weather might have spoiled some crops or depressed yields, but there are several productive weeks of the growing season left. And next year is a fresh opportunity.

**LAST SOWINGS** Don't relax yet! Unless you garden in a very cold site with a short growing season, there is still time in late summer to sow a range of crops for harvesting before everything shuts down for winter.

▶ Lettuce, rocket and salad leaves; repeat-sow in early autumn
▶ Oriental vegetables like pak choi, choi sum, compact Chinese cabbages and Chinese broccoli
▶ First early dwarf peas, for picking in mid-autumn
▶ Fast-growing dwarf French beans, for cropping from early autumn
▶ Summer radishes, ready in 6 weeks, and winter (Chinese) varieties for early autumn onwards
▶ Kohlrabi, turnips and early carrots, for lifting throughout autumn
▶ Sweet fennel, which will mature in mid-autumn

In a good year, climbing beans will crop late with their tips pinched out to encourage more flowers.

Lettuces, radishes, pak choi and beetroot are perfect late summer fillers for cleared patches of ground.

### TRY THIS...

Grow a tall fuchsia like 'Lady Boothby' at one end of the greenhouse and train it into the roof to provide summer shade as well as a floral ceiling. Harvest the luscious berries to pickle in red wine vinegar, marinade in brandy and icing sugar for cheesecake, ice-cream or soufflé omelettes, or turn into wine, 'marmalade' or fuchsia berry dumplings.

### IT'S NOT TOO LATE TO...

Sow a dwarf French bean variety, like 'Delinel' or 'Tendergreen', 6–8 plants in a 25cm (10in) pot, to extend the harvest late into the autumn. Grow them on outdoors and then bring into the greenhouse when temperatures drop much below 10°C (50°F).

### IF YOU HAVE TIME...

Sow red cabbages and a first early Brussels sprout variety such as 'Oliver' in a seedbed, cover over winter with cloches (*see left*), and transplant early next spring. They will crop a month or more sooner than plants that were started in late winter or early spring.

**LATE SOWINGS**

There will still be enough residual warmth and day-length in the weeks to come for several crops to mature during autumn, especially if you extend their harvest by using cloches or some other kind of insulating cover. Sowing or transplanting in a greenhouse border, cold frame or used growing bag for moving indoors later can prolong pickings still further.

Crops to sow now include all salad leaves and oriental greens, short peas ('Kelvedon Wonder', 'Ambassador'), small beetroot ('Detroit', 'Golden Detroit' – *see below*, 'Red Ace'), first early carrot varieties, kohlrabi, a fast-growing dwarf French bean ('Maxi', 'Aiguillon'), summer radishes, salad onions, and leafy 'broccoli raab', a turnip relative with spicy leaves that are ready for picking in 40 days.

# HARVEST HIGHLIGHTS

**APPLES** Guard the first early dessert apple varieties such as 'Discovery', 'Epicure', 'George Cave', 'Merton Knave' and 'Irish Peach', which could be ready 3–4 weeks after the longest day in favoured areas and seasons. Birds often peck reddening patches, inviting wasps to follow, and some years fruit starts to drop unusually early. Test often for readiness by 'palming' – gently lifting a fruit in the palm of your hand (*see picture, page 88*) to see if it comes away easily (no twisting!). Eat straight from the tree, as the first varieties rarely keep for more than 2–3 weeks, or use up in Waldorf salads, turnovers, fritters and open tarts with plenty of cinnamon. For true cooking apples this early in the year, grow 'Early Victoria' ('Emneth Early'), which ripens and drops very quickly so be prepared to freeze, dry or bottle, or the less precipitate 'Grenadier'. (*See also page 214.*)

**MELONS** There are several ways to test if a melon is ripe, but the most immediately obvious is the heady sweet fragrance that greets you as you enter the greenhouse or open the cold frame. Inspect the stalk end, where you should find signs of cracking around the junction with the fruit – if you gently press a ripe melon at this point, it will give slightly. Cut with some of the stalk and keep in a cool airy place for a few days if necessary, or on a warm windowsill if it is not quite ripe enough. Do not adulterate with flavourings, such as ginger or port, but eat and admire as a trophy. If you have several melons ripening together, turn the extras into sorbet or ice cream. Young small fruits left at the end of the season can be pickled like gherkins, or candied. (*See also page 200.*)

**NEW ZEALAND SPINACH** Conventional summer spinach is inclined to bolt in the summer sun and needs frequent repeat-sowing for a long season's use. A drought- and heat-tolerant alternative is New Zealand spinach, which creeps into a low mat of lush trailing foliage up to 1.2m (4ft) across. Soak seeds overnight, sow in late spring 90cm (3ft) apart (in pots in cold gardens) and pinch out growing tips when 15cm (6in) high. Harvest complete stems all summer and autumn, stripping the leaves and shoot tips indoors: these make the most alarmingly green spinach koftas. Frost eventually kills the plants, but self-set seedlings often appear the following year. (*See also page 205.*)

Ripe redcurrant strig.

**Mixed runner beans.**

## REDCURRANTS & WHITECURRANTS

Net ripening redcurrants from predatory birds and squirrels, for whom they are an irresistible treat; whitecurrants are less appealing and often escape raids. Gather complete strigs (trusses) when fully ripe and translucent, but don't rush: most varieties will hang for a few weeks without deteriorating. Redcurrants have many uses: they add tartness and pectin to raspberries in jam and jelly, make an authentic summer pudding or a fruity rosé wine, and are a delicacy on their own if whole strigs are dredged in egg white and icing sugar for stripping between the teeth. Less acid whitecurrants (which turn pink when cooked) can be eaten in the same way, or make classic little tarts. (*See also page 217.*)

**A perfectly ripe, ready-to-eat sweetcorn.**

**RUNNER BEANS** Disdained by gourmets in favour of their French cousins but eagerly anticipated by most plot-holders, the first plateful of tender runner beans is a certain sign high summer has arrived. Pick before they become rough and lumpy, and gather regularly and thoroughly until the last are cleared in early or mid-autumn. For a change, try them Indian-style, cooked with mustard or as major ingredient of a vegetable *biryani*; baby runner beans may be cooked whole for serving in a vinaigrette dressing. Once the initial euphoria is past, a constant and lavish supply may become tedious, in which case preserve some for winter. Sliced beans were once laid down in crock pots between layers of crushed block salt, but this is now rare – don't use ordinary kitchen salt, which includes easy-pouring additives and soon turns to brine. Sea salt sometimes works, or you can freeze or dry any surplus; dry mature beans from aged pods for winter stews and seed. (*See also page 189.*)

**SHALLOTS** The bulbs are ready to lift when their leaf tips first show yellow. Ease each cluster from the ground with a fork and leave intact on the surface (or transfer under glass in a wet season) to colour up and fall apart naturally. Save medium-size bulbs as fat as a 10p coin from healthy plants (no yellow virused leaves, for example) to grow next year, and eat the rest. Store completely dried bulbs in trays in a cool but frost-free shed, and use them up by the end of winter. They are a vegetable for the discerning, so treat them with respect rather than as a substitute for onions: cook them gently to preserve their delicate distinctive flavour, and never brown them like onions, which turns them bitter. (*See also page 197.*)

**SWEETCORN** Time to maturity claimed in some seed catalogues can be misleading, as it usually refers to North America, where corn cobs ripen 50–60 days sooner than in Britain. Here, it is always prudent to sow a fast variety, such as 'Swift' (a super-sweet kind that doesn't need growing apart from others), as early as possible, and watch ripening carefully from the moment tassels start to shrivel. When they resemble scorched hair, peel a cob cautiously to expose a few kernels and press with your thumb nail: a thin white fluid shows the cob is 2–3 days away from harvest, while milky contents are just right. Then cut and run, because the sugars begin turning to starch after just 20 minutes. Ignore fancy recipes: simply plunge into boiling water until tender, and eat dripping with butter and sea salt. (*See also pages 210–11.*)

## EAT NOW

Although the days are still long and lovely, there are intimations of autumn in the odd chilly evening and dewy dawn, and the growing momentum of the fruit season shifts a gardener's thoughts to harvesting and storing. Not so many years ago the preserving season meant Kilner jars to fill with plums and cherries, and loaves of block salt for crocks full of runner beans. Methods might change but the squirrel instinct is the same, reawoken by the sight of a typical late summer glut (runner beans go wild) and the irresistible urge to save surpluses for leaner times. Gluttony becomes forgivable now as you scuttle home with sweetcorn to enjoy at its succulent best and bags of French beans or blackberries to pack in the freezer. (*See* In season now, *page 86*.)

## RECIPES

seasonal planner

## CUCUMBER SOUP WITH SPICY POTATO CAKES

**SERVES 4**

This a very pretty, refreshing Thai-style cold soup that takes minutes to make. It is soft and green with a subtle aniseed taste from the Thai basil. The potato cakes are similar to latkes, but spicy. Leave out some of the chilli if you prefer them less hot.

1 large cucumber, peeled and grated

large bunch of Thai (holy) basil, finely sliced

500ml (17fl oz) plain yoghurt

300ml (10fl oz) double cream

salt and freshly ground pepper, to taste

### Potato cakes

1kg (2¼lb) waxy new potatoes, peeled and grated

1 large shallot, finely sliced

1 medium red chilli, deseeded and finely sliced

handful of fresh mint leaves, finely sliced

2.5cm (1in) piece root ginger, peeled and cut into very thin strips

1 tbsp plain flour

1½ tsp sea salt

2 tbsp vegetable oil

- Put all the soup ingredients in a large bowl and whisk together. Season with salt and pepper. Chill for at least 1 hour to allow the flavour to develop.
- In a bowl, combine all the ingredients for the potato cakes, except the oil, and mix together with your hands. Shape into eight flat cakes. Don't make them too thick or they won't cook through.
- Heat the oil in a frying pan. Add the cakes and press them down with a fish slice as they cook. Turn them over when they are golden on the underside. They take about 5 minutes on each side.
- Serve the soup in individual bowls, each with a couple of potato cakes alongside.

## GAZPACHO VERDE WITH LEMON CROÛTONS

**SERVES 6**

This simple chilled soup is based on the classic Gazpacho but without tomatoes, and with a strong green hue.

1 white onion, roughly chopped

3 garlic cloves, chopped

6 tbsp extra virgin olive oil, plus extra for drizzling

900ml (1½ pints) water

175g (6oz) baby spinach

several ice cubes

salt and and freshly ground pepper, to taste

100g (3½oz) crustless white bread, soaked in 3 tbsp red wine vinegar

2 celery sticks, finely chopped

1 green pepper, finely chopped

⅓ cucumber, cut into small cubes

2 salad onions, white and green parts, thinly sliced

3 tbsp finely chopped fresh mint

2 tbsp finely chopped fresh flat-leaf parsley

1 green chilli, deseeded and finely chopped

3 slices of brown bread

grated zest of 1 lemon

- Soften the onion and half the garlic in 2 tablespoons of oil in a saucepan. Pour in the water and bring to the boil. Remove from the heat and stir in the spinach until it wilts. Blitz in a food processor or blender with a few ice cubes until smooth. Season and put into the fridge to chill.
- Blend the vinegar-soaked bread into the chilled soup base. Stir in the rest of the garlic, vegetables, herbs and chilli. Add the remaining oil and more salt and pepper if necessary. Return to the fridge while you make the croûtons.
- Preheat oven to 180°C/350°F/gas 4. Cut each slice of brown bread into small squares or triangles and sprinkle with the lemon zest and a drizzle of oil. Bake for 10–12 minutes until browned. Serve warm in the chilled soup.

## GREEN SOUP

**SERVES 6**

Another attractively verdant chilled soup, this is made thicker and greener with the addition of a non-home-grown ingredient.

1 green pepper

2 cucumbers, peeled, deseeded and diced

2 celery sticks, diced

4 salad onions, white and green parts, thinly sliced

60g (2oz) fresh coriander, roughly chopped

1 avocado

4 limes

475ml (16fl oz) skimmed milk

1 tsp coarse salt

½ tsp freshly ground black pepper

1 tsp ground cumin

- Preheat the grill to high. Put the whole pepper on a baking tray and grill until blistered and blackened on all sides. Put in a plastic bag, (the steam made in the bag softens the skin) cool for 5 minutes, then remove the skin and seeds and chop into small pieces.
- Place 2 tablespoons each of pepper, cucumber, celery, salad onions and coriander into small bowls. Set aside.
- Peel and stone the avocado and cut into small pieces. Squeeze over the juice of 2 limes and toss to coat. Put 2 tablespoons of the avocado in a bowl and cover tightly.
- Put the remaining vegetables and herbs in a bowl. Stir in the milk, salt, pepper, cumin and juice of 1 lime.
- Transfer half of the mixture to a food processor or blender and process for about 30 seconds or until creamy but not completely smooth. Pour back into the bowl with the remaining ingredients and stir together. Cover and chill until ready to serve.
- Serve the soup in bowls, with wedges of the remaining lime and the little bowls of garnishes.

## GLUT BUSTER
### TOMATOES

Tomatoes are probably the one vegetable of which a glut is a blessing. They are so versatile and there are so many ways to use and cook them: the basic tomato sauce for pastas and pizzas, soups, salads, tarts... You can also store them for winter – they freeze easily, can be slowly dried or be made into chutneys. At the end of the season, when there are green tomatoes remaining on the vines, they can still be harvested, brought indoors and ripened in a drawer, made into chutney or fried as a side dish.

## HENRY'S TOMATO SOUP
### SERVES THE MASSES!

This is Henry's (*see page 15*) favourite soup to put away for the winter, hence the enormous quantities! The bucket? It's the same bucket for measuring both.

> 1 garlic head, cloves peeled and chopped
> 6 large onions, chopped
> 55ml (2fl oz) vegetable oil
> 1 bucket tomatoes, peeled and chopped
> 1 bucket water
> salt and freshly ground pepper, to taste

- Put the garlic and onions in a large pan with some oil and cook until translucent. Add the tomatoes and water and cook until the soup is reduced by half. Season with salt and pepper.
- Enjoy the first bowl of soup of the season straightaway. Freeze the remainder so that you can warm it up in the depths of winter and remind yourself how easy and essential it is to grow tomatoes.

## GAZPACHO
### SERVES 6

The quintessential Spanish summer soup which exists in hundreds of variations. This is the perfect soup to make if you have masses of very sweet tomatoes. It also uses up your stock of cucumbers, peppers and onions. You can do all the chopping by hand, but a food processor makes short work of the preparation.

> 2 garlic cloves
> 1 large onion, chopped into quarters
> 900g (2lb) tomatoes, peeled and chopped
> 2 red peppers, deseeded and chopped
> 1 cucumber, peeled and chopped
> 115g (4oz) fresh white breadcrumbs
> 110ml (4fl oz) extra virgin olive oil
> 2 tbsp sherry or white wine vinegar
> 110ml (4fl oz) water
> salt and freshly ground pepper, to taste

**Garnish**

> 3 slices crustless white bread, cubed
> 2–3 tbsp olive oil
> 2 tomatoes, peeled and finely chopped
> 1 green pepper, deseeded and finely chopped
> 3 salad onions, very finely chopped
> 2 tbsp finely chopped fresh flat-leaf parsley

- Put the garlic and onion in a food processor and process until finely chopped. Add the tomatoes, red peppers, cucumber, breadcrumbs, oil, vinegar and water. Blitz until almost smooth, then pour into a bowl. Add some iced water if the soup is too thick. Season with salt and pepper and chill.
- To make the garnish, fry the bread cubes in the oil until browned. Drain on kitchen paper. Put these croûtons and all the other finely chopped garnishes into small bowls.
- Ladle out the soup and serve with the croûtons and garnishes alongside to add at will.

## COOL TOMATO JELLIES
### SERVES 6 AS A STARTER

Make this elegant, refreshing starter at the height of the tomato season when they are juicy and full of flavour. The almost clear water you extract is the pure essence of the tomato. The waste can be put on the compost heap. Use whole small tomatoes as decoration – if you have the pear-shaped ones, even better.

> 2.7kg (6lb) very large, very ripe tomatoes
> 1 tsp salt, or more to taste
> 2 tsp sherry or white balsamic vinegar
> leaf gelatine to set 1 litre (1¾ pints) liquid
> 36 very small red and yellow tomatoes, plus extra to decorate
> 1 small bunch chervil leaves
> tomato flowers, to decorate (optional)

- Cut up the tomatoes and purée in a food processor. Set a sieve over a bowl and line with two layers of muslin. Pour in the tomato pulp and leave to drip through overnight or until there is 1 litre (1¾ pints) of tomato water. If the tomatoes don't release enough water, lift the sides of the muslin and gently squeeze the bag of tomatoes to yield more liquid.
- Pour the tomato water through a fine sieve into a measuring jug. Stir in the salt and vinegar. Put aside.
- Soften the gelatine in cold water for 5 minutes. Squeeze dry. Warm a little of the tomato water in a small pan and melt the gelatine in this. Cool, then mix with the rest of the water.
- Fill six glasses one-third full with the tomato water. Put in a few small tomatoes and a few chervil leaves. Chill for 45 minutes to set. Add another layer then chill again. Repeat until the glasses are full. (If the jelly in the jug sets, sit it in a bowl of hot water until it liquefies.) Garnish with tomato flowers and whole small tomatoes.

## SLOW-ROASTED TOMATO HALVES

### MAKES 36

Plum tomatoes roast well because of their dense flesh. The best variety to grow and use are San Marzano – nearly all canned plum tomatoes are this variety. Slow roasting intensifies the flavour of the tomatoes and gives them a sweet, earthy taste. They're a delicious addition to pasta, soups or stews.

18 plum tomatoes, sliced in half lengthways and core removed

2 garlic cloves, finely sliced

3 tbsp extra virgin olive oil

1½ tsp salt

¼ tsp freshly ground black pepper

1 tbsp chopped fresh oregano

- Turn your oven to its lowest setting – probably 110°C/225°F/gas ¼.
- Arrange the tomatoes, cut side up, in a single layer on a baking tray and sprinkle with the garlic, olive oil, salt, pepper and oregano.
- Roast for 3–4 hours or until the tomatoes are gently shrivelled and dry (the drier they are, the longer they will keep). Cool and use immediately, or refrigerate in an airtight container with a layer of oil on top.

## SLOW-ROASTED TOMATO SALAD

### SERVES 6

A fragrant way to roast tomatoes. The principle is the same as normal roasting, but the addition of spices and shallots makes this suitable to serve as a salad or starter on its own. Will keep for 2–3 days.

3 garlic cloves, finely sliced

2 shallots, finely sliced

½ tsp ground coriander

¼ tsp ground cinnamon

pinch of ground cloves

pinch of caster sugar

salt and freshly ground pepper, to taste

12 plum tomatoes, halved lengthways

4 tbsp extra virgin olive oil, plus extra for drizzling

1 tbsp finely chopped fresh parsley

- Preheat oven to 140°C/275°F/gas 1.
- Put the garlic and shallots in a bowl with the spices, sugar, salt and pepper. Add the tomatoes and oil and mix together.
- Take the tomatoes out of the bowl and arrange, cut side up, on a baking tray. Pour over the rest of the oil, shallot and garlic. Roast for 1½ hours until tender. Transfer to a serving dish and drizzle with a little extra olive oil. Eat at room temperature.

## MOROCCAN TOMATO SALAD

### SERVES 6

This salad uses the sweetest tomatoes, heated up with fresh chilli, spices and fresh herbs. Try to mix two different colours of tomatoes for a pretty dish. The salad goes wonderfully with barbecued meats and fish.

3 tbsp extra virgin olive oil

1 tbsp balsamic vinegar

1 tsp ground cumin

1 tsp ground coriander

½ red chilli, deseeded and finely chopped

450g (1lb) very ripe, small, yellow and red sweet tomatoes, halved lengthways

salt and freshly ground pepper, to taste

½ bunch fresh parsley, finely chopped

½ bunch fresh coriander, finely chopped

- Make a dressing with the oil, vinegar, spices and chilli.
- Layer half the mixed tomatoes in a serving dish. Season and sprinkle over half the fresh herbs and half the dressing. Repeat. Leave for about 30 minutes for the dressing to infuse before serving.

## TRY THIS
### EDIBLE FLOWERS

Many flowers are not only edible but also valuable as a food ingredient for the colour and unique flavours that they contribute to dishes. Many are an unexpected extra crop from vegetables or herbs and may be used whole, as picked, or with just their green parts or separate petals removed.

Always gather flowers in the morning, when dry and just fully opened, and use or preserve them the same day.

### Preserving flowers

Freezing is preferable, either as loose blooms frozen on a tray and then carefully bagged for storing, or added to ice cubes. Borage is often used in cubes.

For decoration many flowers can be crystallized by dipping in beaten egg white and then dredging them with icing sugar. Layer between greaseproof paper to store. Preserve rose petals in this way.

Flowers may be boiled in sugar syrup or with apples to make a floral jelly, or they can be layered with sugar in airtight jars.

### Familiar flowers to eat

Borage

Calendula (pot marigolds)

Chives

Courgettes

Citrus

Elder

Honeysuckle

Mint

Nasturtiums (see page 73)

Roses (see page 80)

Sweet cicely

Violets

## TOMSATINA CHUTNEY

**MAKES 4 JARS**

This is especially useful when you have
lots of tomatoes, basil and thyme – all
need to be ripe and well flavoured. The
chutney is best eaten with a strong
hard cheese such as Cheddar, but it
can also be served with Vegetable cake
(*see page 102*).

1.8kg (4lb) ripe tomatoes
300g (10oz) shallots, finely chopped
3 tbsp yellow mustard seeds
1 tbsp allspice berries, tied up in
a muslin bag
2 tbsp fresh thyme leaves
125g (4½oz) caster sugar
450ml (15fl oz) cider vinegar
a large bunch fresh basil, chopped
salt and freshly ground pepper, to taste

- Cut the tomatoes in half and chop
  the flesh. Put in a preserving pan
  and add the shallots, mustard seeds
  and allspice berries. Cook over a
  gentle heat until the tomato juices
  start to run. Add the thyme. Increase
  the heat and simmer, stirring from
  time to time, for about 45 minutes
  until reduced by one-third.
- Add the sugar, lower the heat and
  stir until it dissolves. Add the vinegar,
  basil and seasoning. Increase the
  heat again and simmer for about
  30 minutes or until thickened.
  Remove the allspice berries.
- Ladle the hot but not boiling
  chutney into hot, dry sterilized
  jars (*see page 80*) and seal. Leave
  until cold before labelling.

## TOMATO TART

### SERVES 4

A simple and rustic tart suitable as a starter. You could use ordinary pastry instead of the cheese pastry – just add more cheese to the filling.

#### Parmesan pastry

200g (7oz) plain flour

100g (3½ oz) unsalted butter, diced

60g (2oz) Parmesan cheese, freshly grated

salt and freshly ground pepper, to taste

grated zest of ½ lemon

55ml (2fl oz) iced water

#### Tomato filling

2 tbsp Dijon mustard

2 tbsp freshly grated Parmesan cheese

600g (1¼lb) cherry tomatoes, halved

2 tbsp finely chopped fresh basil

1 tbsp finely chopped fresh thyme

1 tbsp finely chopped fresh flat-leaf parsley

2 garlic cloves, chopped

1 tbsp olive oil

1 egg yolk, beaten with 1 tsp water

- Preheat oven to 220°C/425°F/gas 7.
- To make the pastry combine the flour, butter, cheese and a good pinch of salt in a food processor. Blitz to crumbs. Add the lemon zest and water and process just until the dough binds together.
- Press out to a 30cm (12in) disc on a baking tray. Spread over the mustard, leaving a small border clear all round. Sprinkle the Parmesan over the mustard and arrange the tomato halves on top. Mix the herbs and garlic in a bowl, sprinkle over the tomatoes and season.
- Fold in and pleat the edges of the pastry disc. Drizzle the oil over the filling. Paint the pastry edges with the egg wash. Bake for 20 minutes or until the pastry is golden. Leave the tart to cool slightly and serve warm.

## FRENCH BEANS WITH TOMATOES

### SERVES 4 AS A SIDE DISH

This is a classic Greek dish, but variations are found all over the Mediterranean. A glut of beans and tomatoes often occurs at the same time and this is good way to use them both up. You can substitute runner beans for the French beans.

1 tbsp olive oil

1 onion, finely sliced

1 garlic clove, finely chopped

500g (1lb 2oz) tomatoes, peeled, deseeded and roughly chopped

500g (1lb 2oz) French beans, topped only

- Heat the oil in a frying pan. Add the onion and cook gently for about 10 minutes until soft and translucent but not coloured. Add the garlic and cook gently for 1 more minute, then add the tomatoes and beans. Stir well and bring to a gentle simmer.
- Turn down the heat, cover the pan and cook very gently for about 10 minutes or until the beans are tender but still with a little bite – they mustn't be overcooked. Stir frequently and add a splash of water or wine to prevent sticking, if necessary. Serve warm or cold.

## TOMATO COBBLER WITH GRUYÈRE CRUST

### SERVES 8

A cobbler topping is a cross between pastry and scone. Usually plain, here the addition of cheese lifts this tomato pie. It's not too substantial, but best served as a main dish with just a salad.

300g (10oz) plain flour

250g (9oz) cold butter, cut into pieces

125g (4½oz) Gruyère cheese, grated

1 large onion, sliced

3 garlic cloves, chopped

900g (2lb) assorted cherry tomatoes

15g (½oz) fresh basil, chopped

salt and freshly ground pepper, to taste

1 large egg, lightly beaten

- Put the flour, 225g (8oz) butter and 115g (4oz) cheese in a food processor and blitz to crumbs. Add enough iced water to bind to a dough. Wrap in clingfilm and chill for 1 hour.
- Melt the remaining butter in a large frying pan and cook the onion and garlic until soft and translucent. Allow to cool.
- Put the tomatoes in a deep pie dish and toss with the basil and some seasoning. Add the onion and garlic and mix together. Set aside.
- Preheat oven to 190°C/375°F/gas 5. Roll out the pastry dough to a round or oval 2.5cm (1in) larger than the pie dish. Lay the pastry over the dish and press it down on to the rim to seal. Flute or fork the edge. Make four slits in the pastry lid. Brush with the beaten egg and sprinkle with the remaining cheese. Place the pie dish on a baking tray to catch any drips.
- Bake for about 50 minutes or until the pastry is golden and the filling is bubbling. Leave the cobbler to cool slightly before serving.

## PEPERONATA

### SERVES 4

It's no secret that some of the best dishes using tomatoes, peppers and aubergines come from the Mediterranean countries, where long, hot summers make growing these vegetables outdoors very easy. This is a very simple, classic Italian side dish to serve cold with cold meats, warm with steaks or chops, or it could be served cold as an antipasto or starter.

100ml (3½fl oz) olive oil

375g (13oz) onions, finely sliced

2 garlic cloves, crushed

500g (1lb 2oz) red and yellow peppers, quartered and deseeded

400g (14oz) tomatoes, chopped

salt and freshly ground pepper, to taste

- Heat the oil in a heavy-based pan and gently fry the onions and garlic until lightly coloured. Add the peppers, cover and cook over a gentle heat for 8–10 minutes.
- Add the tomatoes and season generously with salt and pepper.
- Continue to cook, uncovered, until the peppers are tender and the tomatoes have reduced to a thick sauce. Serve warm.

## PANZANELLA KEBABS

### SERVES 8

This is based on traditional panzanella – an Italian bread salad – but the ingredients are grilled to intensify their flavour.

6 tbsp extra virgin olive oil

4 tbsp white wine vinegar

1 tbsp clear honey

1 tbsp finely chopped fresh flat-leaf parsley

1 tbsp finely chopped fresh thyme

salt and freshly ground pepper, to taste

450g (1lb) chicken breast fillets, cut into 2.5cm (1in) cubes

3 red onions, quartered

450g (1lb) small courgettes, cut into 1cm (½in) rounds

2 orange or yellow peppers, deseeded and cut into 2.5cm (1in) squares

24 cherry tomatoes

300g (10oz) crustless day-old white bread, cut into 2.5cm (1in) cubes

- Soak 24 wooden skewers in water for 10 minutes. Alternatively, use metal skewers. Preheat the grill or a ridged griddle pan.
- For the marinade, mix the oil, vinegar, honey, herbs, salt and pepper together.
- Thread chicken and onion onto eight skewers; courgettes and peppers onto another eight skewers; and tomatoes and bread onto the final eight skewers. Brush with the marinade.
- Put the chicken and onion skewers under the grill first. After 3 minutes, add the courgette and pepper skewers. After a further 5 minutes, add the tomato and bread skewers. Grill, turning often, until the chicken is cooked, all the vegetables are tender and the bread is toasted.
- Take the grilled ingredients off the skewers and put in a bowl. Add any remaining marinade, plus extra oil if it seems dry, and season. Toss well to mix. Serve slightly warm.

## RED PEPPER, CHILLI & FETA COILS

### MAKES ABOUT 20 PIES

In Greece and Turkey they make delicious little pies that usually include feta cheese. This is a slightly spicy pie, which is intriguingly coiled up. Don't attempt to make filo pastry – it is much easier to use shop-bought pastry.

2 tbsp olive oil

2 red peppers, deseeded and finely chopped

2 fresh green chillies, deseeded and finely chopped

250g (9oz) feta cheese, crumbled

salt and freshly ground pepper, to taste

1 standard-sized packet filo pastry

melted butter, to brush

- Heat the oil in a large frying pan, add the peppers and chillies and fry for about 15 minutes or until softened. Allow the mixture to cool, then add the feta and a little salt and pepper. (Remember that feta is quite salty.)
- Preheat oven to 180°C/350°F/gas 4. Lay one sheet of filo, folded in half, on a flat surface. (Keep the remaining filo covered with a damp tea towel.) Spread a heaped spoonful of the filling along one long side of the filo and brush the rest of the sheet with melted butter. Roll up the pastry into a long, thin cigar shape. Tuck in the ends to seal in the filling. Coil the cigar into a flat spiral. Brush with melted butter and put on to an oiled baking tray. Repeat with the other filo sheets and the remaining filling.
- Bake for 15 minutes until the pastry is golden brown. Serve warm.

## AUBERGINE CAPONATA

### SERVES 8 AS A SIDE DISH

Caponata is Sicilian, but has a distinctive Arabic feel to it with the sweet-and-sour flavour of sultanas and capers.

1 large aubergine, roughly chopped

salt and freshly ground pepper, to taste

75ml (2½ fl oz) extra virgin olive oil

1 large onion, finely chopped

3 garlic cloves, finely chopped

400g (14oz) tomatoes, chopped

2 celery sticks, roughly chopped

½ fennel bulb, finely chopped

3 tbsp red wine vinegar

60g (2oz) sultanas

60g (2oz) pine nuts, toasted

60g (2oz) capers

a small bunch of fresh parsley, roughly chopped

2 tsp caster sugar

- Put the aubergine in a colander and sprinkle generously with salt. Leave to drain for at least 2 hours.
- Heat 1 tablespoon of oil in a large, deep frying pan and cook the onion and garlic for 10 minutes until soft. Tip into a large bowl and set aside.
- Lightly rinse off the salt from the aubergine and dry well. Heat the rest of the oil in the pan, add the aubergine, tomatoes, celery and fennel and cook for 1–2 minutes until tender and golden. Add more oil if necessary: aubergines can absorb masses of oil. Scoop out the vegetables with a slotted spoon and drain on kitchen paper.
- Add the vegetables to the onions. Season, then add the vinegar. Stir in the sultanas, pine nuts, capers, parsley and sugar. Cover and chill for at least 2 hours or overnight. Serve at room temperature, with grilled meat and fish.

## VEGETABLE CAKE

### SERVES 6

This is a pretty impressive dish – delicious with some fish or chicken. It is cut into wedges to show the colourful layers, so keep this in mind when you are layering the ingredients in the tin.

3 large aubergines, thickly sliced

12 large peppers: 4 red, 4 green and 4 yellow

6 tbsp olive oil

2–3 garlic cloves, finely chopped

250g (9oz) feta cheese, sliced

salt and freshly ground pepper, to taste

- Salt and drain the aubergines as for Caponata (*see left*).
- When the aubergine is almost drained, preheat the grill and heat the whole peppers until they are blistered and charred all over. Put them in a plastic bag to cool, then peel them and remove the core and seeds. Cut the flesh into large pieces.
- In batches, sauté the aubergine slices in the olive oil until tender, then transfer to a plate and sprinkle with the chopped garlic.
- Layer the peppers, aubergines and cheese in a 25-30cm (10-12in) springform cake tin, in any order you like, seasoning each layer with pepper and a tiny amount of salt (remember that feta is salty). Put a plate and a heavy weight on top. Set the tin in a bowl to catch any juice and chill overnight.
- Turn out of the tin and cut into wedges like a cake. The layers will stay firmly together if you keep the cake cold. Serve with Tomastina chutney (*see page 90*).

## PISTO MANCHEGO

### SERVES 6

This is an easy recipe for a traditional dish, a favourite cooked and served all over Spain, which is similar to the French ratatouille. For the best flavour use plum tomatoes or something similar in taste. It can be served warm to accompany a main dish or cold as a starter. Its uses are varied: it makes a good pasta sauce or a filling for sandwiches – try slicing open a small baguette, put in a wedge of Spanish omelette (*see page 46*) and add a large spoonful of pisto. It freezes well, so you can make a big batch and use as required.

4 tbsp extra virgin olive oil

2 medium onions, sliced

3 garlic cloves, chopped

2 green peppers, deseeded and sliced

1 red pepper, deseeded and sliced

2 courgettes, sliced

4 ripe tomatoes, peeled and cut into pieces

1 tbsp chopped fresh oregano

1 tsp sugar

salt and freshly ground pepper, to taste

- Heat the olive oil in a frying pan and gently fry the onions and garlic until soft. Add the green and red peppers and turn up the heat a little. Cook for 5 minutes, stirring all the time.
- Add the courgettes. Stir and cook for 5 more minutes, then add the tomatoes. Cover the pan and simmer for about 15 minutes.
- Add the oregano, sugar and some salt and pepper. Turn up the heat and stir well. If the pisto has too much liquid, simmer to evaporate it, but keep stirring to prevent catching. Serve warm or cold.

## CUCUMBER & BULGUR WHEAT & FRESH HERBS

**SERVES 4**

Bulgur wheat is made by cooking grains of wheat until they crack, then drying and grinding them. Used all over the Middle East, it makes a brilliant base for this green and herby salad. Serve as a starter or as part of a mixed mezze.

170ml (6fl oz) water

140g (5oz) bulgur wheat

1 large cucumber, peeled, deseeded and chopped

450ml (15fl oz) plain fat-free yoghurt

2 salad onions, green and white parts, chopped

7g (¼oz) fresh coriander, finely chopped

7g (¼oz) fresh chives, finely chopped

7g (¼oz) fresh mint, finely chopped

7g (¼oz) fresh dill, finely chopped

salt and freshly ground pepper, to taste

- Bring the water to the boil in a saucepan. Add the bulgur wheat and bring back to the boil, then cover and remove from the heat. Leave to soak, covered, for 30 minutes.
- Meanwhile, spread the chopped cucumber on kitchen paper and drain for 10 minutes.
- Pour the bulgur wheat into a sieve and press with the back of a wooden spoon to squeeze out all excess water. Transfer the bulgur to a large serving bowl.
- Add the yoghurt, cucumber, salad onions, herbs and seasoning, and stir thoroughly. Cover with clingfilm and refrigerate for at least 3 hours before serving. Serve cold.

## PICKLED CUCUMBERS

**MAKES ONE 1.5 LITRE (2¾ PINT) JAR**

There is very little vinegar in this recipe as the cucumbers will weep copiously and add their own liquid. The taste is very delicate. Slicing the cucumbers with a swivel vegetable peeler makes for a very fine, translucent pickle.

enough washed, small cucumbers to fill the jar, thinly sliced

2 large garlic cloves, peeled

1 tbsp rice vinegar

1 fresh bay leaf

1 tsp black peppercorns

1 tsp coriander seeds

5 allspice berries

2 fresh dill sprigs

- Put the cucumbers in a sterilized 1.5 litre (2¾ pint) Kilner jar (*see page 80*) and fill it with cold water to within 2.5cm (1in) of the top. Add the garlic, vinegar, bay leaf and spices, and shake to mix.
- Leave the pickle in the fridge or a cool place for 2 days for the flavours to develop, then take out the spices and add the dill. The cucumbers will keep for 2–3 weeks in the fridge.

## BLUEBERRY BUCKLE

**MAKES ONE 25CM (10IN) CAKE**

Blueberries, which have long been a favourite in America, are becoming much more popular here and are very easy to grow. This 'buckle' (an old American term for a simple cake made with berries or other fruit) is made in a springform tin so it is easy to release. You could substitute blackcurrants or other small berries for the blueberries.

225g (8oz) plain flour

1½ tsp baking powder

pinch of salt

115g (4oz) soft unsalted butter

175g (6oz) caster sugar, plus extra to sprinkle

1 tsp pure vanilla extract

1 egg, beaten

140ml (5fl oz) milk

500g (1lb 2oz) blueberries

- Preheat oven to 180°C/350°F/gas 4. Butter and flour a 25cm (10in) springform cake tin and set aside.
- Sift the flour, baking powder and salt into a bowl and put aside.
- In another bowl, cream together the butter and sugar until light and fluffy. Add the vanilla extract and then the egg and mix well.
- Add a little of the flour mixture and then a little of the milk and continue alternately, ending with the flour mixture. Gently fold in the berries.
- Pour the mixture into the prepared tin and sprinkle some sugar over the top. Bake for 60–70 minutes or until a skewer inserted into the centre comes out clean. Leave to cool in the tin for 15 minutes before removing the side of the tin and sliding the cake on to a serving plate. Serve with a generous dollop of whipped cream on top of each helping.

## BLUEBERRY COBBLER

**SERVES 8–10**

Here's another traditional American way to enjoy blueberries. A cobbler is made from fruit baked with a scone-dumpling top. The topping could be used for any fruit – blackberries and apples especially.

800g (1¾lb) blueberries

grated zest and juice of 1 lemon

175g (6oz) caster sugar, plus 2 tbsp and extra to sprinkle

2 tbsp cornflour

½ tsp ground cinnamon

350g (12oz) plain flour

1½ tsp salt

1¾ tsp baking powder

115g (4 oz) cold unsalted butter, diced

225ml (8fl oz) milk

- Preheat oven to 180°C/350°F/gas 4.
- Combine the blueberries, lemon zest and juice, 175g (6oz) sugar, the cornflour and cinnamon in a bowl, and toss together. Tip into a 2 litre (3½ pint) baking dish and set aside.
- Put the flour, salt, baking powder and the remaining 2 tablespoons of sugar in another bowl. Add the butter and rub in until the mixture resembles breadcrumbs. Gradually add the milk, only adding enough to bind the crumbs into a dough. Form the dough into a ball, wrap in clingfilm and chill.
- Bake the blueberry mixture for about 20 minutes. Remove from the oven and increase the temperature to 220°C/425°F/gas 7. Place blobs of the dough on top of the blueberry mixture, covering the surface. Sprinkle with sugar. Bake for about 15 minutes until the scone topping is browned and the fruit filling is bubbling. Allow to cool a bit, then serve with cream.

## BLUEBERRY SHORTCRUST CUPS

**SERVES 6**

These are really very deep tarts, but because they are cooked in muffin tins the filling can be more substantial. When cooked, soft fruit becomes very juicy, so you don't need to add anything but sugar. You could substitute blackcurrants or raspberries mixed with redcurrants for the blueberries, but be sure to check for sweetness.

600g (1¼lb) blueberries

2 tbsp caster sugar

1 packet (375g/13oz) ready-made sweet shortcrust pastry

1 egg, beaten

icing sugar, to sprinkle

- Preheat oven to 220°C/425°F/gas 7. Butter a six-hole muffin tray.
- Toss the blueberries with the caster sugar.
- Roll out the pastry and cut out six discs large enough to line the muffin cups. Press them in gently, rippling the sides to flute the edge. Fill with the sugared berries. Brush the pastry with the beaten egg, making sure to get some between the pastry folds
- Bake until the pastry is golden. Dust lightly with icing sugar, and serve warm with cream or ice cream.

## BLACKBERRY JELLY 1

**MAKES 3 JARS**

A good way to use soft fruit is to make jellies – not the children's party kind but the classic recipe to serve with roast meat and poultry. A home-made jelly will be a revelation compared to the commercial varieties. Redcurrants, rowan berries and crab apples are the usual choices, but blackberries, which are coming into season around the end of the summer, are there for the taking. The easy thing about making jellies is that you don't need to strip the berries from the stalks.

1.8kg (4lb) blackberries
600ml (1 pint) water
caster sugar (see recipe for quantities)

- Put the washed fruit, stalks included, and water in a preserving pan, bring to the boil and stir. Reduce the heat and simmer for 30 minutes, pressing the fruit frequently to release the maximum amount of juice.
- Leave to drain in a cone-shaped commercial jelly bag, or a sieve lined with a muslin, suspended over a large bowl. For the maximum amount of juice, it's best to leave overnight. Don't be tempted to squeeze the bag dry as this will make the jelly cloudy.
- Measure the amount of juice made. You will need 450g (1lb) caster sugar for every 600ml (1 pint).
- Put the measured juice back into the clean preserving pan and add the sugar. Stir until until it is completely dissolved. Then bring to the boil and cook rapidly for 15 minutes. Test for setting point (*see page 80*).
- Pot into hot, dry sterilized jam jars (*see page 80*). Leave to cool before labelling the jars.

## BLACKBERRY JELLY 2

**SERVES 6**

This is the grown-up version of the children's favourite. Blackberries will give you the richest coloured jelly, and with the addition of some frosted berries on top it will be fit to grace a posh party. Any soft fruit can be substituted, and for an extra kick use half wine and half water.

700g (1½lb) blackberries, hulled
3 tbsp water
juice of ½ lemon
110g (4oz) caster sugar, plus extra for frosting
20g (¾oz) powdered gelatine, softened
10 blackberries with stalks

- Place the hulled blackberries in a saucepan with the water. Simmer until the fruit is becoming pulpy. Purée in a blender or food processor, then pass through a sieve. Return to the saucepan.
- Measure the lemon juice and add enough water to make 600ml (1 pint). Add to the pan with the sugar. Heat gently, stirring, until the sugar has dissolved. Add the gelatine and stir until the gelatine has completely dissolved. Allow to cool slightly. Turn into a glass serving dish or mould. Leave until cold, then chill until set.
- Meanwhile, holding the blackberries by their stalks, dip them in cold water and then in sugar to coat all over. Leave to dry. Lay the frosted blackberries on top of the set jelly before serving.

## GREENGAGE CLAFOUTIS

**SERVES 8**

From the Limousin region, this French dessert is traditionally made with cherries, but fruits such as pears, peaches and plums can also be used. The batter encases the fruit and, when baked, has a wonderful glossy top.

700g (1½lb) greengages, halved and stoned
3 tbsp plain flour
pinch of salt
60g (2oz) caster sugar
4 large eggs plus 2 large egg yolks
300ml (10fl oz) milk
300ml (10fl oz) double or whipping cream
1 vanilla pod, split open
3 tbsp kirsch (optional)

- Preheat oven to 190°C/375°F/gas 5.
- Generously butter a 25cm (10in) flan or tart dish. Fill with the greengages, cut side down, and set aside.
- Sift the flour and salt into a large bowl. Add the sugar. Gradually whisk in the eggs, egg yolks, milk and cream. Scrape the seeds from the vanilla pod into the mixture (keep the pod for another recipe or to make vanilla sugar). Add the kirsch, if using. Whisk until smooth.
- Strain the batter through a sieve placed over the greengages. Bake for 25–30 minutes or until puffed and browned. Allow to cool (the batter will sink slightly), then serve warm or cold with pouring cream.

# early autumn
# setting the scene

This is harvest festival time, bringing out the latent squirrel in us all and tempting everyone to purr with satisfaction. It might be an overcoat colder at times, and average rainfall tends to increase, but there are usually many soft golden days that are dry enough for gathering in fruit, storing maincrop vegetables and saving seeds to sow next year, all the traditional homesteader's ways of ensuring continuity and food security. Keep an eye open for chilly nights, though: global warming might be evident, but there's still a growing threat of the occasional frost, the cue to make remaining crops safe and keep the harvest going.

The start of the main harvest, with onion bulbs ripening in the sun until dry enough to store for winter.

seasonal planner

**IN SEASON NOW**

apples, aubergines, beetroot, blackberries, blackcurrants, Brussels sprouts, cabbages (autumn), calabrese, cardoons, carrots, cauliflowers (summer/autumn), celeriac, celery, chard, chicory (heading), cucumbers, endive, figs, French beans, grapes, green sprouting broccoli, Jerusalem artichokes, kale, kohlrabi, land cress, leeks, lettuces, melons, onions (bulbing), oriental greens, parsnips, peaches, pears, peas, peppers, perpetual spinach, plums, potatoes, quinces, radishes, raspberries, runner beans, salad onions, salsify, scorzonera, spinach (winter), squashes, strawberries, swedes, sweetcorn, sweet fennel, tomatoes, turnips, winter purslane

**SOW NOW**

**indoors** carrots, lettuces (greenhouse), radishes
**cold frame/nursery bed** cabbages (spring), cauliflowers (summer), chicory (heading), endive, lettuces (hardy), oriental greens, salad leaves
**outdoors** broad beans, peas (hardy), turnips, spinach (winter)

**PLANT NOW**

**indoors** herbs (transplanted), lettuces
**outdoors** cabbages (spring), garlic, onions (autumn)

# SEASONAL TASKS

**GARDENERS AS STEWARDS** Most seed companies are regretful but emphatic about replacing old varieties with new: conserving, registering and testing stocks is expensive, and only those kinds with commercially approved qualities are likely to survive. Fortunately, seed banks and libraries, seed-saving networks and individual gardeners are aware of the risks to established varieties, their genetic value or special flavours, and keeping these in existence is now a high priority for many people.

Bypassing the seed industry is a habit for some gardeners and recommended for all. Saving your own can supply more fresh seed than you are likely to need and at virtually no cost; quality and germination rate can be higher than those of bought seeds; you can preserve unique characteristics if you harvest from unusually vigorous, productive, hardy or drought-tolerant plants; and you could be helping to steward a long heritage of living heirlooms grown for decades, even centuries, by our ancestors, who were often more alert to the value of tradition.

For routine saving from one year to the next, collect ripe seeds from several of the best plants, but *not* F1 hybrids whose progeny will be unpredictable. Dry them thoroughly and keep cool in airtight containers. Do not leave plants to seed freely and invade neighbouring plots (salsify, parsnips and phacelia have become endemic on many allotment sites!).

There are a few important points to note when saving special seeds.

- Check donor plants are free from diseases, which may be passed on via the seeds.
- Make sure the plants are true to type, if you are helping to maintain a specific named variety.
- Grow self-pollinating crops, such as peas, lettuces and tomatoes, at least 2m (6ft) from another variety.
- Be aware that cross-pollinators, like brassicas, carrots and sweetcorn, need growing in total isolation, ideally in special crop cages.
- Collect seed from several plants in the same batch to maintain genetic vigour and diversity.
- Make sure that seeds are fully ripe when gathered, or ripen them (tomatoes and squashes, for example) soon after harvest.
- Store dried seeds somewhere cool, dry and as airtight as possible.

**Harvesting ripe borlotti beans left to dry on the vine.**

**PROPAGATING FRUIT PLANTS** Whole gardens have been created from cuttings taken from other people's plants and, even at unorthodox times of year, many gardeners habitually view any wayward or accessible shoot as a potential cutting to root by one method or another – thrust into the ground, stood in water on a windowsill or struck conventionally in a potful of cuttings compost.

Inspect fruit prunings for potential propagating material, which are always valuable for replacement or surplus bartering stock, provided that the donor plants are totally healthy.

Spring and summer trimmings can supply soft and semi-ripe cuttings for rooting in a frame or greenhouse (even raspberry cane tips are successful), while hardwood cuttings are routinely taken at this time of year. These are the simplest of all to root: essentially the process involves little more than pushing a stick into the ground.

**Autumn leaf-fall is time to select hardwood cuttings.**

seasonal planner

Giving up chemical pesticides means using other, less environmentally harmful methods of protecting crops, such as camouflage, deterrence, interception or simple vigilance and understanding (winged fruit pests, for example, are hard to avoid except by exploiting features of their lifestyles).

▶ Fruit moth grubs and females that pupate or hibernate in the soil over winter can be waylaid with sticky grease bands applied to tree trunks and their stakes now, and left in place until late spring.

▶ Various moths that lay their eggs in flowers or immature fruits can be lured to sticky pheromone traps hung in the branches of fruit trees from mid-spring onwards (*see right*).

▶ Keep the area at the base of fruit clear of weeds. Gently loosen mulches or the soil surface in the autumn to expose grubs to foraging blackbirds.

▶ Pick and destroy mummified fruits to prevent the spread of disease, trim broken branches back to sound tissue, and remove any diseased or dead wood whenever seen.

▶ Only prune stone fruits like plums and cherries between spring bud-burst and autumn leaf-fall so that wounds heal faster, preventing the entry of pathogens like silver leaf disease spores.

Plants to try from hardwood cuttings include nearly all the woody soft fruits: blackcurrants, red- and whitecurrants, gooseberries and grapes outdoors now; blueberries, loquat and citrus fruits in a cold frame or greenhouse in late summer. Among top fruits, quinces, damsons, myrobalan plums, mulberries and figs (under glass) are more variable but always worth trying.

**PLANTING PERENNIALS** There are various sound arguments for preferring autumn to spring for planting new perennials like rhubarb, most woody herbs and all soft and top fruit.

▶ The ground is still warm and receptive, allowing roots to start working before winter sets in.
▶ There will be fewer demands next season than there would be from spring-planted stock, which could need water and shelter in a dry or windy season until they are growing strongly.
▶ Nursery plants are usually lifted and delivered in autumn, as soon as their foliage has died down, making planting them now another job completed at a time when there is less pressure than in spring.

**A selection of young herbs gathered together in a window box for easy picking over winter.**

About a month before you expect plants to arrive, dig planting sites two spades' deep and about 90cm (3ft) across each way for individual plants or as a continuous 90cm (3ft) wide strip for fruits (like cordon apples) grown in rows. Remove perennial weeds, as it's easier to do now than after new plants are settled in. Work in plenty of garden compost or a tree planting mixture (nothing richer), especially for raspberries, which enjoy slightly acid conditions; stone fruits, like cherries and plums, prefer an alkaline soil, so lime acid ground to pH6.5–7.2. Then leave the site to settle until you are ready to plant.

**Perennials to delay planting until spring include asparagus and globe artichokes, except on the lightest soils, because autumn transplants are notoriously vulnerable to rotting in cold, wet conditions. As a winter crop, Jerusalem artichokes are most easily divided and replanted in spring.**

ask the
EXPERT

## POTTING UP HERBS FOR WINTER

Although you might have a comprehensive stock of dried and frozen herbs for winter use (*see pages 68–9*), a fresh supply is always welcome. Basil, chives, parsley, marjoram, mint and tarragon can all be kept in pots in a cold frame or sheltered place outdoors, in a greenhouse bed or used growing bag, or assembled in a sunny window box, close to hand for convenient harvest.

Choose small bushy plants from cuttings taken last spring, divide established clumps of chives, marjoram and tarragon, or make special sowings of basil and parsley early in autumn to make young clumps for growing on indoors. Use a free-draining compost that is not too rich at this time of year (*John Innes No. 2* is ideal), and keep plants cool in a cold frame or close to the greenhouse glass (remove all shading first) to avoid soft leggy growth. Prepare several pots of each kind to use in circulation, allowing cropped samples to recover for subsequent picking. Plant out next spring to augment or replace existing stocks.

**Supermarkets often sell pots of young herb plants for immediate use. Buy now, harvest the leaves over winter, then move the pots to the greenhouse or cold frame. Feed and divide in early spring to plant outside for a head start.**

ask the
EXPERT

### START TIDYING THE PLOT

With less sowing and maintenance to fit into your visits to the plot, start tidying here and there while conditions are still mild and inviting – later on, everything might be sodden or frozen, and the work could seem dreary and unappealing.

▶ Cut down exhausted topgrowth.

▶ Check for overlooked produce or seedheads to salvage.

▶ Add all soft and green waste to the compost heap.

▶ Dry any woody material and store under cover for improvised supports next season.

▶ Use tougher stems and lifted plant roots as the base layer of your next compost heap.

▶ Collect dead and yellowing leaves for making *leafmould* or adding carbon to your compost heap.

▶ Trim grass paths and edges, and add the clippings to collected leaves to accelerate decomposition.

▶ Compost soft annual weeds or dig them into bare ground.

▶ Fork up perennial weeds and pack in a black bin bag, sealing it when full so the roots will rot safely. (During summer, spread these roots on a path or hard surface to dry until brittle and then add to compost as a source of minerals.)

▶ Pull up stakes and canes, brush them clean and store in the dry.

▶ Collect up string and labels, and recycle or discard.

▶ Roll up netting and pack away safely off the ground (frogs, slow worms and small mammals are easily trapped in plastic mesh).

### TRY THIS...

Dig up healthy runner beans (especially heritage kinds, like black-seeded strains) and store over winter exactly like dahlias. Runner beans are true perennials, and will survive in a frost-free place for replanting in late spring to give earlier and heavier crops.

### IT'S NOT TOO LATE TO...

Plant early potatoes (save some from bought supplies) in pots, 3–4 in a container 45cm (18in) wide and deep (*see left*). Tend pots outside until frosts threaten, then bring under glass and harvest when in flower, or cut off fading topgrowth and store the potful dry, dark and frost-free until needed.

### IF YOU HAVE TIME...

Propagate the best blackberries and hybrid berries for planting on fences and in hedges. Bury the end 8–10cm (3–4in) of a new (unfruited) cane in the ground or simply anchor it to the soil with a brick. The cane will root and produce a new shoot next spring, when it can be severed and grown on for transplanting in the autumn.

**TRY THIS**

**HERB HARVEST**
The fully stocked home herbarium contains seeds and roots, as well as the leaves gathered and dried in summer (*see pages 68–9*). Don't wait until the seedheads of dill, fennel (*see picture*) or aniseed are fully ripe, as they could suddenly shed while your back is turned. In early autumn, look out for a change of colour, darkening stalks or papery skins on pods, gently tuck the heads in paper bags and then cut them off to hang in a warm, airy place to finish drying for 2–3 weeks. Later, as their foliage shows signs of dying down, you can dig up the roots of angelica, lovage, liquorice and marshmallow to dry whole, with larger pieces split lengthways. Dry in the oven at 50°C (120°F) or in a microwave (full power for 30-second bursts) until light in weight but not discoloured.

# HARVEST HIGHLIGHTS

**GRAPES** There are many incidental reasons to make do without garden chemicals: organic tomatoes are higher in precious antioxidants, for example, and there's no need to wash unsprayed grapes and spoil their fragile bloom. Check maturing bunches regularly, keeping those under glass warm and dry but regularly ventilated to deter moulds. Outdoor kinds and nominal wine varieties can be harvested as they ripen, using them for jams, jellies, wine-making or pickling in anis, brandy or vodka. Don't process fine dessert kinds like 'Muscat of Alexandria', though, as these should be savoured just as they are. Preserve surplus bunches by cutting each with 30cm (12in) of main stem. Insert the lower end of this in a jar half-filled with water and wedged at an angle on a shelf so the grapes hang free: they will keep for 2–3 months like this in a cool room. (*See also page 215.*)

**ONIONS & LEEKS** Maincrop onions are ready to lift about the same time as the first leeks. Ease onion bulbs out of the ground with a fork to dry for a week or two on the surface (under glass if wet), then store in trays or plaited into ropes and suspended. Use split, damaged and flowering bulbs first – if they start to deteriorate, make onion soup and freeze. Begin forking up early leek varieties, which will be sweet and tender – perfect as buttered leeks with pot-roasted beef. Even their soft leaves can be chopped for flavouring soups and stock. Finish these early plants before midwinter, when it's time to move on to hardy varieties with their sturdier constitution, darker leaves and more robust flavour. (*See also pages 194 and 196.*)

**TOMATOES** Depending on when they were planted and whether they grow indoors or out, you might have been picking tomatoes from midsummer onwards, but in late summer and early autumn the trickle becomes a flood. Greenhouse plants can be left to continue naturally for a few more weeks, possibly with 8–10 trusses on vigorous kinds like 'Mirabelle' and 'Sungold'. Outdoor plants should be stopped in late summer and might need help with ripening now: cover plants with cloches, first laying down cordon types on a bed of straw, or suspend complete plants or trusses under glass. Use up blemished fruits of all varieties to make tomato conserve for the winter stock-cupboard, for thickening and flavouring, or as a basis for sauces and pizza toppings. (*See also page 211.*)

**Preserving ripe grapes in water until needed.**

**Ripening tomatoes by covering with cloches.**

**Drying onions in sunshine until their skins are papery.**

### HEDGEROW HARVEST

You may have so much maturing on the plot that it's easy to overlook boundary hedges (as well as the open countryside), where a whole larder of fruits could be ripe for gathering. Elderly gardeners sometimes avoid elderberries because wartime memories of collecting them for ersatz currants linger long, but these are a choice and often profuse crop to turn into richly flavoured preserves. Or you could simply gather all the hips, haws, sloes, blackberries and elderberries you can find to mix together for hedgerow wine or add to apples to make hedgerow jelly to spread on toasted teacakes by the winter fireside. You might even discover hazelnuts overlooked by squirrels – eat the nuts before they dry and lose their fresh subtle flavour – or the papery cones of wild hops to harvest for home-made beer and festive garlands. (*See pages 128–9 for some hedgerow recipes.*)

### STORING FRUIT ODDMENTS

Surplus and spoiled cultivated fruits can be mixed and preserved for the winter store-cupboard. Clean up any apples, pears, plums and cherries that are bruised, cracked or invaded by pest larvae, cut into pieces and add to the last soft fruits like strawberries, blackcurrants and blackberries. Either pack all together in large bags or plastic containers (useful for adding any extras later) or separate into meal-size portions and freeze. Then, whenever needed, a couple of handfuls can be cooked into a rich fruit 'cocktail' for pies and crumbles, compôtes and brûlées, or a full-bodied topping for steamed puddings.

## EAT NOW

Not everyone relishes the approach of autumn with its lengthening shadows, mellow twilight and early drawing down of blinds, but for gardeners, tuned to the rhythm of the seasons, it is the climax of the year and a time for celebration. The air is full of sweet or spicy perfumes: ripening melons, apples sweating out their field heat in store, the penetrating scent of blackcurrant bushes, and even the earthy and opulent fragrance of parsnip foliage. Gather in everything that might be harmed by an early frost or the mildew that's fed by morning mists. Load the table with good things, store the rest, and take time out to harvest the hedgerows. (*See* In season now, *page 108*.)

## RECIPES

## CHILLED BEETROOT SOUP

**SERVES 4**

It is still enjoyable to have a chilled soup at this time of year. This recipe and the soup with goat's cheese (*see right*) are just as good hot or cold. Use small beetroots for this recipe as they are sweeter.

- 2 tbsp extra virgin olive oil
- 1 small onion, peeled and finely chopped
- 1 leek, white part only, washed and chopped
- 2 garlic cloves, crushed
- 900g (2lb) beetroot, peeled and finely chopped
- 1 litre (1¾ pints) hot vegetable or chicken stock
- salt and freshly ground pepper, to taste
- crème fraîche, to garnish

- Heat the oil in a pan and cook the onion slowly until it is translucent.
- Add the leek and garlic to the onion and cook until soft. Add the beetroot and stock. Bring to the boil, then reduce the heat, cover and simmer until tender, about 30 minutes.
- Blend the mixture in a blender or food processor. If you prefer a finer consistency, pass it through a sieve. Leave to cool, then chill in the fridge.
- Check the seasoning. It is best to do this when it is cold as the flavour can change from warm soup.
- Pour into bowls, spoon on some crème fraîche and use a skewer to make a pattern on the top.

## BORSCHT WITH PICKLED ONIONS & DILL

**SERVES 6**

This is a classic beetroot soup but with a kick of orange juice and 'pickled onions' added to it.

- 250ml (8fl oz) red wine vinegar
- 2 tsp caster sugar
- ½ red onion, peeled and cut into 6mm (¼in) half moons
- 675g (1½lb) beetroot
- 120ml (4fl oz) orange juice, freshly squeezed
- 500ml (16fl oz) hot vegetable or chicken stock
- 500ml (16fl oz) water
- 1 tsp coarse salt
- ¼ tsp freshly ground black pepper

**Garnish**

- fresh dill sprigs
- sour cream

- Place the vinegar and sugar in a small saucepan over a medium heat. Bring just to the boil, then remove from the heat, and stir until the sugar has dissolved. Put the onion in a bowl, pour over the vinegar mixture, and marinate for 1 hour.
- Preheat oven to 200°C/400°F/gas 6. Put the beetroot in a small roasting pan, cover with aluminium foil and roast until tender, about 1–1½ hours. Allow to rest until cool enough to handle, then remove the skins and cut the beetroot into bite-sized wedges.
- Put the beetroot in a saucepan with the orange juice, stock and water. Bring just to the boil, then turn off the heat, cover and leave for 30 minutes to let the flavours combine.
- Remove the onions from the marinade with a slotted spoon, add to the saucepan with the beetroot mixture and stir in. Add the salt and pepper. When ready to serve, garnish with the dill sprigs and a dollop of cream.

## LINDA'S BEETROOT & GOAT'S CHEESE SOUP

**SERVES 6**

Linda Tubby, the well-known food writer and celebrated cook, donated the recipe for this earthy beetroot soup with melted goat's cheese discs.

- 4 tbsp olive oil
- 6 small onions or 375g (13oz) finely chopped onion
- 4 garlic cloves, finely chopped
- 5 beetroot, cooked then peeled
- 1 litre (1¾ pints) hot vegetable or chicken stock
- salt and freshly ground pepper, to taste
- 3 x 100g (3½oz) portions of round goat's cheese
- 1 tsp fresh thyme leaves

- Heat the oil in a pan and cook the onions and garlic slowly until they are translucent. Slice the beetroot and add to the onion and garlic with the stock, adding salt to taste.
- Bring to the boil, then reduce the heat, cover and simmer for about 35 minutes until the beetroot are really soft.
- Pour the mixture into a blender or food processor and blend, then return to the pan to heat further.
- Meanwhile, preheat the grill to high. Cut the goat's cheeses in half horizontally, place on a foil-lined grill pan and scatter with pepper and thyme. Put under the grill until the cheese is bubbling and golden.
- Pour the soup into bowls, lift off the cheese slices with a spatula and place one in the centre of each bowl, then serve.

## SWEETCORN & CHILLI CHOWDER

**SERVES 4**

A chowder is a thick soup. It also has the addition of milk, so the soup is always a creamy colour. By processing the soup and not leaving the sweetcorn kernels whole, you get a yellow- and red-flecked soup.

5 sweetcorn cobs, husks and threads removed

30g (1oz) butter

2 leeks, white parts only, coarsely chopped

1 stalk celery, diced

1 small red chilli, deseeded and finely chopped

750ml (1¼ pints) hot vegetable or chicken stock

juice of 2 lemons

450ml (16fl oz) milk

salt and freshly ground pepper, to taste

6 tbsp coarsely chopped fresh coriander, to garnish

- With a large knife, cut the kernels off the sweetcorn cobs. With the blunt side of the knife, scrape off the pulp.
- In a large pan, melt the butter over a medium heat. Add the leeks, celery and chilli. Sauté until the leeks are translucent and the celery and chilli are soft. Add the corn and pulp and stir for 2–3 minutes, making sure that it is thoroughly combined. Add the chicken stock and lemon juice and bring to the boil, then reduce the heat and simmer for 15 minutes.
- Pour the soup into a food processor or blender in small amounts, and blend.
- Return the soup to the pan and stir in the milk slowly. Cook for 5 minutes or until heated through. Season with salt and pepper.
- Ladle into four bowls, garnish with the coriander and serve.

## SWEETCORN & CHICKEN FLOWERPOTS

**SERVES 6**

Make this in six small flowerpots or individual bowls, or one deep 20cm (8in) pie dish. Terracotta flowerpots are perfect for this kind of pie, as they are ovenproof and a good one-person serving. If you are using them, half line the bottom with foil to stop the filling falling through the hole in the bottom. Inside it is a very creamy, delicate pie. The corn crust on top has a delicious crispness to it. Note that the crust should be used as soon as it is made, as waiting around will spoil it.

6 sweetcorn cobs, husks and threads removed

3 tbsp olive oil

600g (1lb 5oz) chicken thighs, skinned and meat removed from bones

3 leeks, white parts only, coarsely chopped

1 garlic clove, chopped

2 bay leaves

pinch each of nutmeg and cayenne

1 tbsp plain flour

2 tbsp chopped fresh thyme

300ml (10floz) hot vegetable or chicken stock

250ml (8fl oz) double cream

salt and freshly ground pepper, to taste

**Cornmeal dough**

210g (7½oz) plain flour

30g (1oz) yellow polenta

2 tsp baking powder

¾ tsp bicarbonate of soda

¾ tsp salt

1½ tbsp caster sugar

100g (3½oz) chilled unsalted butter, cut into pieces

90ml (3fl oz) skimmed milk

- Preheat oven to 230°C/450°F/gas 8.
- With a large knife, cut the kernels off the sweetcorn cobs. With the blunt side of the knife, scrape off the pulp.
- Heat the oil in a large pan, add the chicken and sear until golden. Add the leeks and the garlic and stir until the leeks are translucent.
- Add the bay leaves, nutmeg, cayenne and flour and cook for 1 minute, stirring all the time.
- Add the sweetcorn kernels and pulp plus the thyme and cook for a further minute. Stir in the stock and cream. Bring to the boil, then reduce the heat and simmer until the liquid has thickened and reduced by a third and the chicken is just cooked.
- Pour the mixture into a sieve set over a dish, then pour the liquid back into the pan and boil to reduce it by a third. Return the chicken to the pan, remove the pan from the heat and take out the bay leaves. Season with salt and pepper.
- To make the dough, mix together the flour, polenta, baking powder, bicarbonate of soda, salt and sugar.
- Rub the butter into the dry mixture with your fingertips until it resembles breadcrumbs. Add enough of the milk until it holds together.
- On a floured surface, roll out the dough to a 28 x 35cm (11 x 14in) rectangle. Cut out six small circles or one large one, using the dish/pots as a guide.
- Spoon the corn and chicken mixture into the dishes and place the pastry circles on top. Cut two slits in the top to let the steam out. Crimp the edges and brush with the remaining milk.
- Place the pots on a baking sheet and bake for around 12 minutes or until the crust is golden brown. Serve with a simple green salad (see page 73).

## SWEETCORN SOUP

**SERVES 4**

This is another sweetcorn soup, but this one has a kick of ginger and herbs and a potato added to make a really thick and warming soup.

2 tbsp olive oil

1 onion, peeled and chopped

1 leek, white part only, chopped

4 salad onions, white part only, chopped

1 tbsp peeled and grated fresh root ginger

3 sweetcorn cobs, husks and threads removed, cooked

1 potato, peeled and chopped

500ml (16fl oz) hot vegetable or chicken stock

2 tbsp finely chopped fresh basil

1 tbsp finely chopped fresh mint

salt and freshly ground pepper, to taste

- Heat the oil in a pan. When it is hot, add the onion, leek, salad onions and ginger. Sauté until soft, stirring frequently.
- With a large knife, cut the kernels off the sweetcorn cobs. With the blunt side of the knife, scrape off the pulp. Add to the mixture with the potato, vegetable stock and herbs.
- Simmer for around 30 minutes or until the potato is soft.
- Pour all the soup into a blender or food processor and blend, then return to the pan, warm through and season with salt and pepper. Alternatively, if you prefer to keep some chunks, blend just half the soup.

## SWEETCORN FRITTERS

**MAKES TEN 10CM (4IN) FRITTERS**

Fritters use a batter mixture with added fruit or vegetables. Sweetcorn can be made into really delicious fritters, and the addition of beaten egg white makes them very light. Serve with a salad and one of the following puddings for a really good autumnal lunch.

3 large sweetcorn cobs, husks and threads removed, cooked

1 large egg, separated, plus 1 large egg white

1 tbsp plain flour

1½ tsp caster sugar

¼ tsp salt

pinch of freshly ground pepper

4 tbsp vegetable oil

- With a large knife, cut the kernels off the sweetcorn cobs. With the blunt side of the knife, scrape off the pulp. Put the kernels and pulp into a bowl, add the egg yolk, flour, sugar, salt and pepper, and stir to combine.
- In a clean bowl, whisk egg whites until stiff but not dry. Fold into the sweetcorn mixture. Heat half the vegetable oil in a large cast-iron or non-stick frying pan over a medium-high heat.
- Drop spoonfuls of batter into the oil, spaced a few centimetres (a couple of inches) apart. Cook until golden on the bottom, 1-2 minutes. Turn over using a spatula, and cook until golden on the other side, 1-2 minutes more. Keep the fritters warm while you repeat with the remaining batter and oil. Serve immediately.

## SPICY FRYING-PAN CORNBREAD

**SERVES 8**

This recipe uses ground dried maize known as polenta. This is a popular ingredient used a great deal in America (where it is called cornmeal) and Italy. You make this recipe in the same way as muffins. The mixture is lightly folded in to create a sloppy mixture. Ideally, use a cast-iron ovenproof frying pan, although you could use a loaf tin or cake tin.

2 large sweetcorn cobs, husks and threads removed, cooked

30g (1oz) unsalted butter

1 onion, peeled and chopped

250g (9oz) polenta

300g (10oz) self-raising flour

30g (1oz) caster sugar

2 tsp baking powder

1 red chilli, deseeded and finely chopped

1 tsp salt

4 eggs

400ml (14fl oz) milk

100g (3½oz) hard cheese, grated

3 salad onions, trimmed and chopped

- Preheat oven to 190°C/375°F/gas 5.
- With a large knife, cut the kernels off the sweetcorn cobs. Melt the butter in a large frying pan and fry the onion until softened. Add the corn and fry for a few more minutes.
- Tip into a food processor or blender and blend to a purée.
- Combine all the dry ingredients in a large bowl. Whisk together the eggs and milk and stir in the corn purée, then tip the mixure into the dry ingredients and combine loosely.
- Pour the batter into a large ovenproof frying pan. Scatter the cheese and salad onions over the surface. Bake in the oven for 45 minutes until golden and a skewer inserted into the middle comes out clean.
- Serve straight from the pan with a spicy chilli con carne or similar.

# SWEETCORN & COCONUT PUDDINGS

### SERVES 6

These sweetcorn puddings are made with coconut milk. Reducing the sweetcorn to a purée and adding cornflour gives custard-like puddings, which will keep, covered, in the refrigerator for up to three days.

3 large sweetcorn cobs, husks and threads removed, cooked

250ml (8fl oz) unsweetened coconut milk

250ml (8fl oz) whole milk

115g (4oz) caster sugar

1 tbsp cornflour

1 tsp vanilla extract

pinch of cinnamon, plus more to spinkle

3 tbsp desiccated coconut

- With a large knife, cut the kernels off the sweetcorn cobs. With the blunt side of the knife, scrape off the pulp.
- Put the sweetcorn, pulp and remaining ingredients, except for the desiccated coconut, into a food processor and blend until smooth.
- Force the mixture through a sieve into a heavy saucepan, pressing the solids hard to extract as much as liquid as possible. Discard the waste.
- Bring the mixture to a boil, then whisk constantly for 5 minutes, keeping the mixture at boiling point.
- When the mixture has thickened, add the coconut. Pour into 6 teacups and leave to cool, then chill. Sprinkle with cinnamon before serving cold.

## TRY THIS
### BBQ SWEETCORN

Keep the husks on the sweetcorn, dampen with water and place on a barbecue. The husks protect the ears inside from burning and let them cook to perfection. The smoky taste is irresistible.

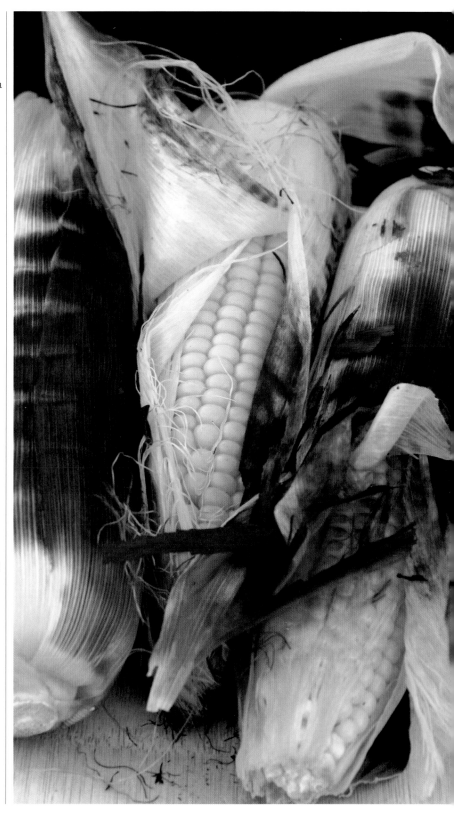

## APPLE ALMOST PIE

### SERVES 6

This is an apple upside-down pie if you
care to invert it to serve. Use any kind of
nuts instead of walnuts. It is just as good
served with cream or ice cream.

butter, for greasing

225g (8oz) cooking apples, peeled, cored
and sliced

60g (2oz) chopped walnuts

115g (4oz) soft light brown sugar

2 eggs

225g (8oz) caster sugar

115g (4oz) butter, melted

115g (4oz) self-raising flour

- Preheat oven to 170°C/325°F/gas 3.
  Grease a 25cm (10in) pie dish.
- Spread the apples over the bottom of
  the dish. Sprinkle with the nuts and
  the brown sugar.
- In small bowl beat the eggs well,
  using an electric mixer, then add the
  caster sugar and beat until well
  mixed in. Add the melted butter and
  beat again. Fold in the flour gently.
  Pour over the apples in the dish.
- Bake for about 1 hour or until the top
  is golden brown.
- Serve hot with cream or warm with
  ice cream.

## SPICED APPLE & TREACLE TART

### SERVES 6

This is a take on the classic treacle tart. The
addition of apples, cinnamon and sultanas
cuts down any excessive sweetness. Why
treacle and not syrup tart? Sounds better.

450g (1lb) packet ready-made sweet
shortcrust pastry

3 large cooking apples, peeled, cored and
finely chopped

115g (4oz) sultanas

175g (6oz) fresh breadcrumbs

1 tsp mixed spice

½ tsp ground cinnamon

6 tbsp golden syrup

finely grated rind and juice of 1 lemon

1 egg yolk, beaten

- Preheat oven to 190°C/375°F/gas 5.
- Roll out the pastry to fit a 20cm (8in)
  diameter shallow tart tin. Lift the
  pastry into the tin and press it gently
  over the base and up the sides,
  making sure not to stretch it. Trim
  the edges and reserve the trimmings.
- To make the filling, mix together all
  the ingredients and spoon the
  mixture into the pastry case.
- Roll out the pastry trimmings and
  cut into thin strips. Use them to
  make a lattice pattern on top of the
  tart. Brush the lattice with a little
  beaten egg, then bake the tart in the
  oven for about 30 minutes or until
  cooked through and golden brown.
  Serve warm.

## APPLE RICE

### SERVES 6

This is rice pudding with a difference.
It is served cold, which is common
practice in the Mediterranean. You add
the uncooked fruit, including some late
strawberries, to the rice and serve it
piled high with some strawberry sauce
poured around it.

65g (2¼oz) short-grain rice

600ml (1 pint) milk

45g (1½oz) sugar

1 eating apple, peeled, cored and diced

1 tbsp lemon juice

125g (4½oz) strawberries, hulled and
quartered

150ml (5fl oz) crème fraîche

### Sauce

125g (4½oz) strawberries

1 tbsp icing sugar

- Put the rice in a heavy-based
  saucepan with the milk. Bring to
  the boil, then reduce the heat and
  simmer gently for 20 minutes or
  until tender. Stir in the sugar, remove
  from the heat and leave to cool.
- Toss the diced apple in the lemon
  juice to prevent browning. Mix the
  apple and the strawberries into the
  crème fraîche, then fold into the
  cooled rice. Turn into a bowl and chill.
- To make the sauce, purée the
  strawberries in a blender or food
  processor with the icing sugar.
  Spoon the rice into individual bowls,
  spoon the strawberry sauce around
  and serve.

seasonal planner

## APPLE BROWN BETTY

**SERVES 6**

Every American cook could give you a recipe for Brown Betty. It consists of apples baked between layers of buttered crumbs. A 'Betty' is an English pudding closely related to the French Apple Charlotte. It was a popular baked pudding during colonial times in America.

60g (2oz) butter, plus extra for greasing
115g (4oz) fresh wholemeal breadcrumbs
1 tsp ground cinnamon.
2 tbsp soft light brown sugar
450g (1lb) cooking apples, peeled, cored and thinly sliced
60g (2oz) sultanas
2 tbsp golden syrup
1 tbsp water

- Butter a large pudding basin. Add a few of the breadcrumbs and swirl around the basin to coat.
- Melt the butter and add to the rest of breadcrumbs, mix thoroughly and cook in a frying pan over low heat until golden brown.
- Mix together the cinnamon and sugar. Put layers of apple, breadcrumbs, sultanas, and the cinnamon mixture in the basin. Blend the syrup and water and pour over everything. Cover with a double thickness of greased greaseproof paper or foil. Twist and fold under the rim of the basin to secure. Steam for 2 hours.
- Serve warm with cream or custard.

## APPLE & DAMSON TANSY

**SERVES 4**

An old favourite. The dish is like an omelette and should be served straight from the pan. This recipe is no longer flavoured by the herb tansy, which was very bitter and also gave it its name, but instead uses a splendid combination of spices that is much more appealing to modern tastes. If you can't find any damsons, increase the amount of apples. You could sprinkle some flaked almonds on top before grilling.

2 large Cox apples, peeled, cored and thinly sliced
225g (8oz) damsons, stoned and quartered
30g (1oz) butter
60g (2oz) sugar
pinch of ground cloves
pinch of ground cinnamon
4 eggs, separated
3 tbsp sour cream or natural yoghurt

- Place the apples, damsons, butter and half the sugar in a large frying pan. Cook over a gentle heat for 10–15 minutes or until the fruit is soft, stirring all the time. Stir in the cloves and cinnamon and remove from the heat.
- In a large bowl, beat together the egg yolks and cream, then stir in the fruit.
- In another bowl, whisk the egg whites until stiff, then very gently fold into the fruit mixture. Put back in the frying pan and cook over a low heat until set.
- Preheat the grill to high. Sprinkle the fruit mixture with the remaining sugar, place under the grill and brown. Serve immediately.

## GRAN'S APPLE PUDDING

**SERVES 4–6**

Murdo's gran – Murdo is the art editor on this book – used to make this recipe, which has been handed down to him. Although there is suet in the pastry, it doesn't make the pudding heavy. Gran always served it with clotted cream.

butter, for greasing
225g (8oz) plain flour
pinch of salt
1 tbsp baking powder
85g (3oz) shredded vegetable suet
750g (1lb 10oz) cooking apples, sliced
30g (1oz) demerara sugar
pinch of ground cloves

- Grease a large pudding basin. Sift the flour, salt and baking powder into the basin. Stir in the suet and mix with enough cold water to form a soft but not sticky dough. Knead gently on a lightly floured surface.
- Cut off a quarter of the dough, roll it out to the size of the top of the basin and reserve for a lid. Roll out the remaining dough and use to line the basin.
- Mix together the apples, sugar and cloves and use them to fill the basin. Add 2 tablespoons water. Dampen the dough edges with a little water and place the lid in position. Press the edges together well to seal. Cover with a double thickness of greased greaseproof paper or foil, with a pleat in the centre to allow for rising. Twist and fold under the rim of the basin to secure. Steam for 2½–3 hours.
- Remove the greaseproof paper or foil. Tie a clean napkin around the basin and serve straight from the basin with clotted cream.

## APPLE & CARROT SALAD WITH GINGER-MINT DRESSING

**SERVES 4-6**

This is an invigorating and refreshing Southeast Asian-style salad. It combines matchsticks of apples and carrots with a simple dressing. It is very low in both calories and fat, yet still satisfying. Prepare the apples just before you need them, so that they don't go brown. This dish needs to be served immediately after preparation to keep the colours fresh.

3 tbsp seasoned rice wine vinegar

2 tbsp peanut oil

2 large, crisp apples, peeled, cored and cut into matchsticks

2 carrots, peeled and cut into matchsticks

2.5cm (1in) piece fresh root ginger, peeled and grated

2 shallots, peeled and thinly sliced

salt and freshly ground pepper, to taste

20g (⅔oz) fresh mint, finely chopped

65g (2¼oz) roasted peanuts, coarsely chopped, to garnish

- In a large bowl, whisk together the vinegar and oil to form a smooth dressing.
- Add the apples, carrots, ginger and shallots to the dressing and mix together. Season with salt and pepper.
- Add the mint and mix in gently. Serve immediately, garnished with the peanuts.

## POTATO & APPLE PANCAKES WITH BEETROOT RELISH

**SERVES 6-8 AS A STARTER**

A combination of pancake and rosti, this recipe needs crisp apples, especially in the relish. Beetroots don't just come in purple. There are some pretty coloured ones around, too – yellow, orange, and white with red stripes. Try to mix the colours for this fresh-tasting dish. You could serve this dish with some smoked eel or mackerel on the side. Their strong flavours won't overwhelm the delicious pancakes.

500g (1lb 2oz) floury potatoes, peeled

1 crisp apple, peeled, cored and quartered

1 tsp salt

freshly ground pepper, to taste

4 tbsp plain flour

2 large eggs, beaten

2 tbsp snipped fresh chives

1 tbsp chopped fresh dill, plus sprigs to garnish

vegetable oil, for shallow-frying

about 6 tbsp crème fraîche

### Beetroot relish

½ small onion, peeled and very finely chopped

½ tsp golden caster sugar

4 small cooked beetroots, cooled, peeled and very finely chopped

1 crisp apple, peeled, cored and finely chopped

2 tbsp white wine vinegar

1 tbsp finely chopped fresh dill

salt and freshly ground pepper, to taste

- Make the relish first. Put the onion and sugar in a bowl and leave for 5 minutes. Then stir in the beetroot, chopped apple, vinegar and dill. Season with salt and pepper.
- To make the pancakes, grate the potatoes coarsely, rinse, dry well and put into a bowl. Grate in the apple, season with 1 teaspoon of salt and lots of pepper, then stir in the flour, eggs and herbs to make a thick batter.
- Put plates in a low oven to warm. Meanwhile, heat a small amount of oil in a large frying pan and add 2 tablespoons of mixture, flattening to make into a pancake about 10cm (4in) in diameter. Cook for 3-4 minutes on each side. Remove from the pan and add 2 tablespoons of mxture for the next pancake. Continue to make pancakes until the mixture is used up. As you finish each pancake, keep warm on crumpled kitchen paper or in a low oven while you cook the others.
- Serve the pancakes on warmed plates, topped with the relish and a dollop of crème fraîche. Garnish with the dill sprigs and some black pepper.

## APPLE DUMPLINGS

**SERVES 4**

Not really a dumpling, but a pastry with a secret. The secret? When you break open the pastry shell you'll find a whole, peeled apple inside.

225g (8oz) plain flour

175g (6oz) chilled butter, diced, plus extra for greasing

2 tbsp caster sugar

1 egg, separated, white beaten

115g (4oz) soft light brown sugar

pinch of ground cloves

grated rind of 1 lemon

4 large cooking apples, peeled, cored but left whole and covered with lemon water

- Put the flour in a bowl and rub in 115g (4oz) of the butter with your fingertips until the mixture resembles fine breadcrumbs. Stir in the caster sugar. Add the egg yolk and enough cold water to form a soft but not sticky dough. Turn out onto a lightly floured surface and knead gently. Wrap in clingfilm and chill for 30 minutes.
- Meanwhile, mash the remaining butter with the brown sugar, cloves and lemon rind and pack into the holes in the centres of the apples.
- Preheat oven to 200°C/400°F/gas 6 and grease a baking sheet.
- Cut the pastry into four equal pieces and roll out each piece to a 25cm (10in) circle. Place an apple in the centre of each. Use the beaten egg white to brush the edges of the pastry. Gather up the pastry over the apples to enclose them completely. Pinch the edges together firmly to seal.
- Place, sealed-sides down, on the greased baking sheet. Brush the dumplings with some more egg white to glaze. Bake for 20 minutes, then reduce the heat to 180°C/350°F/gas 4 for about 30 minutes until golden brown. Serve with custard.

## INDIAN PUDDING

**SERVES 10-12**

Using polenta instead of flour in this apple pudding gives it a wonderful crunchy texture. There is a simple apple sauce to pour over it.

40g (1½oz) polenta

1.4 litres (2½ pints) milk

pinch of salt

3 tbsp treacle

140g (5oz) caster sugar

3 eggs, beaten

350g (¾lb) apples, peeled, cored and chopped

140g (5oz) raisins

2 tsp cinnamon

½ tsp ginger

### Apple sauce

350g (¾lb) apples, peeled, cored and sliced

60g (2oz) caster sugar

½ tsp cinnamon

- Preheat oven to 170°C/325°F/gas 3
- In a saucepan heat the polenta with 450ml (¾ pint) of the milk. Keep stirring until slightly thickened, then leave to cool.
- Combine the remaining ingredients (not including those for the sauce) in a large ovenproof dish and add the cooked polenta. Bake for 2 hours.
- To make the sauce, put the apples, sugar and cinnamon in a heavy pan and cook on a low heat until they have reduced to a mushy state. As there is no water, you'll need to keep an eye on it to make sure it doesn't burn. For a smoother sauce, either liquidize or pass through a sieve. Keep warm.
- Serve the pudding warm with the apple sauce and some pouring cream.

## SPICED APPLE CAKE

**SERVES 8**

A simple cake recipe with a slightly spicy kick to it. The apples are carefully laid on the bottom of the tin so that after baking and inverting it you will have an apple topping. Serve as a cake or a pudding. Don't prepare the apples until you need them, or they'll turn brown.

140g (5oz) unsalted butter, softened, plus extra for greasing

225g (8oz) caster sugar

2 eggs, beaten

225g (8oz) self-raising flour

1 tsp mixed spice

450g (1lb) cooking apples, peeled, cored and sliced into circles

2 tbsp chopped walnuts

2 tsp apricot jam, warmed, to glaze

- Grease a 20cm (8in) deep, loose-bottomed cake tin. Preheat oven to 170°C/325°F/gas 3.
- Beat together the butter and sugar in a bowl until light and fluffy. Add the eggs, a little at a time, beating well after each addition. Sift in the flour and spice and fold in carefully with a metal spoon.
- Place the circular apple slices on the bottom of the tin and scatter the walnuts over the top. Pour the cake mixture in carefully so you do not disturb the apple slices.
- Bake for 1½ hours or until risen and golden. A skewer inserted in the centre should come out clean.
- When cooled, carefully invert the cake on a plate and brush over some warmed apricot jam to glaze the apples. Serve warm with some thick cream.

## APPLE CIDER CAKE

**SERVES 8-10**

This recipe from the West Country uses one of its favourite exports – cider – to increase the appley flavour. It can be served warm as a pudding or cold as a cake. Don't prepare the apples until you need them, or they'll turn brown.

115g (4oz) butter, plus extra for greasing

200g (7oz) plain flour, plus extra for dusting

3 eggs

225g (8oz) caster sugar

140ml (5fl oz) cider

1 tbsp baking powder

25g (about 1oz) caster sugar

¼ tsp ground cloves

zest of 1 large lemon

- Grease and flour a large roasting tin. Preheat oven to 200°C/400°F/gas 6.
- Whisk together the eggs and sugar in a bowl until thick and pale.
- Melt the butter in a saucepan with the cider. Bring to the boil, then remove from the heat and set aside to cool. Once cool, stir into the eggs and sugar. Sift in the flour and baking powder and fold in with a metal spoon. Pour into the roasting tin. Place the apple slices on the top. Mix the remaining sugar with the ground cloves and lemon zest, and sprinkle this mixture over the top.
- Bake for about 40 minutes until the cake is golden and the centre springs back when lightly pressed. Turn out onto a wire rack to cool, then cut the cake into squares and serve.

## APPLE BUTTER

**MAKES 2 JARS**

Apple butter is a preserve of highly concentrated apples, produced by long, slow cooking with juice to a point where the sugar in the apples caramelizes. It comes out as a thick, dark, spicy purée that is delicious spread on toast. The concentration of sugars gives it a long shelf life as a preserve, though it is best kept in the refrigerator.

1.8kg (4lb) tart dessert apples, peeled, cored and sliced

85ml (3fl oz) fresh apple juice

900g (2lb) soft dark brown sugar

2 tsp vanilla extract

1 tbsp fresh lemon juice

½ tsp ground cinnamon

½ tsp ground nutmeg

½ tsp ground ginger

pinch of ground cloves, to taste

- Place the apples, apple juice, brown sugar, vanilla extract, lemon juice and spices in a large heavy pot with a tight-fitting lid.
- Bring the mixture to the boil. Reduce the heat to medium-low and simmer for 15–25 minutes until the apples are soft enough to mash.
- Remove the apple mixture from the heat and purée in a food processor or pass through a sieve until smooth.
- Pour into hot jars (*see page 80*) and cover when cold.

## FRIED GREEN TOMATOES

**SERVES 4-6**

Heard of the film *Fried Green Tomatoes at the Whistle Stop Café*? Well, here's the recipe – a favourite from America's Deep South. The polenta gives a crispy coating and, if you use the residue fat from cooking bacon, it will add to the taste. Delicious in a Sunday fry-up!

4–6 green tomatoes

salt and freshly ground pepper, to taste

polenta (loose grains), to coat

bacon grease or vegetable oil, for shallow-frying

- Slice the tomatoes into 6–12mm (¼–½in) slices, season with salt and pepper, then dip into the polenta.
- Heat the bacon fat or oil in a frying pan and fry the tomato slices for about 3 minutes or until golden on the bottom. Gently turn and fry the other side.

## GREEN TOMATO JAM

**MAKES 4 JARS**

If you tire trying to ripen those last stragglers, then make this tangy jam. It will use up a large quantity of green tomatoes at the end of the season.

2.25kg (5lb) green tomatoes, chopped

1.8kg (4lb) golden granulated sugar

zest of 1 large lemon

- Put the tomatoes and sugar in a preserving pan. Bring slowly to the boil and turn down to soften the tomatoes.
- Add the lemon zest, and boil fast for 20 minutes or until the jam sets when tested (*see page 80*).
- Pour into hot jars (*see page 80*) and cover when cold.

## ROSEHIP CURD

**MAKES TWO 175G (6OZ) JARS**

Rosehips have 20 times more vitamin C than any other fruit. Both the following recipes come from an old Ministry of Food booklet. Rosehips make an interesting, thick, highly coloured curd with a sweet but sharp taste. The curd will quickly lose its vitamin content if it is not kept in the dark or the refrigerator to preserve it.

900g (2lb) very ripe rosehips
1.1 litres (2 pints) water
225g (8oz) golden granulated sugar

- Wash the hips and take the tops off. Boil them in the water in a stainless steel pan until they are mushy – about 1 hour.
- Rub through a sieve or a mouli. The pulp will have reduced by half and should weigh around 450g (1lb).
- Put the pulp and sugar back in the pan and bring to the boil, then turn down slightly and cook for around 10 minutes, stirring to prevent sticking.
- Pour into hot, sterilized jars (*see page 80*). Add waxed discs and cover.

### TRY THIS
### HEDGEROW HARVEST

There is so much free food for the taking on an allotment (*see page 115*). You can make the usual sloe gin or elderflower cordial (*see The Allotment Book*), but there are less-familar foods that deserve a place. Rosehips were found to contain so much vitamin C that older plot-holders may remember being sent out as school children to harvest them. Every allotment should have a rowan tree, not just for harvest but to keep small birds happy. It will certainly keep our friends the blackbirds from stealing your grapes by supplying alternative nourishment.

## ROSEHIP SYRUP

**MAKES FOUR 150ML (5FL OZ) BOTTLES**

Here's another wartime recipe using free food. Take it by the spoonful and put it on your morning porridge or evening ice cream for a quick vitamin boost. The syrup has a sweet but sharp taste, and, as before, will quickly lose its vitamin C content if not preserved properly. If you think you might need to keep it longer, freeze it in ice-cube trays.

900g (2lb) very ripe rosehips
2.6 litres (4½ pints) boiling water
450g (1lb) golden granulated sugar

- Top and tail the rosehips and either process them in a food processor or mince in an old-fashioned mincer.
- Pour 1.7 litres (3 pints) of the boiling water into a pan, add the fruit and bring back to the boil. Remove from the heat and leave to cool.
- Pour through a sterilized jelly bag or muslin square over a sieve and allow the liquid to drip through.
- When it has stopped dripping, put the liquid aside. Return the pulp to the pan, add the remaining amount of boiling water and bring back to the boil. Remove from the heat and leave to cool.
- Strain through the jelly bag or sieve again. Don't be tempted to squeeze, or you will cloud the syrup.
- Pour both extracted liquids into a clean pan and boil to reduce the liquid eventually to 900ml (1½ pints).
- Add the sugar and boil rapidly for about 5 minutes. Pour into small hot sterile bottles (*see page 80*) and seal.
- If you want to freeze the syrup, cool first, then pour into ice-cube trays.

## HEDGEROW JAM

**MAKES 3 JARS**

This has an amazing taste, like bramble jelly but sharper. Come winter, toast crumpets, spread with butter and jam, sit back, read the seed catalogues and enjoy your hedgerow harvest.

225g (8oz) crab apples, chopped
225g (8oz) very ripe rosehips
225g (8oz) hawthorn berries
225g (8oz) sloes
225g (8oz) rowan berries
450g (1lb) blackberries
450g (1lb) elderberries
900g (2lb) golden granulated sugar, plus extra, as needed

- Wash and clean all the fruit. The only ingredients that need chopping are the crab apples. Put the rosehips, hawthorn berries, sloes, rowan berries and crab apples in a pan and cover with water. Cook for about an hour until the fruit is mushy.
- Now for the messy bit! Sieve the mixture, then weigh the sieved pulp (noting the weight) and put it back into the pan. Add the blackberries and elderberries and simmer for around 15 minutes.
- Add the sugar, plus extra to equal the weight of the earlier sieved pulp. Cook gently until the sugar has dissolved, then boil rapidly. Test for setting point (*see page 80*)
- Pour into sterilized jars (*see page 80*), cool and label.

## BLACKBERRY CORDIAL

**MAKES ABOUT 1 LITRE (1¾ PINTS)**

A cordial is a concentrated mixture of just fruit, cooked and sieved to get the maximum amount of natural juice and sugar. In America, alcohol is added, which acts as a preservative. This is an option here but it makes it an adult drink. You can sustitute elderberries, which have a greater vitamin content than blackberries. All cordials are delicious diluted with still or fizzy water.

450g (1lb) blackberries or elderberries
225g (8oz) golden caster sugar
glass of brandy (optional)

- Pick the fruit on a dry day and wash in cool water, but don't pick over them or remove their stems. The cooked fruit is sieved to leave all the bits behind.
- Place the washed fruit in a heavy-based pan with just enough water to cover it. Place over a medium heat and bring to the boil.
- Turn down to a simmer and stew until the berries have become mushy.
- Remove from the heat and pass through a sieve, pressing down heavily on the cooked berries to extract the maximum juice. Place the pulp in a piece of muslin and squeeze thoroughly to get as much juice out as possible.
- Add the sugar and boil again for 10 minutes. Allow to cool. Add the brandy now if you are using it.
- Pour into sterile bottles with plastic screw-on tops and store in a cool place. The cordial can be used immediately, and will keep for a month in the refrigerator.
- This cordial is renowned as a guard against colds, and a spoonful each day in winter is a wise precaution.

# late autumn
## setting the scene

This is the end of one practical gardening year and the start of the next. The weather generally assumes a wilder mood, with squally rain and roaring winds ripping the last leaves from trees, and only hardy crops, winter vegetables and those planted for next spring remain in the ground. All else should be gathered in as the winter season of dormancy approaches, and either eaten or stored. You might be able to press on with clearing and cultivating, or need to keep off the ground except in prolonged dry spells. Begin your assessment of how the year went – your triumphs and disappointments. The pressure's off and there's time to reflect.

**Maincrops are harvested and compost heaps fatten with cleared topgrowth and fallen leaves.**

**IN SEASON NOW**
apples, Brussels sprouts, cabbages (winter), carrots, cauliflowers (summer/autumn), celeriac, celery, chard, endive, grapes, chicory (heading), Jerusalem artichokes, kale, kohlrabi, lamb's lettuce, land cress, leeks, lettuces, oriental greens, parsnips, pears, perpetual spinach, potatoes, pumpkins, salsify, scorzonera, spinach (winter), squashes, swedes, sweet fennel, turnips, winter purslane, winter radishes

**SOW NOW**
**indoors/cold frame** lettuces, radishes, salad leaves
**outdoors** broad beans, peas (hardy)

**PLANT NOW**
cabbages (spring), fruit, garlic, herbs (perennial), onions (autumn sets)

# SEASONAL TASKS

**GATHERING IN** Pick and store or preserve all your hard-won produce before frost or prolonged wet weather can spoil it but, no matter how urgent their harvest, take care to avoid mishandling crops if you want them to keep well. Make sure they are fully mature but not overripe (late apples and pears finish ripening in store, however). Plan how you intend preserving a crop before any mass harvest, and have all your equipment/space ready in advance.

Crops that survive outdoors, at least through the first light autumn frosts, include beetroot, Brussels sprouts, cabbages, carrots, cauliflowers, kale, kohlrabi, leeks, parsnips, perpetual spinach, salsify, scorzonera, spinach (winter), swedes, turnips and winter radishes. Regular winter and spring vegetables like cabbages, leeks and sprouts withstand most winter hazards without protection, but roots benefit from earthing up or a mulch of straw, leaves, bracken or fleece. Most of the other vegetables should be used up steadily or protected from the worst weather with cloches.

Useful storage tips include:

- ▶ Use maincrop or late-maturing varieties for keeping, as they last longer than 'early' kinds.
- ▶ Label different varieties clearly with their name and the months when they are at their best.
- ▶ Never store unripe, diseased or damaged produce, which should be used up quickly.
- ▶ Leave stalks or short tufts of foliage on crops to avoid wounding their skins when handling.
- ▶ Allow crops to dry and cool down before storing them. Handle and clean them gently, and never wash them.
- ▶ Use clean packing materials, arrange plenty of ventilation in the store, and check for the first couple of weeks that conditions are not too warm or humid.
- ▶ Keep different varieties separate, especially if they mature at different times, and isolate any that have strong flavours or aromas.
- ▶ Inspect crops regularly for ripeness, rotting, shrivelling and attacks by pests or diseases.
- ▶ Produce near the end of its storage life can often be preserved for longer if cooked and then frozen.

## RENEWING RHUBARB

Established clumps of rhubarb often become overcrowded after 5–6 years and start to produce thinner stems. Splitting the oldest crowns now will rejuvenate plants and give you surplus portions that can be forced for a last crop before being discarded. Dig up an entire crown and use the spade to slice it into portions (*see left*), each with a few fibrous roots and 1–2 fat dormant buds. Replant these in fresh, rich ground.

Leave the remaining root on the surface for a few days to chill and break its natural dormancy, and then replant in a greenhouse bed, or pack in soil or straw in a large box or black plastic bag. Keep evenly moist at a temperature of about 10°C (50°F), and check for usable stems after 5–6 weeks. Cut up and compost the exhausted root after forcing.

Divide only healthy, productive plants. Dig up and destroy any with crinkled or misshapen leaves and soft crowns, yellowish leaf patterns and streaks, or soft brown patches and root cavities – these may have stem eelworms, virus diseases or crown rot respectively.

**TRY THIS...**
If you find any sturdy sideshoots while clearing out tomatoes, pull them off, stand them in water for a couple of days and then root in pots of compost. Keep them in a warm, well-lit spot indoors. If you are lucky, they could flower and even fruit, but they are more likely to make useful greenhouse plants for a head start next spring.

**IT'S NOT TOO LATE TO...**
Force strawberries for early pickings in the greenhouse if you have strong rooted plantlets outdoors. Simply fork up some of the best and transfer them to a greenhouse border or a used growing bag revived with a little balanced fertilizer. Remember to open the door or ventilators at flowering time or hand-pollinate the open flowers with a soft paintbrush.

**IF YOU HAVE TIME...**
Monitor acidity levels in several places on the plot, especially where you are planning to grow brassicas. Use a basic soil-test kit to measure the pH (*see left*) and to find out how much lime to add, if necessary, to adjust levels to nearly neutral (or higher for brassicas).

**PREPARING THE GREENHOUSE** Begin tidying up the greenhouse ready for overwintering tender plants and early sowing. Pull up and compost tomatoes and other exhausted plants, gather up their fallen leaves, and clear weeds or moss from beds, paths and staging. Outside, clear leaves from guttering once trees are bare; drain and scrub out tanks and water butts with warm soapy water. You should also amend any sources of draughts, and insulate at least part of the house with bubble polythene or a thermal screen.

**SOWING PEAS & BROAD BEANS** Autumn sowing is often recommended for the first spring peas and broad beans, but success is unpredictable and depends on where you garden as much as on choosing a bone-hardy variety ('Aquadulce' or 'The Sutton' broad beans or a round-seeded pea like 'Pilot' or 'Meteor'). Good results might be expected in a district with consistently mild winters on soil that drains well (prospects could improve further as winters become warmer), but you should keep cloches at the ready for covering rows from late autumn or early winter until early or mid-spring. Elsewhere, sow the same varieties towards the end of winter, outdoors under cloches or in a greenhouse or cold frame for transplanting: crops often mature just a week or two after autumn sowings.

**FORCING EARLY PRODUCE** It is not too early to start forcing Witloof chicory, seakale and rhubarb for harvest from late winter onwards, especially if you heat your greenhouse.

The following crops can all be forced where they are growing in the ground: chicory under a 15cm (6in) mound of soil covered with cloches; seakale beneath an upturned bucket or large pot; and rhubarb inside a large box, traditional forcing pot or a tripod of sticks wrapped all round in sacking. For winter heads, chicory is normally forced and *blanched* indoors, and you can do the same with seakale and rhubarb if you have spare older plants due for lifting and splitting (*see box, opposite*).

Darkness is essential for best results – the best place is under greenhouse staging, on the ground on a bed of straw or in a large pot or box of compost.

Using containers allows you to keep the plants outside in the cold, and then move one or two at a time indoors approximately 6 weeks before you want supplies. Keep plants evenly moist once forcing starts, and screen them on all sides with old blankets or black plastic to exclude light.

Indoor forcing exhausts plants, which are then discarded, so make sure you have stock to spare (outdoor plants are simply rested for a season after forcing to build up their strength before being used again).

**TRY THIS**

**GREEN TOMATOES**

When the time comes to clear tomato crops because of frost, pick fruits and spread them in boxes lined and covered with newspaper, each containing a ripe tomato, orange or banana to gently ooze ethylene gas and speed ripening. Completely green fruits often refuse to colour up (make sure they are not naturally green varieties, such as 'Green Grape' or 'Green Sausage'), so use them unripe in preserves like chutneys, relishes and pickles, or explore the huge repertoire of traditional tomato dishes in America's Southern cuisine, especially the classic *Whistle Stop Café* version of fried green tomatoes. (*See also page 127.*)

**FRENCH & RUNNER BEANS** When clearing French or runner beans at this time of year, you will often find overlooked pods studded with ripening seeds. Pick them off and spread on newspaper until crispy dry, when the seeds are easily shelled out for storing. When bulk-harvesting beans like dwarf 'Chevrier Vert' or tall 'Cherokee Trail of Tears' for pulses, pull up entire plants and hang them upside down in a warm place until all the pods are dry. Shelling these by hand can be tedious, so pick all the pods and stuff them in a clean sack or pillowcase, tie the end shut and either jog up and down on it, flail it with a rolling pin or hang it from a washing line and use a carpet beater. Pick out the seeds manually, or pour everything repeatedly from one bowl into another outdoors in a stiff breeze to winnow seeds from the lighter chaff. Tossing the mixture in a garden sieve is also effective, or a hair dryer can be used to blow away the chaff. Then store the dry, clean seeds in glass jars with airtight rubber seals on their lids, and keep in a cool, dry, dark place for up to a year (older pulses do not cook well). (*See also pages 186 and 189.*)

**These seeds may be used successfully for sowing next year, but don't expect varietal purity, especially from runner beans, which can cross-pollinate with other kinds up to half-a-mile away, unless you isolate their flowers with cloth blossom bags.**

ask the **EXPERT**

**SQUASHES** The difference between summer and winter squashes becomes confusing in the autumn, when all types are harvested before frost spoils them, and the terms are often used indiscriminately. Summer squashes (including marrows, courgettes, patty pans, crooknecks and a few pumpkins) keep only for 2–4 months and should be used first. When grown in Britain, their flesh is often soft and needs careful cooking to stop it disintegrating into a wet nothingness. Winter squashes, which include most pumpkins, acorn and butternut types, have smooth firm flesh, especially 'Hubbard' varieties and Italian or Japanese kinds, like 'Marina di Chioggia' and 'Uchiki Kuri'. Temper these after harvest by laying them in the sun for 2–3 weeks (under glass in a wet season) to harden the skins. They can then be stored in a well-ventilated place at about 8–10°C (45–50°F) for up to 6 months. (*See also page 201.*)

**LEFT** Storing borlotti beans that have been dried on the vine for use in cooking and sowing.

**TRENCH CELERY** Once an essential winter crop on every allotment, trench celery has generally been ousted by green and self-blanching kinds, which are less laborious to grow but must all be used before the frosts. Varieties like 'Solid White', 'Giant Red' and 'Clayworth Pink' are planted in trenches and progressively earthed up as they grow, a process that blanches the stems and insulates them from frost, so that heads can be harvested right through to the spring, their flavour improving as time passes. Dig up a plant whenever needed and resettle the soil firmly around those left. If possible, leave the last plant to flower and set seeds next year: save and dry these for sowing future crops and for use as a pungent condiment to lift soups, stews and rice dishes. They can also be turned into celery salt for seasoning roast meat and root vegetables or enlivening salad dressings. (*See also page 207.*)

**BELOW** Tempering winter squashes and pumpkins in the sunshine to harden their skins for storage.

**WINTER ROOTS** Some find maincrop roots dull fare after summer feasts of exotics, but winter crops like carrots, parsnips, turnips, swedes and celeriac are all wonderful packages of low-calorie nutrients and intense flavours. Explore them individually – as carrot nut rissoles or war-time carrot cookies, for example, buttery swede and potato topping for a cottage pie, or the classic turnip recipe Meg Dods' Bashed Neeps – or mix them together to make vegetable pakoras or for roasting in a tray of olive oil to accompany the Sunday joint. (*See also pages 182–5.*)

In mild areas, most roots keep successfully in the ground if tucked under a blanket of autumn leaves (parsnips are rugged and can be left uncovered as they improve with frost), but where winters are very cold or wet it is advisable to lift and store them under cover. American colonists used a home-spun version of the modern veggie-box scheme, packing a selection of all the different kinds in layers of straw inside wooden boxes or kegs, which were then buried in a trench and unearthed at regular intervals throughout the winter. Sinking a plastic dustbin (with a secure lid) up to its rim in the ground makes an alternative root store.

**EASY MUSHROOMS** Growing white cap mushrooms on kits of straw or composted manure in a greenhouse requires delicate husbandry. An easier way is to scatter spawn in a corner of the plot on ground that has been enriched with well-rotted horse manure, and simply forget about them.

## EAT NOW

Another time of transition, as one allotment year closes and makes way for the next. The last of the season's crops need salvaging – over-mature lumpy peas and beans to shell and dry for winter casseroles, stubbornly green tomatoes to finish off on windowsills or turn into preserves, and maincrop potatoes, lowly but rewarding when baked in autumn bonfires. These merge now with the first true winter vegetables, such as leeks, maincrop turnips and all the oriental greens that thrive on the shortening days. Above all, it is time to harvest the main apple varieties for storing through to the spring, grapes that seem to colour almost overnight, and pumpkins galore to cook or carve as the fancy takes you. (*See* In season now, *page 130*.)

## RECIPES

seasonal planner

## RIBOLLITA

**SERVES 8**

This is a famed Tuscan soup, and every Italian cook has their own version. In Tuscany, when the *cavolo nero* (black Tuscan kale) is harvested in autumn, it coincides with the new season's olive oil, an important ingredient in this recipe. Make sure to use the best oil you can find. Traditionally, this dish uses cannellini beans, which you will have dried earlier on in the season. You can use other dried beans, but cannellini are the authentic choice. The soup is very hearty with slices of ciabatta bread laid in it, which soak up the juices. These quantities make a large amount which needs to be eaten fresh. Eat for lunch – you probably won't need anything else afterwards.

1 large onion, thinly sliced

4 tbsp olive oil

4 carrots, peeled and finely chopped

4 celery stalks, trimmed and chopped

4 small leeks, trimmed and finely chopped

250g (9oz) black Tuscan kale, trimmed

400g (14oz) tomatoes, peeled and deseeded

2 garlic cloves, finely chopped

1 bay leaf

1 dried chilli, crumbled

400g (14oz) dried cannellini beans, soaked and drained

1–2 tbsp finely chopped fresh herbs, such as parsley, chervil, rosemary

salt and freshly ground pepper, to taste

**To serve**

8 slices ciabatta, toasted

good-quality extra virgin olive oil

3 tbsp finely chopped fresh parsley

- In a saucepan gently cook the sliced onion in 2 tablespoons of the oil until soft and translucent. Add the carrots, celery, leeks and kale and stir them in with the onions and oil until they are coated lightly.
- Place the tomatoes in a sieve over the cooking pan and press them until their flesh and juices ooze out into the vegetable mixture. Add one of the garlic cloves, the bay leaf and the chilli with its seeds to the mixture.
- Add the beans and enough water to cover all the ingredients in the pan. Bring to the boil, then reduce the heat, cover and cook gently for at least 30 minutes.
- Remove a third of the soup and blend to a purée in a food processor. Return to the cooking pan.
- In another, smaller pan, warm the remaining oil and fry the rest of the garlic and chopped herbs. Add to the the vegetables in the pan and season to taste. If you want the flavours to really mature, leave the soup for 6–8 hours. When you are ready to serve it, reheat the soup and season well. The consistency should be sloppy but not too runny at this point.
- To serve, ladle the ribollita into individual soup bowls. Lay a slice of toasted bread on the top of each and drizzle with a generous quantity of the extra virgin olive oil. Finally, sprinkle over some chopped fresh parsley and serve.

## BLACK TUSCAN KALE WITH CHILLI & GARLIC

**SERVES 4 AS A SIDE DISH**

As well as being very good-tasting and extremely healthy for you, kale can take on other flavours without losing its own. Try cooking any kind with bacon, for instance. Here it is cooked with some chilli and garlic. You can cut down the amount of chilli if it seems too much, but it should have some bite still. This dish goes well with a plain grilled chop, chicken breast or fish.

400g (14oz) black Tuscan kale

2 small fresh red chillies, finely sliced

2 garlic cloves, crushed

2 tbsp extra virgin olive oil

salt and freshly ground pepper, to taste

- Put the kale in enough water to just cover it and steam for about 2 minutes until tender. Don't overcook – it must still have some bite to it. Drain and set aside.
- In a large frying pan, sauté the chillies and garlic in the oil. Add the cooked kale and cook for another couple of minutes. Season to taste.

## BASIL PESTO

MAKES ONE 175G (6OZ) JAR

Basil is not in full flight now, but if you sowed your seeds in succession and brought it into the greenhouse you will still have plenty left. This classic Italian sauce made with fresh basil can't be beaten to use with pasta but also as an accompaniment to many other dishes. It originates from northern Italy and not only is good basil essential, but extra virgin olive oil and pinenuts are too. You really need a food processor to make this. Pesto is not long lasting – it will keep for a week at the most refrigerated in a tightly sealed jar – so make it when you need it.

2 large garlic cloves, peeled and chopped
85g (3oz) pinenuts
150g (5½oz) Parmesan cheese, finely grated
2 large bunches of basil, without stems
300ml (½ pint) extra virgin olive oil
salt and freshly ground pepper, to taste

- Put the garlic and pinenuts in a food processor or blender and blitz. Add the cheese and process briefly. Add the basil and blend until you have a vivid green mixture.
- With the processor still running, add the olive oil gradually, making sure that the oil is well incorporated with the basil mix.
- Add salt and pepper. Blend again, then taste to check the seasoning. Serve immediately on hot pasta or pour into a sterilized jar (*see page 80*), seal and refrigerate.

## PASTA, GREEN BEANS, POTATOES & PESTO

**SERVES 4**

Ready in 20 minutes or less, lunch couldn't come quicker than this. If you planted your beans late you should get a last harvest in before the frosts, and now they are ready to pick and put in the pot. You don't need a lot of pesto and this dish is substantial enough to stand alone without accompaniments.

1kg (2¼lb) small or new potatoes, halved
500g (1lb 2oz) pasta (penne or fusilli)
350g (12oz) ) green beans, halved and par-boiled
4 tbsp fresh basil pesto (*see left*)
salt and and freshly ground pepper, to taste
fresh basil, torn into large shreds, to garnish

- Cook the potatoes in a large pan of boiling water until nearly done. Add the pasta and cook for 5 more minutes. Now add the green beans and cook for a further few minutes. The pasta and the beans should be al dente.
- Remove from the heat and drain well. Put back in the pan and stir in the pesto. Warm over a low heat for a few minutes, tossing the ingredients to mix. Season with salt and pepper. Divide between bowls and garnish with some fresh basil.

## SQUASH & GREEN BEAN COCONUT CURRY

**SERVES 4**

Your squashes will be ready now, as will your cauliflowers. A tasty curry is just what you need when the nights draw in.

1 tsp cumin seeds
1 tsp coriander seeds
2 tbsp vegetable oil
1 onion, chopped
500g (1lb 2oz) winter squash, peeled, deseeded and diced
½ red chilli, deseeded and chopped
½ tsp turmeric
400g (14oz) tin coconut milk
300ml (10fl oz) hot vegetable stock
100g (3½oz) fine green beans, halved
200g (7oz) cauliflower, trimmed and cut into small florets
2 handfuls of baby spinach leaves, washed
a few coriander leaves

- In a small frying pan, dry-fry the cumin and coriander seeds for 1 minute until lightly toasted. Grind together in a mortar and pestle.
- Heat the oil in a saucepan over a medium heat, add the onion and cook for 5 minutes. Add the squash, toasted spices, chilli and turmeric and cook, stirring, for a further 5 minutes. Pour in the coconut milk and stock and bring to the boil, then reduce the heat and simmer for 10 minutes, or until the sauce has reduced and thickened slightly.
- Meanwhile, blanch the beans in boiling water for 1 minute, drain them and then refresh under cold running water to keep their vivid colour. Put aside.
- Add the cauliflower florets to the curry and cook for 5 minutes. Add the spinach and cook until wilted. Season to taste and stir in the coriander leaves.
- Serve with steamed basmati rice.

## MINT & PARSLEY PESTO

**MAKES ONE 175G (6OZ) JAR**

Not strictly a pesto, but more a strong-tasting posh mint sauce that can be used in a similar way. The garlic is roasted first, which gives it a softened flavour.

3 garlic cloves, unpeeled

30g (1oz) fresh mint leaves, no stems

30g (1oz) fresh flat-leaf parsley, no stems

2 tbsp balsamic vinegar

¼ tsp caster sugar

120ml (4fl oz) extra virgin olive oil

salt and freshly ground pepper, to taste

- Preheat oven to 180°C/350°F/gas 4. Put the garlic cloves in a roasting tin and roast in the oven for 15 minutes. Pop the roasted garlic cloves out of their skins and put aside while you make the sauce.
- Put the mint, parsley, vinegar and sugar together in a food processor and blend until finely chopped. Add the cooked garlic and combine.
- Pour in the olive oil slowly and gradually, making sure it combines thoroughly with the rest of the mixture. Season with salt and pepper.

## MARINATED LAMB WITH MINT PESTO

**SERVES 6**

A Sunday roast with a difference. Lamb and mint is, of course, a classic, but this recipe uses mint as a marinade as well as a sauce. Serve with the usual vegetables.

2.25kg (5lb) leg of lamb

**Marinade**

120ml (4fl oz) extra virgin olive oil

4 garlic cloves

90ml (3fl oz) freshly squeezed lemon juice

zest of 1 lemon

20g (¾oz) fresh mint leaves, no stems

salt and freshly ground pepper, to taste

- Mix together all the ingredients for the marinade in a food processor or with a pestle and mortar.
- Put the lamb in a shallow baking dish and spread over the marinade, keeping any excess for later. Cover with clingfilm and marinate for at least 4 hours or overnight in the refrigerator.
- Preheat oven to 180°C/350°F/gas 4.
- Take the lamb out of the refrigerator and bring it to room temperature.
- Baste with any extra marinade and roast for about 1½ hours. Continue to baste while the lamb is cooking in order to keep the meat as moist as possible. Take the lamb out of the oven and let it sit for 20 minutes before you carve.
- Slice the lamb and place on a serving dish. Using the juices from the lamb, make a gravy. Serve with some mint pesto.

## STIR-FRIED MIXED VEGETABLES

**SERVES 4-6**

Chinese leaves are easy to grow and will carry on right through the season. A quick stir-fry, served with noodles, makes a nutritious lunch or light supper.

1½ tbsp peanut oil

2 tbsp coarsely chopped shallots

2 large garlic cloves, chopped

2 tbsp finely chopped fresh root ginger

2 tsp salt

225g (8oz) carrots, peeled and cut into thin diagonal slices

450g (16oz) Chinese green leaves, such as pak choi, cut into strips

2 tsp caster sugar

1 tbsp rice wine or dry sherry

2 tsp sesame oil

- Heat a wok over a high heat. Add the oil and, when it is very hot and slightly smoking, add the shallots, garlic, ginger and salt and quickly stir-fry for a minute.
- Add the carrots and stir-fry for another minute. Add 1 tablespoon of water, cover and cook over a high heat for 2 more minutes.
- Lastly, add the Chinese leaves and greens with the sugar and rice wine or sherry. Stir-fry for 3 minutes or until the greens are really wilted.
- Sprinkle over the sesame oil and serve at once with some Chinese noodles.

## BORLOTTI BEAN STEW

### SERVES 6

Borlotti beans are an Italian staple. Fresh, they take only an hour to cook, but if you have dried your beans, leave them to soak overnight before draining and using. The beans absorb all the flavours you put with them. Do use the best-quality olive oil, though the wine can be cheaper without affecting the quality of the dish.

- 200g (7oz) packet of lardons (optional)
- 1 onion, peeled and finely chopped
- 1 garlic clove, crushed
- 1 celery stalk, finely chopped
- 120ml (4fl oz) extra virgin olive oil
- 2kg (4½lb) fresh borlotti beans, podded
- 3 large tomatoes, chopped
- 1 tbsp tomato purée
- 5 sprigs fresh sage
- 250ml (8fl oz) water
- 250ml (8fl oz) white wine
- salt and freshly ground pepper, to taste

- Fry the lardons, if using, in a heavy pan and put aside. Put the onion, garlic and celery in the pan with a splash of oil and sauté until translucent.
- Add the beans, tomatoes, tomato purée and sage, followed by the water, wine and oil. The liquid should be just enough to cover the beans. Bring to the boil, then simmer for 45–60 minutes. Don't let it dry out – add more water or wine if necessary. Towards the end add the cooked lardons and season with salt and pepper
- Serve with some herby sausages – Italian fennel ones go particularly well with this dish.

## MOROCCAN TAGINE OF CHICKEN & QUINCES

### SERVES 4

The tagine is a Moroccan speciality that nearly always includes the same fruits: apples, quinces, prunes and apricots. Quinces are often mistaken for pears and in fact the taste is between an apple and a pear. They keep their shape and texture when cooked even for a long time, but still absorb all the spices and flavours.

- 2 tbsp extra virgin olive oil
- 1.8kg (4 lb) free-range chicken, cut into 8
- 1 onion, peeled and chopped
- 1 tsp ground ginger
- 1 tsp ground cinnamon
- 2 tsp cumin seeds
- 1 tsp paprika
- ½ tsp freshly ground pepper
- 225g (8oz) cooked quinces, chopped
- 800g (1¾lb) tomatoes, chopped
- 2 tbsp honey
- 250ml (8fl oz) water
- salt, to taste
- 400g (14oz) chickpeas, cooked
- 1 bunch fresh coriander leaves, finely chopped

- Preheat oven to 150°C/300°F/gas 2.
- Heat the oil in a frying pan, add the chicken pieces and cook until brown all over. Transfer to an ovenproof casserole or tagine.
- Fry the onion in the same frying pan until soft. Add the spices and the pepper and stir to blend. Put in the quinces and stir and then add the tomatoes, honey and water and season with salt. Bring gently to the boil, then simmer for about 3–4 minutes. Stir in the chickpeas and adjust the seasoning if necessary.
- Pour the mixture over the chicken in the casserole. Cover and put in the oven for a further 40 minutes or until the chicken is cooked. Scatter with the coriander and serve with couscous.

## TRY THIS
### JUICING

Raw fruit and vegetables made into juices are good for you, as there is no loss of vitamins. You do need to invest in an electric juicer, though, for the best results. A glass of one of the following combinations will set you up for the day. Wash your ingredients thoroughly with filtered or distilled water before juicing. Depending on the season, you might have to resort to the shops for some ingredients.

**recipe 1** beetroot, watercress, carrot, celery

**recipe 2** apple, carrot, fresh basil

**recipe 3** carrot, mint

**recipe 4** apple, watercress

**recipe 5** apple, beetroot

**recipe 6** fennel, red pepper, carrot, apple

**recipe 7** carrot, spinach, celery, parsley

**recipe 8** cabbage, celery

## PEAR COMPOTE

**SERVES 4-6**

Stewing pears in wine is quite common, but you can also achieve a tasty dish by slowly stewing them with a sugar syrup. If you are partial to the taste the alcohol gives, add a small glass of dessert wine or Poire William liqueur to the liquid.

> 1kg (2¼lb) firm, ripe pears, peeled but kept whole with stalks intact
>
> 225g (8oz) caster sugar
>
> 450ml (15fl oz) water
>
> 7.5cm (3in) cinnamon stick
>
> grated zest of ½ lemon

- Place the pears in a saucepan with the rest of the ingredients. Bring slowly to the boil, then reduce the heat to low and cook for 10-15 minutes, until the pears are soft but still hold their shape. Don't be tempted to overcook them, as they must remain whole.
- Remove from the heat, cover and allow to cool a little.
- Serve the pears individually with the cooking syrup spooned over them until they glisten.

### TRY THIS
### PICKLED GRAPES

This is a traditional Spanish delicacy, prepared in autumn to keep for Christmas indulgence.

- De-stalk, wash and dry 1.3kg (3lb) ripe sweet grapes, and prick each one with a needle; pack in sterilized jars.
- Boil 120ml (¼ pint) water and 115g (4oz) caster sugar to make a syrup, and then stir in 1 teaspoon of aniseed.
- Leave to cool, mix with 1.2 litres (2 pints) brandy and pour over the grapes.
- Seal and store in a cool dark place for about 3 months.

## PEAR DUMPLINGS

**SERVES 4**

Dumplings are normally associated with savoury dishes, but in Eastern Europe they are commonly used as puddings. Cooking the dumplings in fruits and juices ensures a moist and fragrant dish. Other orchard fruit would work just as well as pears.

> 30g (1oz) chilled butter, diced
>
> 115g (4oz) self-raising flour
>
> 85g (3oz) caster sugar, plus extra to decorate
>
> 450g (1lb) ripe pears, peeled, cored and cut into large pieces
>
> 450ml (¾ pint) water

- In a bowl, rub the butter into the flour with your fingertips until it resembles fine breadcrumbs. Stir in the sugar and add enough water to form a soft dough. Make into dumplings about the size of a golf ball.
- Place the fruit in a large saucepan with the measured water. Bring to the boil and cook briefly until the pears have softened and their juices have started to flavour the water. Carefully drop the dumplings into the boiling liquid, turn down the heat and simmer. Cook steadily for 20 minutes.
- Transfer to a warmed serving dish, sprinkle with sugar and serve hot.

## PEAR & GINGER CAKE

**MAKES A 20-22CM (8-9IN) ROUND CAKE**

Although it's never been clear why, pear and ginger makes a successful pairing. Considering the delicate taste of pears, compared to the sharpness of apples, it is surprising how the ginger adds to the taste rather than overwhelms it.

> 100g (3½oz) unsalted butter
>
> 100g (3½oz) self-raising flour
>
> 100g (3½oz) ground almonds
>
> 2 tsp baking powder
>
> 2 tsp mixed spice
>
> 115g (4oz) golden caster sugar
>
> 3 pieces preserved stem ginger, chopped
>
> 3-4 firm ripe ripe pears (about 300g/10oz chopped weight if using windfalls), peeled, cored, quartered and diced
>
> 3 large eggs, beaten
>
> 20g (¾oz) flaked almonds

- Preheat oven to 180°C/350°F/gas 4. Grease and flour a deep 20-22cm (8-9in) loose-bottomed sandwich tin. You need to use a loose-bottomed tin, as the cake is quite juicy and some of the juice will leak out and cause the cake to stick to an ordinary tin.
- Melt the butter in a pan and remove from the heat. Put the flour, ground almonds, baking powder, mixed spice and 100g (3½oz) of the sugar into a large mixing bowl.
- Add the ginger, pears, eggs and melted butter to the dry ingredients. Stir well and pour into the prepared tin. Scatter the flaked almonds over the top. Put the baking tin on a baking tray and bake for about 45-55 minutes, until golden brown and springy to the touch.
- Leave to cool for 5 minutes, remove from the tin and put on a cooling rack. Before serving, dust the top with the rest of the sugar.

## PUMPKIN & CHESTNUT SOUP

### SERVES 4

Pumpkins are ready to eat now as well as to use for Halloween. Here, two rich autumn flavours and textures are put together. If you don't want to cook chestnuts, use tinned instead.

1.5 litres (2¾ pints) hot chicken stock

750g (1lb 10oz) pumpkin, peeled, deseeded and chopped into small pieces

4 tsp lemon juice

2 tbsp cornflour

1 tbsp caster sugar

2 pinches grated nutmeg

salt and freshly ground pepper, to taste

75ml (2½ fl oz) crème fraîche

250g (9oz) chestnuts, cooked

- Bring the chicken stock to the boil, add the pumpkin and leave to simmer for 15 minutes.
- Remove the pumpkin and blend in a food processor or blender with the lemon juice.
- Mix the cornflour in 200ml (7fl oz) of the cooking juice and pour back into the pan with the blended pumpkin. Season with the sugar, nutmeg and add salt and pepper to taste. Add the crème fraîche and stir in well.
- Keep the soup warm over a low heat while you crush the chestnuts into small pieces with a fork.
- Pour the soup into bowls and sprinkle with the chestnut pieces.

### ROASTING PUMPKINS

Preheat oven to 325°F/190°C/gas 5. Oil a roasting pan. Quarter the pumpkin, scoop out the seeds and fibrous tissue and discard. Cut the pumpkin into large pieces and place skin-side up in the pan. Roast for 1¼ hours.

## PUMPKIN BREAD

### MAKES 3 MEDIUM LOAVES

Pumpkin and sweet potato are used all the time in America for sweet puddings, breads and cakes. They add bulk and cut down on the amount of sugar you need.

butter, for greasing

350g (12oz) plain flour

250g (9oz) light brown sugar, plus extra for sprinkling

350g (12oz) granulated sugar

2 tsp baking powder

1 tsp salt

1 tsp ground cinnamon

½ tsp grated nutmeg

4 eggs

250ml (8fl oz) sunflower oil

150ml (5fl oz) water

4–8 wedges roasted pumpkin (*see box, below left*)

125g (4½oz) raisins

125g (4½oz) chopped walnuts

- Preheat oven to 325°F/190°C/gas 5. Grease 3 medium-sized loaf tins.
- Remove the skin from the roasted pumpkin wedges and process the flesh in a blender. Line a sieve with muslin and set it over a bowl. Let the purée drain.
- Combine all the dry ingredients in a large mixing bowl. Make a well in the centre then break in the eggs. Add the oil, water and pumpkin purée and beat until thoroughly mixed. Add the raisins and nuts and mix again.
- Sprinkle a little brown sugar into the prepared tins. Pour in the mixture and bake for 1 hour or until a skewer inserted in the centre comes out clean. Cool for 5 minutes in the tins before turning onto wire racks to cool.

## SWEET POTATO MUFFINS

### SERVES 24

Surprisingly, the colour of the sweet potato is retained, even when cooked, so there is a wonderful orange treat when you break these muffins open. Pumpkin can be used instead of sweet potato.

115g (4oz) butter, softened, plus extra for greasing

225g (8oz) caster sugar

300g (10oz) sweet potato, peeled, boiled and mashed

2 large eggs

350g (12oz) plain flour

2 tsp baking powder

1½ tsp cinnamon

¼ tsp grated nutmeg

pinch of salt

300ml (½ pint) milk

115g (4oz) raisins

60g (2oz) chopped nuts

- Preheat oven to 200°C/400°F/gas 6. Grease 2 muffin trays and line with doubled-up muffin cases. (This makes them easier to release from the tray.)
- Beat together the butter and sugar in a bowl until smooth, then add the mashed sweet potato and blend well. Add the eggs and mix thoroughly.
- Sift together the flour, baking powder, spices and salt into another bowl. Fold into the sweet potato mixture, alternately with the milk, stirring lightly to blend. Do not over-mix: it should still be lumpy. Fold in the raisins and nuts.
- Spoon into the muffin cases.and bake for about 25 minutes. Remove from the oven and allow to cool slightly but do try to eat them while still warm, when they are absolutely delicious!

# early winter

## setting the scene

With cool temperatures, low light levels and the shortest day imminent, there is little or no active growth at this time of year. You might find yourself spending much of the time sheltering from rude and boisterous blasts, although the season can also bring long, mild interludes and still, sunny spells when it's a pleasure to be on the plot. Pace yourself through the winter chores – clearing finished plants, reviving exhausted soil, overhauling paths or repairing equipment – because there are still several weeks before any crucial spring deadlines, and make time to stop and enjoy winter on the plot, which has its own pleasures and rewards.

**A good frost helps crop remains to decompose, as well as adding flavour to winter vegetables.**

**IN SEASON NOW**
Brussels sprouts, cabbages (winter), cauliflowers (winter), celeriac, celery, chicory (forced + heading), endive, Jerusalem artichokes, kale, kohlrabi, land cress, perpetual spinach, leeks, lettuces, oriental greens, parsnips, rhubarb (forced), salsify, scorzonera, seakale, spinach (winter), swedes, sweet fennel, turnips, winter purslane, winter radishes

**SOW NOW**
broad beans

**PLANT NOW**
fruit (top + bush), garlic, globe artichokes, rhubarb, shallots

# SEASONAL TASKS

**TRYING SOMETHING NEW** Use this year's experience to help you decide your seed and plant lists for next year. Some varieties will have performed well and deserve repeating, while others may need replacing with an alternative kind, perhaps an older well-established variety or a recent introduction that might be better suited to your soil, climate or cropping plan.

Catalogue descriptions of new introductions should be read with caution – even if claimed qualities are realistic, they might be attainable only in perfect conditions. No one, though, should be fearful of investigating new or unknown crops: allotment gardening is an adventure, and trying out novelties adds spice to the practical routine. In addition to the latest varieties, there are many traditional and ethnic crops that deserve trying. Neighbouring plot-holders may grow plants from other cultures, such as okra, carosella or sorghum, or historical

## CONSULTING CATALOGUES

Keep all the new seed catalogues in the allotment shed, and when the weather drives you indoors, seize the opportunity to browse and select your supplies for next season. Being on the spot, able to scan your patch of ground at a glance and recall which vegetables and varieties did best, can help you plan what to grow and where. Remember that it is always a sound idea to grow two varieties of any crop, the best of last season's performers, together with a new one for comparison.

Consider trying something each year that is novel to you – perhaps a cereal like quinoa, amaranth or teff, tomatillos or huckleberries or cape gooseberries for unusual fruits, or an old crop like skirret or Hamburg parsley, which is rarely grown today. Now-familiar crops, such as garlic, aubergines and rocket, once made their debut on a single allotment and were then taken up by other plot-holders. You might just discover a new favourite to share with your neighbours.

Red perilla is a colourful anise-flavoured cousin of green shiso. Both have a spicily seasoned taste when cooked.

Callaloo is a popular Caribbean vegetable, easily grown for salads or as a spinach substitute.

seasonal planner

crops, like pigeon peas, skirret, Chinese artichokes (*see page 209*) and good king henry (*see page 56*).

There is a whole range of unfamiliar hardy fruits to explore, too: treacle berries, Nanking cherries, saskatoons or juneberries, or recently fashionable goji berries. The risk is little more than disappointment, whereas the reward could be an agreeable discovery.

**SOURCES OF FERTILITY** In a natural system, plant death and decay feed the growth of others and maintain a steady, if meagre, supply of nutrients, but allotment cropping is intensive and requires a relatively large input of fertility to compensate for what is taken from the ground. Finding enough organic sources of fertility can be a challenge, and most gardeners supplement the limited quantity of compost made from kitchen and crop waste with bought-in manure or mushroom compost and the occasional judicious boost of fertilizer.

There are several ways to increase your supplies of organic fertility.

▶ Use a well-designed insulated container that can speed up decomposition and separate liquid – to use as a potent and targeted feed – from the solids, applied as a physical soil improver.
▶ Expand the range of raw materials: collect other people's weeds and lawn mowings and add these to plenty of crumpled newspaper, torn cardboard, shredded prunings and tree leaves (glean the pavement outside your house for extra supplies).
▶ Explore sources such as a local stable or anyone who keeps rabbits, poultry, pigeons, or pets that use paper, hay or straw bedding; approach local restaurants, greengrocers and market stall-holders, who might have discarded vegetable waste.
▶ Grow your own fertility: green manure crops are soil improvers but add some fertility, especially if dressed with dried blood or urine to speed decomposition. Mineral-rich 'weeds', such as nettles and comfrey, can be cropped several times a year for compost material or to make liquid feeds.
▶ Avoid disturbing the soil deeply, which can liberate nutrients into the atmosphere. Ration supplies by manuring planting sites rather than entire beds. Grow more perennial crops to trap and absorb nutrients all year round that might otherwise leach from the soil. Keep the surface mulched to stabilize humus levels as a slow-release source of plant foods.

**DEBRIEFING THE SEASON** Don't berate yourself or lose confidence if some crops have not done as well as you expected – reasons beyond your control are just as likely to be the cause of failure as any lapse or oversight on your part.

Weather is a constant influence, for example, and it takes only a cold spring to prompt onions to bolt and flower or a hot and dry midsummer for runner bean flowers to drop fruitlessly. A long wet summer leaches nutrients from the soil and leaves plants starved, while a poor set of fruit is almost certain to result if pollinating insects were discouraged by cold or windy weather.

Disappointing results on a new plot may be caused by exhausted soil that can take more than a season to restore to high fertility; nutrients like calcium (lime) or magnesium might be lacking, causing stunted growth or poorly developed fruits or roots. Frequent rotavation by a previous tenant or constant trampling could leave a legacy of compacted subsoil or a hard, polished pan buried out of sight, impeding roots and stunting growth.

You might be growing the wrong varieties – a long parsnip or carrot in shallow topsoil, or iceberg lettuces in a district with cool dull summers. Cold ground, soil pests like wireworms and leatherjackets, or an unsuitable pH level can all cause poor or non-existent germination (*see page 53*), or maybe the crop was simply in the wrong place, in full sun, deep shade or a particularly windy spot, when it would have preferred the opposite.

**An active heap of compost or fresh manure generates a lot of heat, often letting off steam on frosty mornings.**

Opinion these days favours minimal cultivation and low-intervention techniques that benefit soil organisms and various complex soil processes, as well as making life a lot easier for gardeners who find bending or mobility difficult. There are many practical alternatives to regular digging, which satisfy the principles of good soil management while still ensuring prolific crops.

**IMPROVE LOCAL AREAS** Instead of digging the whole plot every year, fork an 8cm (3in) dressing of grit into the top 15cm (6in) of seed- and nursery beds on heavy soil, and move these areas to new ground annually. Adding lime to brassica planting sites satisfies their calcium needs but also stimulates earthworms and the breakdown of humus.

**MAKE RAISED BEDS** A frame of edging boards filled with topsoil from intervening paths or elsewhere on the plot will increase the workable soil depth, countering problems of poor drainage, shallow soils and low fertility. Cultivate only the surface, and work from paths at the sides to avoid compacting the growing area.

**TREAT SOIL WITH RESPECT** Disturb the ground as little as possible and only when conditions are suitable: trampling and working wet soil causes compaction and loss of aeration, while trying to cultivate dry soil can result in greater evaporation from below and the loss of dusty topsoil in a breeze. Stand on a board between rows or work from adjacent paths, loosen the ground after stepping on it, keep the surface covered with an organic mulch (which feeds the soil as well as protects it) and plant through this. Compost all waste to return some of the fertility removed as produce.

**IMITATE NATURAL PROCESSES** Encourage earthworms and natural biological cycles to do the digging for you by adding plenty of organic matter as a *top-dressing* to the soil each year and whenever planting or clearing a crop. Spreading organic matter as a mulch shields the soil from weather extremes: light soils retain nutrients and a crumbly soil structure, while clay avoids physical changes between mud and concrete.

There will have been triumphs, though, probably many more on balance than failures, and every successful harvest is a challenge to the fast food and supermarket culture. Each year is different and tests the most experienced plot-holder, the majority of whom return full of optimism every spring, so there's every reason to feel encouraged by your past season's results.

**RULES FOR WINTER PRUNING** Although possibly daunting if you have never done it before, pruning fruit in winter is a simple routine, as long as you remember some basic general guidelines.

▶ Make sure you feel comfortable, allow plenty of time to stand back often to assess the tree or bush as a whole, and stop pruning while you're still enjoying the job.

▶ Use sharp tools and leave clean wounds.

▶ Think twice and cut once to avoid mistakes.

▶ Never prune in frosty weather.

▶ Always cut out dead and diseased growth first, then remove thin weak branches and any that cross each other or spoil the shape (*see right*).

▶ A few bold cuts are more value than endless snipping; pruning should finish just above a bud facing the way growth is to continue.

▶ It is better not to prune at all than to remove too much or the wrong parts. However, most plants are forgiving and respond to pruning with new growth.

**Trimming a dead apple sideshoot back to live healthy tissue – a sound starting point for pruning any woody fruit.**

**TRY THIS...**
Treat the whole plot as a single ecosystem and expand the variety of plants you grow, because research shows that greater diversity stimulates beneficial growing conditions in the soil and surroundings. Balance crops with flowers, annuals with perennials, herbaceous vegetables with woody fruit, and everywhere mingle in a wide range of herbs (*see left*).

**IT'S NOT TOO LATE TO...**
Dig a runner bean trench: stop adding garden waste to the compost heap now, as cold weather inhibits decomposition, and bury it instead a full *spit* deep to rot and help create a moist root run for the beans. Dig out the next stretch of trench and backfill over the waste at the same time to save effort.

**IF YOU HAVE TIME...**
Drape a sheet of clear polythene over wall- and fan-trained peaches and nectarines to ward off spores of peach leaf curl disease and to encourage a slightly warmer microclimate at flowering time. Keep the material clear of the branches, and leave the ends open for ventilation.

# HARVEST HIGHLIGHTS

**BRUSSELS SPROUTS** In the days when Savoy cabbage varieties proliferated, there were just two kinds of Brussels sprouts: tall and dwarf ('Early Half-Tall' is an old, reliable semi-dwarf choice for windy gardens). Now there are hundreds, mostly F1 hybrids, bred for uniform commercial production and easy mass harvest, with whole stems being pulled from the field and stripped clean in sheds; the sprouts themselves are small and hard with a mild, even bland, flavour. Picking sprouts no larger than hazelnuts is infanticide, with a waste of many weeks' growth and meagre servings on the plate. Older, open-pollinated varieties like 'Evesham Special', 'Fillbasket' and 'Seven Hills' can give a sequence of pickings from early autumn to late spring, producing large, hearty, well-flavoured sprouts to relish with crisply fried bacon or even grate raw into salads. Harvest from the bottom upwards, at the same time removing all leaves (green or yellowing) below that level to encourage the sprouts above to fatten. (*See also page 190.*)

**PARSNIPS** The other classic allotment wine apart from dandelion is made from the last of the parsnip crop, usually in spring when surviving roots break into leaf again and develop an unwelcome central core down the root. Until then they are a key maincrop root, easy to grow

---

### DANDELIONS

Noisome weed or versatile crop, depending on your outlook, dandelions have been valued since medieval times for their leaves, blanched for 2–3 weeks under soil, pots or plates at any time between spring and autumn, then gathered as a bracing and mineral-rich salad ingredient. The seed of superior forms is available, and you can improve quality further by dressing plants with rotted manure during winter.

Before they lose their leaves in late autumn, mark the strongest specimens and dig them up now carefully, so as to extract the maximum amount of root. This can be dried to make a caffeine-free 'coffee' or an alternative to chicory for blending with real coffee. Scrub off all the soil, leave small roots whole and slice larger ones lengthways, and spread on paper to dry in a warm room (or greenhouse) before roasting until brittle, when they can be crushed or ground coarsely. If you fear the dandelion's ability to seed promiscuously, chop off the flowers in spring to make one of the best country wines.

---

### FESTIVE PRODUCE

Plot-holders often make a special pilgrimage to the allotment on Christmas morning to gather fresh vegetables for the main meal, sometimes taking considerable pride in collecting as many different kinds as possible. This is the time to pick the very best – uniform unblemished sprouts, exhibition-quality carrots and perfectly shaped shallots – and smugly celebrate the results of a whole year's work on the plot. Remember the special red onions safely squirrelled away and the new potatoes planted in pots in late summer and stored dry under the staging for safe keeping or buried in a biscuit tin in the ground. Gather parsley, horseradish and other fresh herbs for stuffings and sauces, cut salad leaves from the cold frame, and fetch a bottle or two of parsnip or parsley wine from the store. Christmas dinner can be the climax of the allotment year and a final flourish before starting all over again. Boxing Day is the traditional date for sowing maincrop onions.

p. 59 *see* Onion marmalade
p. 159 *see* Parsley wine
p. 175 *see* Roasted, herbed new potatoes
p. 176 *see* Brussels sprouts with breadcrumbs

seasonal planner

if given a sufficiently long season (although a midsummer sowing will still yield fashionable 'baby' roots), safe all winter in any soil except the wettest or stoniest, and maturing pleasantly in flavour as times passes, especially after a frost or two to convert more starch to sugar.

Old varieties are still unsurpassed. They range from deep-rooting 'Hollow Crown', its superior offspring 'The Student', or 'Tender and True', which lives up to its name and can shrug off canker, to abbreviated kinds like 'White Gem' and 'Half-Long Guernsey', for shallower soils. Dig up with a spade or fork, carefully to avoid damaging the roots, and use for a range of dishes, from toothsome and irresistible deep-fried parsnip chips to parsnip sauce (an old Ash Wednesday garnish for salt cod) and a host of traditional country desserts such as parsnip flans and puddings. (*See also pages 183–4.*)

**Inspect stored maincrop potatoes regularly for damp patches, indicating blight or rot, which can surge through a complete stock of winter's finest comfort food. If you do find decay starting, empty out the whole batch, discard badly affected tubers and repack perfect specimens for use before any others. That will leave some tubers just lightly blemished, and there are many ways to cook with them after cutting out infected portions.**

ask the **EXPERT**

**SAVOY CABBAGES** These heavy, solid cabbages with dark crimped leaves are the hardiest of all and, if you sow an early and late variety at the same time, can crop from mid-autumn almost to the end of spring. You need to hunt for varieties, though: most catalogues list modern hybrids, often crossed with a white cabbage for a paler product, or one or two older kinds, like 'Best of All', 'Early Ormskirk' or 'Late Drumhead', worthy survivors from an earlier age. Nineteenth-century Paris markets offered dozens: French, Belgian and Italian, flat-headed or tubular, blue or almost golden yellow, plain or tightly curled. The city gardeners sowed them lavishly, saving seedbed leftovers to plant late between other vegetables, as densely as lettuces, for pulling as 'coleworts' or greens in winter and spring. This practice should be revived, for Savoys are the choicest of cabbages: they contain more minerals and vitamins than other kinds, taste milder and less sulphurous, make the best kind for stuffing and, with their huge surface area of blistered leaves, are supreme for soaking up an ocean of good gravy. (*See also page 191.*)

## EAT NOW

If all has gone to plan, the store should be bursting with preserves and the allotment full of fresh vegetables all approaching perfection. Winter produce is neither bland nor boring – inspiration grows in the kitchen, not on the plot – and there is a multitude of superior foods to enjoy at this season, such as a medley of roots to roast in dripping and the heartiest cabbages for inventive combinations with this year's crop of mushrooms, garlic and sunflower seeds, all seasoned with a bouquet garni of home-grown dried herbs. Given a little cover against frost, there might also be fresh salads for milder sunny spells, while all those autumn fruit preserves are on the menu for warming winter steamed puddings and fruit cobblers. (*See* In season now, *page 146*.)

## RECIPES

seasonal planner

## LEEK & SORREL SOUP

**SERVES 4**

This is a basic leek and potato soup with the addition of sorrel, a much under-used leaf that adds a lemony taste. The soup should be thick with dark flecks of green and will make a filling lunch or supper.

115g (4oz) haricot beans, soaked overnight and drained

60g (2oz) butter

large handful of sorrel, washed and chopped

4 large leeks, chopped into rings

4 large potatoes, peeled and sliced into rounds

1.4 litres (2½ pints) hot water

salt and freshly ground pepper, to taste

1 tbsp single cream

- Cook the soaked beans for 2 hours without salt at this stage. When the beans are ready, melt the butter in a heavy pan and add the sorrel, leeks and potatoes. Cover with the hot water and simmer for 30 minutes.
- Add the beans, heat through and season to taste. Stir in the cream and serve immediately.

## CABBAGE SOUP

**SERVES 4**

Called *garbure* and produced in different versions all over France, this is a thick and savoury soup. This adaptation includes an unsalted bacon joint, which turns the soup into more of a casserole and makes it filling enough for a hearty lunch.

2 tbsp olive oil

2 onions, peeled and chopped

3 turnips, peeled and chopped

4 potatoes, peeled and chopped

½ cabbage, shredded

450g (1lb) unsmoked bacon joint

600ml (1 pint) water

salt and freshly ground pepper, to taste

**To serve**

8 thin slices of French bread

60g (2oz) Gruyère cheese, grated

- Heat the oil in a casserole, add the onions and cook until translucent. Add the vegetables, bacon joint and water. Bring to the boil, then reduce the heat, cover and simmer the soup until the bacon is tender. Taste for seasoning and adjust accordingly – you won't need a lot of salt as the bacon, although unsmoked, will still be salty.
- Remove the bacon and slice it thinly.
- Preheat the grill to high. Place a few slices of the bacon in the bottom of four heatproof bowls and pour in the soup. Put two slices of bread on top of each bowl and sprinkle with the Gruyère, going right to the edge of the bread to prevent the crust from burning under the grill. Put the bowls under the grill until the cheese bubbles and starts to brown. Serve immediately.

## MINESTRONE

**SERVES 4**

No vegetable recipe book could overlook a minestrone without good reason. A classic soup, it combines vegetables with rice or pasta. This recipe also includes pesto. Adapt the vegetables according to what's in season.

115g (4oz) haricot beans, soaked overnight and drained

2 tbsp extra virgin olive oil

1 large onion, peeled and sliced

1 leek, white part only, sliced in rings

2 garlic cloves, chopped

2 carrots, peeled and sliced in rings

2 large potatoes, peeled and cubed

1 turnip, peeled and cubed

a few basil leaves

2 tbsp tomato purée, diluted in a full cup of hot water

salt and freshly ground pepper, to taste

2.4 litres (4 pints) chicken or vegetable stock

handful of rice or soup pasta

handful of spinach

2 tbsp pesto (*see page 138*)

**To serve**

ciabatta bread

1 garlic clove

extra virgin olive oil, to drizzle

- Cook the soaked beans for 2 hours without salt at this stage.
- Heat the oil in a heavy frying pan and sauté the onion, leek and garlic until translucent. Add the carrots, potatoes and turnip and sprinkle on the basil. Now add the diluted tomato purée and a shake of salt. Transfer to a large pan and add the beans, stock and rice or pasta. Simmer for 1 hour.
- After 40 minutes add the spinach and put in the pesto when everything else is ready. Season to taste with salt and pepper.
- Toast the ciabatta, rub with a cut garlic clove, drizzle with olive oil and serve alongside the soup.

## FENNEL SOUP & ROASTED GARLIC CROÛTONS

**SERVES 4**

This unusual soup will be a talking point at any dinner party or event. It is creamy and subtle with a slight aniseed taste.

2 tbsp olive oil

15g (½oz) unsalted butter

4 fennel bulbs, trimmed and thinly sliced

1 leek, trimmed and coarsely chopped

1.2 litres (2 pints) hot vegetable or chicken stock

salt and freshly ground pepper, to taste

30g (1oz) Parmesan cheese, freshly grated

### Croûtons

1 garlic bulb, outer skin removed

3 tsp extra virgin olive oil

4 x 1cm (½in) slices ciabatta bread

freshly ground pepper

- Preheat oven to 200°C/400°F/gas 6.
- Prepare the croûtons first. Drizzle the garlic bulb with 1 teaspoon of the oil and wrap in foil. Roast for 45 minutes until the garlic is very soft. When the garlic is cool, squeeze the cloves out into a small bowl. Discard the skins. Mash with a fork, mix the remaining oil into the purée and set aside.
- Toast the bread until slightly golden and set aside.
- Now prepare the soup. Heat the oil and butter in a large saucepan. Add the fennel and leek, and sauté until softened. Add the stock and bring to the boil. Reduce the heat and simmer until the vegetables are very soft.
- Remove the vegetables with a slotted spoon and purée in a blender. Put the purée back into the soup and simmer just until heated through. Season to taste with salt and pepper.
- Spread the toasted bread slices with the garlic purée. Ladle the soup into four bowls, place a toast on top of each and sprinkle Parmesan over them. Drizzle with some oil and pepper and serve.

## BAKED FENNEL & LEEK PANCAKES

**SERVES 4**

Baking these pancakes rather than frying cuts down on the calories. The vegetables are puréed and added to the batter – any other ingredients such as potatoes and carrots could be used instead. Eat these pancakes as an accompaniment to soup or alongside a salad.

2 tsp extra virgin olive oil

1 fennel bulb, trimmed and chopped

2 large leeks, white parts only, thinly sliced

3 tbsp water

1 large egg, beaten

250g (9oz) plain yoghurt

115g (4oz) plain flour

115g (4oz) Cheddar cheese

1 tbsp chopped fresh chives

- Heat the oil, add the leeks and fennel and sauté until the vegetables are soft. Add the water to prevent the vegetables burning and to make sure that they are soft enough to purée.
- Preheat oven to 375°F/190°/gas 5.
- In a mixing bowl, beat the egg, yoghurt and flour to form a smooth paste.
- Purée the leek and fennel mixture in a food processor or blender. Stir the purée, Cheddar and chives into the batter until smooth.
- Drop the batter, a tablespoon at a time, on to a greased baking sheet, leaving a good space between them. Bake for about 15 minutes until the top has set and the bottoms are golden. Serve hot.

## FENNEL & HERB RISOTTO

**SERVES 4**

This risotto is made more sophisticated with the addition of wine as well as stock.

30g (1oz) butter

1 tbsp olive oil

2 garlic cloves, thinly sliced

½ onion, peeled and finely chopped

1 fennel bulb, trimmed and sliced into thin rounds

350g (12oz) arborio (or risotto) rice

360ml (12fl oz) dry white wine

900ml (1½ pints) hot vegetable or chicken stock

30g (1oz) Parmesan cheese, freshly grated, plus more to garnish

1 tsp finely chopped fresh thyme

1 tsp finely chopped fresh marjoram

1 tsp finely chopped fresh flat-leaf parsley

freshly ground pepper

- In a large saucepan, heat the butter and olive oil over a medium heat. Add the garlic and onion and sauté for 2–3 minutes, or until translucent. Add the fennel and sauté for another 2–3 minutes.
- Add the rice to the pan, then add some of the wine, waiting until the liquid is nearly absorbed before adding more. Add some of the stock and more of the wine, alternating between the two and waiting until the liquid is absorbed before adding more. When all the liquid has been added, cook for another 15 minutes. Add the Parmesan and herbs and stir vigorously for 2–3 minutes. The rice is ready when it is firm but tender.
- To serve, spoon the rice into individual bowls, sprinkle with black pepper and garnish with Parmesan.

## MOROCCAN CARROTS

**SERVES 6**

Cooked carrot salad is a popular dish in Morocco and makes a delicious and refreshing starter. Avoid the really large carrots, as they might be woody; the smaller they are, the better.

- 1 tbsp cumin seeds
- 55 ml (2fl oz) extra virgin olive oil
- 12 carrots, peeled and cut into matchsticks
- ½ tsp salt
- 1 tbsp clear honey
- 4 tsp fresh lemon juice
- 12 black olives in oil, pitted and chopped
- 2 tsp chopped fresh mint
- freshly ground pepper
- handful of fresh coriander, to garnish

- Put the cumin seeds in a heavy pan and dry-fry for 4 minutes, stirring a few times. Grind in a mortar and pestle or spice grinder and set aside.
- Put the olive oil in a large pan and add the carrots. Cook for 5 minutes, or until the carrots are soft and golden. Keep shaking the pan to cook evenly. Sprinkle over the salt.
- Drain the carrots on kitchen paper, then put into a bowl. Mix together the honey, lemon juice, olives and crushed cumin seeds, then mix in the mint and a little ground pepper. Serve garnished with the coriander.

## TURNIP SALAD

**SERVES 4**

This seems like an odd mix of ingredients, but it's a great salad with a sweet and slightly sour flavour. Turnips are underrated as a vegetable, but with this dressing their taste is intensified.

- 4 turnips, peeled and chopped
- 1 bunch salad onions, all parts, chopped
- 2 crisp apples, peeled, cored and chopped
- 115 g (4oz) caster sugar
- 55ml (2fl oz) sunflower oil
- ½ tsp salt
- ¼ tsp freshly ground pepper

- Bring a large pot of salted water to the boil. Add the turnips and cook until tender but still firm. Drain and leave to cool.
- In a large bowl, combine the turnips, salad onions, apples and sugar. Stir to coat evenly with the sugar.
- Whisk together the oil, salt and pepper. Pour the dressing over the fruit and vegetables, toss and refrigerate overnight before serving.

---

**TRY THIS**
**CELERY SALT**

Flavoured salts for seasoning roast meat or poultry, sauces and salad dressings can be made with almost any dried and powdered herb. Seeds need to be pulverized using a pestle and mortar, which adds exercise (at least 10 minutes of pounding) and a hint of alchemy to the preparation. You need 225g (8oz) fine salt, 1 tablespoon celery seeds and 1 teaspoon white peppercorns. Simply grind all the ingredients together using a pestle and mortar to form a fine-blended powder. Store in an airtight jar.

## MEG DODS' BASHED NEEPS

**SERVES 6**

Turnips and swedes, known as 'neeps' in Scotland, have not attracted a huge repertoire of recipes, and those that exist usually involving mashing or 'bashing' them with various flavourings. Indeed, this is a classic 'bash', to serve with sausages or, authentically, with haggis. Meg Dods? This was the pseudonym of the popular cook at an infamous 19th-century diners' club.

- 900g (2lb) swedes or maincrop turnips (preferably yellow), peeled and cubed
- 30g (1oz) butter, plus extra to serve
- pinch of grated nutmeg
- generous sprinkle of freshly ground pepper or ½ tsp ground ginger
- pinch of salt

- Put the swedes into a saucepan and cover with water. Bring to the boil, then reduce the heat, cover and simmer for 30 minutes or until very soft, then drain.
- Add the butter, nutmeg, pepper or ginger, and salt, and mash until the mixture is smooth.
- Put in a large bowl or serving dish, crease the surface with a fork and serve topped with a knob of butter.

## PEA FRITTERS

**SERVES 4**

These have been made for generations with Carlin or Maple peas (*see page 189*), but any dried pea or fresh mealy pea can be substituted. Serve as an interesting vegetable accompaniment to a plain fish or chicken dish.

> 115g (4oz) dried whole peas, soaked overnight and drained
> ½ tbsp extra virgin olive oil
> 1 egg
> 60g (2oz) self-raising wholemeal flour
> 75ml (2½ fl oz) milk
> salt and freshly ground pepper, to taste
> sunflower oil, for shallow-frying

- Put the soaked peas in a saucepan, cover with water and bring to the boil. Reduce the heat and simmer for 45 minutes or until soft.
- Drain the peas and mash well. Add the olive oil, egg, flour, milk and salt and pepper, and mix thoroughly.
- Heat the oil in a frying pan, then drop spoonfuls of the mixture into the hot oil and fry until crisp and brown on both sides. Drain well on kitchen paper.

## BOSTON BAKED BEANS

**SERVES 4**

Any kind of dried common or haricot bean will work here, although 'Dutch Brown' has usually emerged as the supreme variety for this rich and moreish dish, which is also ideal for preparing in a slow cooker all day or overnight.

> 225g (8oz) dried haricot beans, soaked overnight and drained
> 225g (8oz) piece of streaky bacon, cut into small cubes, or 'bacon bits'
> 1 tbsp treacle
> ¼ tsp black pepper
> 4 tbsp tomato ketchup
> 1 tbsp malt vinegar

- Preheat oven to 180°C/350°F/gas 4.
- Layer half the beans in a casserole, add the bacon and then cover with the remaining beans, adding just enough water to reach the top of the beans.
- Fit a tight lid and bake in the oven for 1–1½ hours.
- Melt the treacle in the same amount of hot water, and mix in the pepper, ketchup and vinegar. Add to the casserole.
- Cook for a further 1–1½ hours, stirring occasionally and testing if the beans are soft.
- Serve straight from the pot, with fresh warm granary bread.

## PARSLEY WINE

**MAKES FOUR 75CL BOTTLES**

In a good season a row of parsley can fatten into a robust hedge that easily survives through the winter and remains available for picking for sauces and soups. This recipe turns a surplus into a light and refreshing 'house' wine for all purposes – aperitifs, a Christmas Day tipple, general table use or for the end of a long day. Good wine-making equipment and ingredients are necessary. These can be easily obtained online, from specialist shops and even a large chain of chemists. Otherwise look at car boot sales.

> 450g (1 lb) parsley leaves and stalks
> 4.5 litres (8 pints) boiling water
> 30g (1 oz) fresh root ginger
> rind and juice of 2 oranges
> rind and juice of 2 lemons
> 1.4–1.8kg (3–4lb) caster sugar
> wine yeast (tokay, sauterne or champagne)

- Pull the parsley into pieces, place in an earthenware or plastic bowl and pour over the boiling water. Cover with a clean tea towel and leave for 24 hours.
- Strain into a preserving pan, add the ginger and the orange and lemon rinds, and boil for 20 minutes.
- Pour the liquor onto the sugar (less for a dry wine, more for sweet) in a fermentation bucket or ordinary bucket, stir until dissolved, and add the juice of the oranges and lemons.
- When nearly cool, add the yeast starter according to the packet directions. Cover and leave for 2 weeks, skimming occasionally, until violent fermentation dies down.
- Strain into a demijohn, fit an airlock, and leave until the wine has stopped fermenting (6 months or more).
- Filter into sterilized bottles, cork and keep for at least another 6 months before you drink it.

## BEETROOT FAIRY CAKES

### MAKES 12 SMALL CAKES

These are little moist cakes made in a similar way to carrot cake. Beetroot isn't as moist as carrot, so if the mixture seems a bit dry, add some more milk.

115g (4oz) soft light brown sugar

5 tbsp sunflower oil

60g (2oz) butter, melted

3 eggs

2 tbsp milk

zest of 1 orange

85g (3oz) walnuts, chopped

85g (3oz) sultanas, finely chopped

175g (6oz) beetroot, grated

175g (6oz) self-raising flour

1 tsp baking powder

### Frosting

300g (10oz) cream cheese

2 tbsp clear honey

zest of 1 orange, plus small curls of peel

- Preheat oven to 200°C/400°F/gas 6. Line a 12-cup shallow bun tin with doubled-up paper cases (*see page 144*).
- Put the sugar, oil, butter, eggs and milk in a bowl and whisk together until smooth. Add the orange zest, walnuts, sultanas and beetroot and mix together.
- Sift the flour and baking powder together and fold into the mixture. Do not over-mix. Spoon into the paper cases.
- Bake for 20 minutes. When ready, insert a skewer into the middle of one of the cakes – it should come away clean.
- Cool in the tin then transfer to a wire rack until cold.
- To make the frosting, beat the cream cheese, honey and orange zest in a bowl and spread over the cakes with a knife or the back of a spoon. Decorate each cake with a tiny curl of orange peel.

## JAMAICAN PATTIES

### MAKES 24 PATTTIES

These patties are a Jamaican treasure, with a curry flavour that reflects the British colonial influence of the island. People eat meat patties for lunch or dinner or as a handy snack. They are easy to make, with a wonderful mix of flavours from the lamb, curry, sweet potatoes, chilli and lime. You can substitute minced beef for the lamb. The dough may be kept in the refrigerator for several days before use, but it should be brought to room temperature before being rolled out. Put the patties together in the morning and refrigerate them until you're ready to bake. Serve with Caribbean hot sauce for dipping.

2 tbsp black or brown mustard seeds

350g (12 oz) plain flour

1 tbsp curry powder

1 tsp ground cumin

½ tsp salt

115g (4oz) chilled butter, diced

150ml (5fl oz) iced water

1 tbsp wine vinegar

1 egg yolk, beaten

Caribbean hot sauce, for dipping

1 red chilli, deseeded and sliced, to garnish

### Filling

1 tbsp sunflower oil

½ onion, peeled and diced

½ green chilli, deseeded and finely chopped

½ tsp peeled and chopped fresh root ginger

1 plum tomato, deseeded and diced

½ sweet potato, peeled and diced

115g (4oz) lean lamb, diced

salt and freshly ground pepper, to taste

1 tbsp freshly squeezed lime juice

1 egg, beaten

- First make the pastry. Heat the mustard seeds in a small dry frying pan. Shake occasionally and cook until the seeds are fragrant – about 2–3 minutes. Put the flour, curry powder, cumin, salt and toasted seeds in a food processor and combine. Add the butter and blend until the mixture resembles fine breadcrumbs.
- Combine the measured iced water, vinegar and egg yolk, add gradually to the processor and blend until a ball of dough forms. Wrap the dough in clingfilm and put in the refrigerator.
- Preheat oven to 180°C/350°F/gas 4.
- Now make the filling. Heat the oil in a frying pan and add the onion, chilli, ginger, tomato and sweet potato. Cook until the onion and sweet potato begin to soften. Add the lamb and cook, stirring occasionally, for around 5 minutes or until the lamb is cooked. Season with salt and pepper. Allow the mixture to cool, then add the lime juice.
- Lightly dust a work surface with flour and roll out the dough to a thickness of 3mm (⅛in). Using a 7.5cm (3in) circular cutter, cut out the dough. Place 1 tablespoon of the filling on one half of each pastry circle. Brush the edges with the egg. Fold the dough over the filling to form a semicircle and press the edges to seal. Brush the top with more egg to glaze. Put the patties on an oiled baking sheet and bake in the oven for 10 minutes. Serve immediately with some hot sauce garnished with red chilli slices.

# late winter

## setting the scene

In a good year, spring can tiptoe in and tempt early sowings in the weak, late winter sunshine and gently rising temperatures, or you could just as easily be shovelling snow or sheltering under glass from biting winds and persistent sullen rain. Adapt your plans to the changing weather: there's still plenty of time to complete basic winter tasks outdoors, while under glass and indoors you can get things under way for the new season in comfort. After a few mild dry days, you might even be able to make a start on outdoor seedbeds, confident in the knowledge that spring is only a few weeks away.

**A comparatively dormant season for plots and plot-holders before the new growing year begins.**

**seasonal planner**

**IN SEASON NOW**
Brussels sprouts, cabbages (winter), cauliflowers (winter), celeriac, celery, chicory (forced + heading), Jerusalem artichokes, kale, lamb's lettuce, land cress, leeks, lettuces, parsnips, radishes, rhubarb (forced), salad leaves, salsify, scorzonera, seakale (forced), sorrel, sprouting broccoli, swedes

**SOW NOW**
**indoors** asparagus, broad beans, celery, chives, tomatoes (greenhouse), leeks, parsley, peas, salad leaves, shallots (seeds), strawberries (including alpines), cauliflowers (summer)
**cold frame** beetroot, carrots, radishes, salad onions
**outdoors** broad beans, parsnips

**PLANT NOW**
garlic, globe artichokes, rhubarb, shallots

# SEASONAL TASKS

**GETTING THE GROUND READY** A planting area can be dug and tilled successfully any time of the year, as long as it is not frozen, sodden or dust-dry. Ideally, though, any deep soil treatment should be completed by the end of winter, for a number of reasons:

► Winter and spring rainfall tops up the soil reservoir and infiltrates most easily in loosened ground, especially in places previously compacted or poorly drained

► Heavy clay soils are made up of very fine grains that stick together stubbornly; exposing loosened clods to alternate winter freezing and thawing is a free and effective aid to producing a more workable texture

► There is rarely enough time (and it could be far too warm) to do the job well later on, and disturbed soil needs several weeks to settle into a stable structure for efficient root growth and moisture retention.

Remember that digging isn't always necessary or even beneficial. If the ground drains well and plants grow vigorously, surface cultivation is usually sufficient, especially where annual mulching is practised to keep fertility high and to protect the soil from damage in extreme weather conditions.

Cultivating very light ground can be left until the end of winter because earlier disturbance may cause the

soil to 'slump' and lose nutrients during heavy rainfall. Remember to tread recently dug light soil to firm it before sowing and planting.

Trample and turn in green manures 4–6 weeks before growing any crops to allow the remains of plants time to start decomposing. Plan to finish all major cultivation so that all you need do before planting is loosen the surface with a fork or rake to produce a workable crumbly tilth.

## WINTER HOUSEWORK UNDER GLASS

This is the time to finish all the clearing and cleaning of the greenhouse started in late autumn. Greenhouse work can be a real pleasure now, even the annual chore of cleaning the glass, which is best done while the house is relatively empty. On a mild day, when you can open doors and vents, move the contents outside, and wash the glass with warm soapy water inside and out. Clean and wash cold frames and cloches, too, while you have all the necessary materials and equipment at hand.

Using grubby pots and labels can compromise the most thorough housework under glass. Scrub wooden trays with warm soapy water and, when dry, treat with a plant-friendly preservative. Wash seed labels and scour off old writing with wire wool (use a 2B pencil in future, rather than a pen, for easy reuse). Scrub pots clean and stand to dry before packing away, according to size, to save time later. Don't forget to tidy under staging, which is very often a cache of used, discarded and lost items.

Ventilate the greenhouse until it is dry and then reinstate its contents. Top up supplies of water and fresh seed and potting composts (all kept indoors to warm up), and collect together enough newspapers, fleece or old curtains to cover early seeds and seedlings just in case the weather deteriorates. Loosen gravel on staging, water with mild disinfectant and make level with a board; wash capillary matting in disinfectant and reinstall.

Revive soil borders in a greenhouse or cold frame by removing weeds and forking over the surface, at the same time adding a dressing of general organic fertilizer. Every 2–3 years, exchange the top spit of soil with a fresh 50:50 mixture of mature garden compost and topsoil from your most fertile outdoor bed.

 **ask the EXPERT** **Keep a bowl of water in the greenhouse and load with used pots at the end of the day to soak overnight and loosen any grime. The pots will clean up effortlessly the next day.**

Green manures decompose faster if you trample or cut them down before turning them into the topsoil.

ABOVE Often neglected when washing glass, the overlaps between panes are a safe hiding place for all kinds of unwelcome organisms.

RIGHT Washing off left-over shading when cleaning the glass admits more light into the greenhouse.

ABOVE Top up bare patches with fresh gravel to produce an even depth.

LEFT A layer of gravel on staging makes a good free-draining bed but it must be cleaned and sterilized with a mild disinfectant annually.

**ABOVE** Sprinkle round carrot seeds in modules, for planting out in clusters.

**ABOVE CENTRE** Sow larger seeds like broad beans singly. Plant out when seedlings have developed 2–3 true leaves.

**ABOVE RIGHT** Paper pots will disintegrate in the soil when planted out.

**RIGHT** Use a propagator for additional warmth or cover seed trays with glass and newspaper.

**SOWING INDOORS** Crops that you might want to start now under unheated glass include early leeks, maincrop onions, hardy lettuce, first early peas, hardy broad beans, such as 'Aquadulce' and 'The Sutton', and beetroot and round carrots in cell trays, with a pinch of seed in each division.

Greenhouse tomatoes, strawberries and celery all need heat – a minimum of 15°C (60°F) – and are best started indoors on a warm windowsill.

The seeds of most crops (but not root crops) can be sown in pots or pans for pricking out about 5cm (2in) apart in deeper trays once the seedlings are just large enough to handle safely. You can avoid this stage by sowing in small pots or cell trays, 2–3 seeds in each, and singling the seedlings to leave the strongest to grow on

unchecked. Beetroot, leeks and round carrots sown in pots or modules can be left unthinned and planted out as clusters of seedlings, spacing each group further apart than normal.

In a cold season, stand all these early sowings in a propagator or insulated section of the greenhouse for additional warmth, and keep them in the best possible light once seedlings emerge. Wherever possible, recycle paper and loo-roll tubes to make improvised and biodegradable pots rather than buy new supplies.

**Sow leeks thinly in a pot and leave all the seedlings undisturbed to reach about 15cm (6in) high, when they can be knocked out and separated for planting individually.**

ask the
**EXPERT**

## TAKING STOCK

Before the pace begins to accelerate with the arrival of spring, make sure that all your gardening equipment is in working order and that you have everything you might need for the season ahead, such as fresh seed and potting composts, containers, fertilizers, canes, stakes, string and ties. Don't forget to complete your seed and plant orders in good time.

### TRY THIS...

Sort and pension off your oldest bamboo canes for replacement with new. Cut off rotten portions and divide the sound remnants into equal pieces (open end outwards) to pack into holes in walls or in tin cans to suspend as improvised overwintering and nesting havens for insect allies.

### IT'S NOT TOO LATE TO...

Winter prune fruit by cutting out dead, damaged and diseased wood from fruit trees but leave stone fruit, such as plums and cherries, until late spring. Cut down exhausted raspberry canes and remove one-third of the oldest blackcurrant stems and check for big bud. Shorten the sideshoots on trained fruit (cordons, fans, espaliers) to two buds.

### IF YOU HAVE TIME...

Turn the compost heap to admit air and revive decomposition; check the contents are moist (not wet), and water if they're dry. You can avoid loosening and turning compost by including plenty of screwed-up paper and crumpled card to bulk up and aerate the softer green material as you add it.

**Kale 'Red Russian'**

This perennial edible dock is a common wild herb, enjoyed since early Egyptian times for its cool tangy flavour and early availability – it is one of the first green plants to come back into growth. The best form to cultivate is the less acid French, or round-leaved, sorrel and its more compact variant, buckler-leaved sorrel, both used in stews and soups or to add hints of lemon to salads. The leaves can be cooked like spinach into a purée to accompany bean and fish dishes. Sow in early spring and thin to 30cm (12in) apart. Remove all flower stems as they appear, and divide plants every 2–3 years in spring.

# HARVEST HIGHLIGHTS

**CELERIAC** Whereas trench celery will be nearly finished by now and self-blanching varieties just a distant memory, celeriac should still be usable, either from store or from the open ground, provided that you smothered plants with 15cm (6in) of straw or leaf litter last autumn.

Celeriac is still the best source of fresh celery flavouring when grated in salads or mixed in a mustard mayonnaise as *céleri rémoulade*. You can also start using up the crop as a cooked vegetable, in soups and broths, or puréed with potatoes. In this late season, take care during preparation to remove the coarse fibrous base and outer layer. (*See also page 183.*)

**KALE** Even after the hardest weather, kale normally survives unscathed to greet the end of winter with a steady sequence of young leafy shoots, cut or snapped off when about 10cm (4in) long. Steam or stir-fry small amounts of curled varieties; treat larger quantities and plain-leaved forms like spring greens and cook as a main green vegetable. After particularly savage frosts, cherish notable survivors by allowing them to flower and set seeds for gathering as the nucleus of an extra-hardy strain. Beware, though, the aphids that love to colonize the flowering stems. (*See also page 193.*)

**LAND CRESS** Land (American or Belle Isle) cress is a pungent salad stalwart, so hardy that it is seldom unavailable for picking during winter, especially if it's grown in a cold frame or an unheated greenhouse to ensure superior quality. If you have plenty, you could try the old Swedish custom of boiling the leaves like kale; Cherokees and other Native American tribes ate them ritually as a spring cleanser.

Since land cress is a biennial (although usually treated as an annual), it will soon start throwing out flowering stems, especially in a mild season. The leaves then deteriorate in quality but the clusters of flower buds can be cooked like broccoli. Use plants up steadily, and sow a replacement batch for picking in 8–10 weeks' time. (*See also page 191.*)

**SPROUTING BROCCOLI** As days lengthen, the first young flowering shoots will start to emerge on purple and white sprouting broccoli, especially in sunny sheltered positions. (This applies only to early strains; late varieties are still 4–6 weeks away from harvest.)

**Land cress**

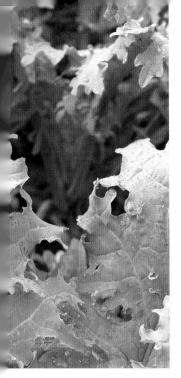

Check plants regularly, and cut or snap off shoots when 10–15cm (4–6in) long, before their buds open. Gather with a few young leaves to bulk up the harvest, and prepare immediately because the tender shoots quickly wilt and lose quality. Pick over every few days to prevent flowering and prolong the harvest for up to 2 months. Any surplus shoots can be frozen. (*See also page 193*.)

**WINTER RADISHES** Unlike their miniature cousins, which mature all summer, winter radishes are ready from late autumn onwards. In well-drained soils, they can be left in the ground all winter, especially if protected with a covering of leaf litter.

Start using them up now if you want their firm mild flesh for a main vegetable or for curries and Japanese tempura. Surplus roots can be pickled. Otherwise, leave unwanted roots in the ground, earth up slightly and harvest the resulting foliage in a few weeks' time in the same way as turnip tops. (*See also page 185*.)

**TRY THIS**
**FIRST SOWINGS**

▶ In mild regions and sheltered sunny gardens on light soil, it could be worth gambling on an early sowing of parsnips, lettuces and hardy peas, especially if you warm the soil for 2–3 weeks first with cloches or plastic film. Otherwise, wait until early spring, when seeds often germinate faster and more fully. These sowings will quickly catch up with earlier batches checked by a cold start in life.

▶ Many vegetable seeds refuse to germinate when soil temperatures are below 5–7°C (40–45°F), so test regularly before sowing by inserting a soil thermometer into the top 8–10cm (3–4in) of the seedbed.

▶ Traditionally, gardeners used makeshift tests to check the soil temperature, such as thrusting a poker in the ground and then holding it against the cheek or even sitting bare-bottomed for a while on the ground, but the accuracy of these methods is debatable. Natural signs, like the emergence of young annual weeds or the fattening of hedgerow buds, are more reliable cues.

**Purple sprouting broccoli**

169

## EAT NOW

All those old earnest handbooks and almanacs advised gardeners to stay indoors and plan the new season at this time of year, to sit by the fire and read seed catalogues or sharpen tools ready for dour battles with weeds and wilderness when the frosts first lift. More enlightened gardeners might prefer to stay indoors and eat. The store-cupboard and pantry should still hold reserves of last year's plenty: sun-dried tomatoes and strings of sweet solid onions, frozen loganberries and bottled plums, boxes of carrots and celeriac, and comforting potatoes for roasting, baking, chipping, mashing... And on mild days there'll be fresh Brussels sprouts to gather, as well as curly kale, early purple sprouting broccoli and all those other green things on the plot that marvellously keep going whatever the weather. (*See* In season now, *page 162*.)

## RECIPES

seasonal planner

## POTATO & SPINACH PUFFS

### SERVES 6

No puff pastry in sight; instead these are little puffed potato cakes, cooked liked muffins. They are quick and simple to prepare, but make a really elegant starter and are also wonderfully aesthetic floated in soup. Feel free to substitute other vegetables for the spinach, including broccoli or carrots and for a stronger flavour swap the Gruyère for mature Cheddar or other strong hard cheeses.

4 medium potatoes, peeled and quartered

225g (8oz) spinach, chopped

butter, for greasing

90ml (3fl oz) skimmed milk

7g (¼oz) chopped fresh parsley

2 tbsp finely snipped fresh chives

2 large eggs, lightly beaten

30g (1oz) Gruyère cheese

30g (1oz) plain flour

1½ tsp baking powder

- Boil the potatoes until soft, drain rinse in cold water. Set aside to cool. Cook the spinach in a very small amount of water, drain thoroughly and chop further – it needs to be extremely fine for this recipe.
- Preheat oven to 190°C/375°F/Gas 5. Grease a 6-hole muffin tin.
- Mash the cooled potatoes with the milk, parsley, chives, eggs and cheese. Sift the flour and baking powder together into the potato mixture. Add the spinach and stir well to make sure the spinach is well distributed.
- Spoon equal amounts of the mixture into each hole in the muffin tin. Bake for about 30 minutes until puffy and golden. Serve immediately.

## POTATO & CAULIFLOWER ALOO

### SERVES 4 AS A MAIN COURSE

This is a delicious side dish to serve with curry but can also stand alone as a vegetarian dish served with rice or naan bread to make a more substantial meal.

1 cauliflower, broken into florets, stalk discarded

2 tbsp vegetable oil

450g (1lb) potatoes, peeled and diced

½ tsp turmeric

½ tsp red chilli, deseeded and chopped

½ tsp fenugreek seeds

½ tsp nigella seeds

½ tsp black mustard seeds

½ tsp cumin seeds

½ tsp fennel seeds

freshly chopped coriander, to garnish

- Cook the cauliflower until tender, drain and put aside.
- Heat the oil in a non-stick frying pan, begin to fry the potatoes and cover. Turn frequently to prevent the potatoes from burning. When the potatoes are half done, add the cauliflower florets, turmeric, red chilli and the whole spices, and mix together. Stir and put the lid back on. When the potatoes are nearly done, take the lid off, turn the heat up and fry to evaporate any excess liquid.
- Garnish with fresh coriander and serve.

## BITTER GOURD CURRY

### SERVES 4

This recipe was given to me by Jay Patel (*see page 17*). He grows bitter gourds quite easily if the summer is hot and dry. They are so bitter that some molasses or brown sugar are required in the recipe. If you prefer, you can substitute courgettes.

1 tsp whole cumin seeds

½ tsp turmeric

1 tsp black mustard seeds

1 large onion, peeled and chopped

2 tbsp sunflower oil

3 garlic cloves, chopped

1 green chilli, deseeded and chopped

½ tsp molasses or brown sugar

knob of fresh ginger, peeled and grated

4 bitter gourds or courgettes, thinly sliced

- Fry the cumin seeds in a dry, heavy frying pan for 1 minute. Grind them with a pestle and mortar. Mix together with the other spices.
- Fry the onion in the oil until soft. Add the spices, garlic, chilli, molasses and ginger. Cook briefly until the onion is coloured with the tumeric.
- Add the bitter gourd and cook gently 20 minutes.
- Serve with rice or naans.

## CARAMELIZED ROOT VEGETABLES

**SERVES 6**

Give roast root vegetables an exciting twist by adding a sugary dressing. They come out of the oven sweet and caramelized and are perfect for serving with a tender joint of meat.

225g (8oz) turnips, peeled and chopped
8 medium waxy potatoes, quartered
225g (8oz) carrots, peeled and chopped
225g (8oz) swede, peeled and chopped
225g (8oz) celeriac, peeled and chopped
12 shallots, peeled and halved
sprig of fresh thyme, leaves only
4 tbsp extra virgin olive oil
4 tbsp balsamic vinegar
2 tsp caster sugar
salt and freshly ground pepper, to taste

- Preheat oven to 220°C/425°F/gas 7.
- Put the vegetables in a large bowl and toss with the other ingredients. Put in a medium roasting pan and bake for 45–50 minutes, or until golden brown. You can check if they are done by pricking with a fork – if it enters the vegetables easily, they are ready.

### TRY THIS
#### SPROUTING SEEDS

You can use most seeds for sprouting, from onions and peas to more specialized seeds such as alfafa and mung. What you achieve are crunchy additions for salads and sandwiches. The flavours can vary from hot, with mustard seeds, to mild with mung seeds.

Do use commercial sprouters – they allow you to sprout lots of seeds at the same time. However, the childhood mustard and cress method, with wet kitchen paper or flannel on a saucer will also work, especially for small seeds.

## CARAMELIZED VEGETABLE PIE

**SERVES 6**

Using the caramelized roasted vegetables from the previous recipe, this has the addition of a cheese sauce and is cooked in a pie. It makes a delicious vegetarian light lunch or supper with a salad.

roasted vegetables from previous recipe
50g (2oz) butter
45g (1½oz) plain flour, plus extra for dusting
600ml (1 pint) whole milk, heated
60g (2oz) Cheddar cheese, grated
handful of fresh parsley, chopped
salt and freshly ground pepper, to taste
375g (13oz) ready-made shortcrust pastry
1 medium egg, beaten

- Preheat oven to 200°C/400°F/gas 6.
- Follow the previous recipe to roast and caramelize the vegetables.
- Meanwhile, make the cheese sauce. Melt the the butter in a pan. Add the flour and cook, stirring, for 1 minute. Gradually stir in the hot milk and cook, stirring all the time until thickened. Stir in the cheese and parsley, and season to taste. Pour over the vegetables and mix together.
- Spoon the mixture into a 2 litre (3½ pint) pie dish. Roll out the pastry on a lightly floured surface, cut out to the shape of the pie dish, allowing a couple of extra centimetres (inches) on all sides. Lay the pastry over the dish and trim off the edges. Brush with the beaten egg and cut a hole in the top for the steam to escape. Place on a baking sheet and bake for 40 minutes, until the pastry is golden and the filling piping hot.
- Serve hot.

## GREEK LAMB

**SERVES 6**

This recipe uses up stores of potatoes and carrots, and broad beans and tomatoes you may have frozen during an earlier glut. It also uses fresh rosemary, a herb guaranteed to be growing all year, and dried oregano, which is more potent when dried. The secret of the dish is its long cooking time in a low oven – the lamb almost drops off the bone. Don't be alarmed at the amount of garlic – when roasted it becomes very sweet. Red wine is ideal with this meal.

1 whole shoulder of lamb, weighing 2–3kg (4½–6½lb)
1 garlic head
6 sprigs of fresh rosemary
1 tbsp dried oregano
1 tsp each of cumin, coriander, cinnamon
salt and freshly ground pepper, to taste
450g (1lb) tomatoes, roughly chopped
450g (1lb) medium waxy potatoes, scrubbed and quartered
450g (1lb) carrots, scrubbed and cut and halved
2 tins chickpeas plus their liquid
½ bottle of red wine
450g (1lb) broad beans

- Preheat oven to 150°C/300°F/gas 2.
- Place the lamb in a very large roasting pan; cut slits in the flesh all over. Insert 4 thinly sliced cloves of garlic, and the sprigs of rosemary. Sprinkle with oregano and the spices, salt and pepper. Add the rest of the garlic cloves.
- Pile in the tomatoes, potatoes and carrots. Pour in the chickpeas and wine.
- Place in the middle of the oven. Cook for 3 hours, occasionally basting. Add more water if it looks too dry. Add the broad beans just before the end.
- Take out the meat and cut into rough slices. Place on individual plates and put a selection of vegetables and some of the garlic cloves around.

## MASHED POTATO

### SERVES 4

Every cook strives for the perfect mash: creamy, buttery and lump-free. Once mastered, there are many variations to try. For each type below, follow the basic recipe, then add the extra ingredients, as given.

450g (1lb) floury potatoes, peeled and halved
30g (1oz) butter
milk, according to taste

- Boil the potatoes until soft. Drain well, return to the pan and add the butter. Mash by hand with a potato masher. Don't do this in a blender, as it will become glutinous. Add enough milk to ensure that the mash is not dry. It should be smooth without lumps.

### Sage & onion mash

- Add a lightly fried chopped red onion and 1 teaspoon of dried sage.
- Ideal with meat and sausages.

### Sweet potato mash

- Exchange half the potatoes with sweet potatoes and follow as above.
- Good with poultry and gammon.

### Swede & potato mash

- Exchange half of the potatoes with swede, add 4 tablespoons of olive oil and some coarse black pepper.
- Delicious with roasts and rich stews.

### Garlic butter mash

- Add 2 large crushed garlic cloves and 3 tablespoons of chopped parsley to the milk and butter.
- Good with grilled fish or roast chicken.

### Saffron mash

- Infuse a good pinch of saffron in the milk prior to mashing.
- Good with fish and tomato stews.

## IRISH COLCANNON

### SERVES 6

A popular Irish dish, traditionally eaten at Halloween. The blend of potatoes, leeks and cabbage makes an easy side dish for a simple supper.

450g (1lb) kale or cabbage, chopped
2kg (4½ lb) potatoes, peeled and halved
2 small leeks, all parts, chopped
365ml (12fl oz) milk
175g (6oz) butter
salt and freshly ground pepper, to taste
pinch of mace

- Cook the kale or cabbage and the potatoes. Simmer the leeks with the milk until soft. Drain the potatoes and mash. Add the cooked leeks and milk with the butter and stir in.
- Over a low heat, add the kale and beat together. Serve in a warmed dish.

## CHAMP

### SERVES 6

Another traditional Irish potato dish, but with chopped chives and parsley this time. In the summer you can also add fresh peas, but don't put them into until the last minute or they'll go soggy.

10 salad onions, all parts, trimmed
75 ml (2½ fl oz) milk
675g (1½ lb) cooked, hot mashed potato (see left)
4 tbsp melted butter
small bunch parsley, chopped
handful of chives, snipped

- Cook the salad onions in the milk until softened. Drain, but keep the milk. Add the drained salad onions to the mashed potatoes, adding some of the cooked milk and the butter. Add the herbs and stir in well. Serve at once. Fry leftovers as potato cakes.

## APPLE & PORK PIE WITH A POTATO CRUST

### SERVES 6

Potato may seem a strange addition to pastry but it makes for a very crisp pie topping. Here it's used to make a cover for a wonderful combination of pork and apple with cider. This pastry can be used for any savoury pie – if making a sweet pie, omit the salt.

### Pastry

115g (4oz) flour
1½ tsp baking powder
¼ tsp salt
450g (1lb) potatoes, mashed and cooled
milk, enough to bind
60g (2oz) butter

### Filling

900g (2lb) pork loin
900g (2lb) apples, peeled, cored and sliced
2 tsp sugar
¼ tsp allspice
2 onions, chopped
900ml (1 pint) dry cider

- First make the pastry. Combine the flour, baking powder and salt and mix into the mash. Add enough milk to produce a light, soft but dry dough. Roll out, dab a third of the butter all over in small pats and fold in three. Roll again, repeat butter and folding and do so twice more. The dough is now ready to use so roll out for a final time and cut slightly larger than the size of your pie dish.
- Preheat oven to 180°C/360°F/gas 4. Cut the pork loin into small pieces. Put a layer of the apple at the bottom of a pie dish, sprinkle with some of the sugar and allspice and arrange the meat and chopped onion on top. Repeat until the apple and meat are used up. Cover with the cider and top with the pastry, making a slit or hole in the top. Bake for 1½ hours.

## POTATO SCONES

**MAKES 12**

Here mashed potato is used to make scones for tea. This recipe was first seen more than 50 years ago and hardly needs to be adapted for today. The scones are not cut out into your usual small rounds, but shaped into three small circular loaves, cut into wedges and cooked on top of the stove. Well worth making for tea if you have some unsalted mash left over from lunch.

450g (1lb) potatoes, mashed and cooled
115g (4oz) plain flour
pinch of salt
¼ tsp baking powder
30g (1oz) butter
1 tbsp milk

- Sift the flour and baking powder into a basin. Rub in the butter, then add the potatoes. Only add milk if the mixture is too dry. Divide into three pieces. Turn out on to a floured board. Roll out each piece thinly and shape into a circle. Prick lightly all over and cut into four wedges.
- These are best baked on a lightly greased flat griddle or heavy frying pan on the hob. Dust each wedge with flour and bake each side until they feel crisp and firm. Keep them warm in a tea towel as you do the next batch. Serve warm and buttered with jam or honey.

## CHOCOLATE POTATO CAKE

**SERVES 8**

Beetroots, courgettes and carrots have already graced our cakes. This time it's the turn of the humble potato. Mixed with spices and chocolate, it makes a moist and moreish cake.

115g (4oz) butter, plus extra for greasing
225g (8oz) sugar
3 eggs, well beaten
225g (8oz) potatoes, mashed and cooled
60g (2oz) cocoa
150ml (5fl oz) hot milk
225g (8oz) plain flour
4 tsp baking powder
½ nutmeg, grated
1 tsp cinnamon
pinch of salt

- Preheat oven to 190°C/375°F/gas 5. Grease two small cake tins with butter.
- Beat together the butter and sugar until creamy. Add the eggs and then stir in the potatoes.
- Dissolve the cocoa in the hot milk. Sift together all the remaining dry ingredients, and add them and the chocolate milk alternately to the potato.
- Pour into the cake tins and bake for 30–35 minutes or until a skewer comes out clean. When cold, sandwich together with chocolate butter cream, chocolate spread or, for absolute indulgence, whipped double cream.

## ROASTED, HERBED NEW POTATOES

**SERVES 4**

If you planted your potatoes in autumn, you could be eating new potatoes for Christmas. And if you potted up herbs on a windowsill or in the greenhouse, you can pretend it's still summer.

900g (2 lb) baby new potatoes, scrubbed and quartered
2 tbsp olive oil
½ tsp salt
½ tsp pepper
1 tbsp fresh flat-leaf parsley, chopped
1 tbsp fresh chives, snipped
1 tsp fresh oregano, chopped

- Preheat oven to 220°C/425°F/gas 7.
- Place the new potatoes in a large bowl and add the olive oil, salt, pepper and herbs and toss together.
- Place the potatoes on a baking sheet, making sure that they don't touch each other. This will help them to crisp up.
- Roast the potatoes in the oven for 40 minutes. Turn the potatoes every now and then to make sure that all sides are becoming crispy and browned on all sides. When ready they should be easily pierced.
- Put the potatoes in a bowl and serve as a side dish.

## BRUSSELS SPROUTS WITH BREADCRUMBS

### SERVES 4

Sprouts are often maligned. If you grow your own, a fresh sprout is delicious just gently steamed. However, to really lift them you could try tossing them with garlic, butter and breadcrumbs.

450g (1lb) small Brussels sprouts

6 tbsp toasted breadcrumbs

1 garlic clove, finely chopped

60g (2oz) butter

salt and freshly ground pepper, to taste

- Steam the sprouts over hot water for about 10 minutes, drain and season.
- Toast the breadcrumbs in a dry frying pan until they are dried out. Add the sprouts, garlic and butter and sauté until golden. Serve immediately.

## BRAISED CHICORY

### SERVES 4

Chicory has a bitter sweet flavour and can be braised as a hot dish as well as used in a salad.

8 heads of chicory

4 tbsp butter

2 sprigs of fresh thyme

2 garlic cloves, sliced

salt and freshly ground pepper, to taste

juice of ½ orange

- Trim the ends of the chicory and wash in cold water. Dry well.
- Heat the butter in a casserole. Add the chicory, thyme, garlic and salt and pepper.
- Cover and simmer over a low heat, turning continually for about 20 minutes. Then remove the thyme and add the orange juice. Cook for a further 20 minutes. Serve as a vegetable side dish.

## RED CABBAGE

### SERVES 6

Red cabbage is delicious raw or cooked. When cooked with apples, vinegar, sugar and spices, it becomes a meal in its own right, but it also makes a good accompaniment to sausages or chops.

1 red cabbage

2 tbsp extra virgin olive oil

3 tart apples, cored and sliced

1 onion, finely chopped

1 garlic clove, chopped

1 tbsp plain flour

4 tbsp red wine vinegar

2 tbsp brown sugar

1 tsp grated orange zest

salt and freshly ground pepper, to taste

grated nutmeg

- Wash and shred the cabbage, removing the central core and battered outer leaves. Sauté in the oil in a large saucepan for 5 minutes. Add the apples, onions, garlic and just enough water to cover, then bring to the boil. Cover with a lid, lower the heat and simmer for about 15 minutes until tender but still crisp. Drain and keep the liquid.
- Mix the flour with the vinegar and brown sugar and add the liquid. Cook until thickened, stirring constantly to stop it from going lumpy. Put the cabbage mixture back in the pan with the liquid. Add the orange zest and season to taste with salt, pepper and nutmeg.

## TRICOLOUR LASAGNE

### SERVES 6

This lasagne uses ricotta instead of béchamel sauce, When you cut into it, you get a glorious coloured display.

**Sauce**

1 onion, sliced and chopped

6 tbsp olive oil

2 garlic cloves, sliced and chopped

1 small chilli, chopped

900g (2lb) tomatoes, chopped

3 bay leaves

handful each of fresh parsley and basil, chopped

salt and freshly ground pepper, to taste

large glass red wine

**Filling**

1 onion, chopped

1 garlic clove

2 tsp olive oil

1.1kg (2½lb) chard, washed and drained

1 packet lasagne, around 6 sheets

350g (12oz) ricotta cheese

Parmesan cheese, grated

- Preheat oven to 190°C/375°F/gas 5.
- To make the sauce, sauté the onion in the oil for a couple of minutes, add the garlic and chilli and cook until softened. Add the tomatoes, bay leaves, herbs and wine. Season to taste. Cook until the sauce thickens.
- In a large pan sauté the onion and garlic in the oil until softened. Add the chard and toss for a minute. Drain, chop roughly and season to taste.
- Grease a large rectangular baking dish. Put in a layer of pasta and cover with a layer of sauce and a layer of cooked chard, followed by the ricotta. Add another layer of pasta, and the rest of the sauce and chard. Finish with a final layer of pasta and a sprinkling of Parmesan. Bake for about 40 minutes and allow to stand for 5–10 minutes before cutting.

# the living larder

The moment you start cultivating an allotment, you stop taking food for granted. You begin instead to really appreciate the many products of the plant kingdom that have been selected, developed and refined, sometimes over many centuries and in various cultures, all with the aim of tempting palates, stimulating digestive juices or simply satisfying hunger. The host of crops you can grow is enormous – confusing even – and ranges from the simplest, such as radishes, potatoes or kale, to luxuries and rarities like asparagus or whitecurrants. Climate change could expand the selection even further, as a longer growing season and milder winters allow many exotics to thrive in our weather. Explore this chapter for some of the many irresistible food plants you could be growing in your first season on the plot.

# the living larder

# crop focus

Exploring and selecting the various kinds of crops to grow can be as stimulating as harvesting their produce. If you aim to grow a wide range of crops, try to balance the different kinds, both for the purposes of soil rotation (*see page 20*) and for a healthy varied diet.

**ROOTS** Noted for their wonderful range of flavours, these are convenient packages of stored foods with long-keeping abilities in many cases, and generally easy to cultivate. As food they are low in calories, and undemanding as a rotation group, happy on soils of low fertility. The most popular roots are potatoes, carrots, beetroot, parsnips and celeriac, plus radishes, swedes and turnips.

**LEGUMES** Some of the most nutritious vegetables belong to the pea and bean family, supplying generous amounts of protein and fibre. Easy to grow, they include shelling peas and mangetout, and a host of different beans – chiefly broad, French and runner beans.

**BRASSICAS** These members of the cabbage family are all rich in vitamins, minerals and proteins, and supply masses of nourishing, non-fattening bulk food with a variety of flavours and textures. The main brassicas are Brussels sprouts, cabbages, calabrese, cauliflowers, kale, kohlrabi and sprouting broccoli.

**ONION FAMILY** Peerless in cuisines worldwide, this family of garlics, shallots, leeks and true onions of all kinds have unique flavours and can often enhance the taste of other vegetables. They are easy and rewarding to grow in a range of soils.

**PUMPKIN FAMILY** Easily grown packages of mild-flavoured, often thirst-quenching flesh that has a variety of uses, both savoury and sweet. They are all greedy plants, transforming water and nitrogen into fruits that range from the smallest gherkin to giant Halloween pumpkins. The main crops are courgettes, cucumbers, marrows, melons, summer and winter squashes.

**LEAVES & SALADS** A whole miscellany of hardy or summer crops that are supplements to the diet rather than essential workhorses. The main crops featured are chicory, lettuce, the leaf beets and various kinds of spinach.

**STEM & PERENNIAL VEGETABLES** Another motley group of crops that includes some of the most important vegetables on the plot, always welcome for adding their unique flavours to seasonal meals. The main crops featured are asparagus, cardoon, celery, Florence fennel, globe artichoke, Jerusalem artichoke and rhubarb.

**SUMMER-FRUITING VEGETABLES** Some allotment favourites are included here, all of them popular but tender crops from warm climates. The main crops featured are aubergines, peppers, sweetcorn and tomatoes.

**HERBS** Most herbs are easy to grow and need very basic and only occasional attention. The main crops featured are basil, bay, chives, coriander, dill, fennel, lemon balm, mint, oregano, parsley, sage, savory, tarragon and thyme.

**FRUIT** These are important crops to start or round off a meal, and are easy to grow once established. Most are perennial and all can be preserved in some way to spread their use over the whole year. Main crops featured include apples, blackcurrant, blueberries, cherries, gooseberries, grapes, pears, plums, raspberries, redcurrants and strawberries.

# ROOTS

Suspense and anticipation surround the harvesting of root vegetables, those buried crops whose qualities are hidden from sight until the moment they are unearthed. Many kinds are biennial and use their roots as storage organs to fuel growth and flowering the following year, and these tend to be packed with accumulated carbohydrates and nutrients for us to enjoy. For best results, root crops need open, well-cultivated soil that is stone-free and easy to penetrate, slightly acid conditions (so avoid recently limed ground), and restrained feeding and watering to concentrate flavour. Let them mop up food residues from a previous crop rather than fatten on fresh fertilizer, and ration watering to encourage them to delve deeply and find their own.

## BEETROOT

Although usually red, the skin and flesh of beetroot can also be white and yellow, but the flavour is always unmistakably penetrating. Fast, round, bolt-resistant varieties like '**Early Wonder**', '**Boltardy**' and '**Red Ace**' are grown for early use, pickling and successional sowings, often as catch crops of 'baby beet', while larger

kinds such as '**Forono**', '**Cylindra**' and '**Cheltenham Green Top**' are heavy maincrops for storing over winter. The young leaves of all varieties can be picked to add colour and a unique flavour to leafy salads, and the raw roots can be grated as an extra ingredient for a cold spread. For most purposes, beetroot needs cooking (before peeling, to prevent the colour bleeding), either in water or roasted in the oven. Maincrop kinds are also excellent baked as crisps and chips.

> **KEY TIMES**
> **SOW IN SITU** late winter to late summer **HARVEST** early summer to late autumn

## CARROTS

The ancestral carrot was a thin purple species, but now there are hundreds of reddish-orange varieties, some producing sweet slender bunching (finger) carrots after just a few weeks (*see page 56*), while maincrops take 4 months or more to mature their large, heavy roots, giving a distinctly strong wintry flavour to add to stews and casseroles. Occasionally, Asian varieties with white,

**Beetroot 'Boltardy'**

**Carrot 'Camestra'**

yellow or gold skins are available, sometimes blended in mixtures such as '**Harlequin**'. All kinds have high levels of sugar and carotene (a source of vitamin A), plus their distinctively aromatic carrot flavour, most of which resides in the skin (always use carrots with moderation if you don't want the flavour to dominate everything else).

The fastest varieties (7–10 weeks to maturity) are suitable for both early and successional sowings, and include various selections of strains like '**Early Nantes**', '**Amsterdam Forcing**' and '**Early Scarlet Horn**'. Round carrots such as '**Paris Market**' are even earlier and can be sown in clusters in cell trays for transplanting. Sowing any of these after midsummer is likely to avoid carrot root fly attention; alternatively, grow resistant hybrids like '**Flyaway**' and '**Resistafly**'.

Maincrop carrots like '**Autumn King**', '**Berlicum**', '**Chantenay**' and classic '**Long Red Surrey**' are often ready in midsummer but continue making weight until lifted in mid-autumn for storing. These are the best kinds for juicing, grating and turning into a host of tasty or hearty winter dishes such as carrot pancakes, rissoles and soups, and desserts like carrot cakes.

> **KEY TIMES**
> **EARLY VARIETIES SOW IN SITU** early spring to late summer **HARVEST** early summer to early autumn
> **MAINCROP SOW IN SITU** late spring **HARVEST** late summer to late autumn

## CELERIAC

Although often regarded as a root crop, the edible part of celeriac is actually the swollen base of the stem. It has a thick gnarled skin that needs peeling with a sharp knife to reveal its smooth white flesh tasting mildly of celery (once peeled, plunge it quickly in water to avoid rapid discoloration). Celeriac is easier to grow than celery, especially on dry soils, and stores well out of the ground. A rich source of vitamin C, it can be grated raw, roasted with other winter vegetables or boiled as a stew ingredient. Sow a variety like '**Prinz**' early under cover, plant out after the frosts into rich moist soil, and mulch lavishly for large melting roots.

> **KEY TIMES**
> **SOW INDOORS** late winter to early spring **TRANSPLANT** late spring **HARVEST** early autumn onwards

**Celeriac 'Prinz'**

## PARSNIPS

A winter vegetable par excellence, with fragrant sweet roots (especially after frost) that can be used for sweet dishes, with added spices, ginger or honey, as well as soups, stews and roasts.

Although it is an ancient crop, relatively few varieties have been bred compared with other vegetables, and most introductions concentrate on resistance to *canker*, which tends to be commonest on acid soils – try modern varieties like '**Avonresister**' and '**Gladiator**' where the disease is prevalent. All share the same unique and penetrating aroma (which makes weeding around the foliage a pleasure) and this is enhanced by exposure to

**Potato 'Red Duke of York'**

frost, so roots are always left in the ground until needed. There is a long sowing season for the crop – a very early start produces the largest roots, although seedlings may take ages to break the surface, while small roots for cooking whole will result from sowings as late as midsummer – and an even longer cropping season.

**KEY TIMES**
SOW IN SITU early spring to early summer HARVEST early autumn to early spring

## POTATOES

Some gardeners like to grow a full year's supply, others just a row or two of earlies for special feasts of 'new' potatoes in summer. Even the poorest soils will produce a useful boiling from each plant, and potatoes are renowned as a pioneer crop to help break up new or neglected ground, but yields increase dramatically with any soil improvement you can make.

First earlies such as '**Arran Pilot**', '**Concorde**' and '**Foremost**' are the most popular ('**Rocket**' and '**Swift**' are extra-earlies, taking only 10 weeks to crop in a good season), and are usually cleared in time to plant a follow-on crop like leeks or brassicas; if prepared carefully (*see pages 39–40*) the same kinds can be planted again in midsummer for a late repeat crop.

Second earlies like '**Estima**', '**Marfona**' and '**Wilja**' mature about a month before maincrops, which can take 6 months to bulk up their heavy yields. These are the kinds to grow for storing, but compare the numerous varieties because their uses differ: '**Desirée**' and '**Cara**' for mashing and baking, for example; '**Maris Piper**' for boiling; '**Picasso**' for chips and roasts. Salad potatoes like '**Lady Christl**' and '**Charlotte**' are firm boiling varieties to eat hot or cold.

Explore some of the less common kinds for their individual qualities and uses: disease-resistant '**Sante**' for organic culture; floury '**Shetland Black**' with inky blue skin; '**Golden Wonder**' for fries and crisps; nutty and knobbly '**Champion**', a classic Irish flavour variety.

**KEY TIMES**
EARLY VARIETIES PLANT early to late spring HARVEST early to late summer
MAINCROP PLANT late spring HARVEST late summer to late autumn

## RADISHES

Most varieties flaunt their colourful roots at surface level, even the long white kinds baring their shoulders so that you can select which to pull. Summer or salad types swiftly produce their round or olive-shaped roots, sometimes only 30 days after sowing, and varieties like 'Sparkler' and 'French Breakfast' make excellent catch crops to sow repeatedly between other vegetables. 'Rudi' and 'Short Top Forcing' are cold-tolerant versions for extra early and winter production under cover.

Long radishes such as white 'Icicle' and red 'D'Avignon' take a little more time to mature, while Japanese radishes (mouli) like 'Minowase' and 'April Cross' are long and heavy, and are sown after midsummer to stay in the ground until needed. True winter radishes (*see page 169*) like 'Black Spanish' and 'China Rose' can survive all winter in a cold frame until pulled for cooking, grating or adding to curries. 'Munchen Bier' also produces long fat seedpods that are crisp and spicy for raw snacks.

### KEY TIMES

SOW IN SITU early spring to early autumn HARVEST late spring to late winter

## SWEDES & TURNIPS

Both vegetables are brassicas and root forms of modern oilseed rape. They are sometimes confused while growing and even on the plate: the maincrop turnip 'Golden Ball', for example, has golden yellow flesh just like a swede. But there the resemblance ends. Swedes are usually grown as a maincrop vegetable with a long growing season for use during winter, especially large varieties like 'Virtue' and 'Best of All'. Early fast turnips are favourites on the plot for sowing under cloches or between other vegetables as a catch crop – 'Atlantic' and 'Snowball' are among the most precocious. Maincrop turnips like 'Giant Limousin' sown in early autumn can yield a heavy crop of tops as 'greens' (*see page 43*), while 'Rapa Senza Testa' is an Italian classic producing useful crops of mild turnip greens just 4 weeks after sowing, right up to late autumn.

### KEY TIMES

SWEDES SOW IN SITU late spring HARVEST early autumn to early spring

TURNIPS SOW IN SITU late winter to early autumn HARVEST late spring to early winter

There are many other root crops that are unfairly overshadowed by the familiar few.

**CHUFA** The small underground stem tubers of this sedge relative are sometimes sold as 'tiger nuts'; some forms of the almost hardy plants produce flowers and few tubers, but the best strains (especially var. *sativa*) are consistently fruitful. In Spain it is sold ground up as a drink, called *horchata di chufa*.

**MASHUA** An almost hardy climbing nasturtium relative, bearing red and yellow flowers and knobbly underground tubers with a very high vitamin C content and a sharp flavour raw. The tubers are best boiled, fried or baked.

**SALSIFY & SCORZONERA** When cooked, salsify and its dusky-skinned cousin scorzonera (also called black salsify) are supposed to taste like oysters, although their delicate nutty taste is equally close to that of asparagus and needs to be enjoyed on its own, away from competing flavours. The slender roots are difficult to peel, so both kinds are usually cooked first and then skinned to expose their pure white flesh. Sow at the same time as parsnips and dig up as needed from autumn onwards.

**SKIRRET** This old European perennial, seldom seen today, is grown from seed or spring offsets from the best plants; roots are pale and slim, gathered in clusters and tasting sweet and mealy when cooked. Grow in moist shade for best results.

**SWEET POTATO** Not a true potato but a relative of morning glory, producing swollen tubers with white, yellow, reddish-brown or purple skins and sweetish, yellow starchy flesh with a high dry-matter content that makes the roots good for mashing, roasting and chipping. Plant sprouted pieces of a bought tuber 15cm (6in) deep in large containers or soil beds under glass during late winter and early spring for harvest from early autumn onwards.

**YAM** There are many kinds of these tropical climbing plants, but the easiest is Chinese yam (cinnamon vine), an almost hardy vegetable that produces swollen roots up to 1m (3ft) long, with a mild floury flavour. Train the twining plants on a strong frame in full sun or under glass, and replant the thin tip of the root for subsequent crops.

**p.144**    *see* Sweet potato muffins

**MORE ROOTS TO TRY**

crop focus: roots

185

# LEGUMES

Legume crops (called 'pulses' once dried) include peas and beans, and are an indispensable source of protein in many cultures and for vegetarians. Globally they are second in importance to grain crops. Combined with cereals, they can provide all the essential amino acid requirements of our diet, together with an impressive range of minerals and vitamins. Most can improve the soil environment for following crops because they host nitrifying bacteria in root swellings (nodules), where nitrogen fertilizer is manufactured from the atmosphere and made available to other plants when the roots of exhausted plants are left to rot in the ground. Plants need little extra feeding but prefer deep, moisture-retentive soil that is slightly alkaline, so prepare sites well with plenty of organic matter, and lime acid ground (*see page 24*) before sowing.

## BROAD BEANS

Also known as horse, field, tick, Windsor or fava beans, this is one of the most ancient crops, often despised in Europe as peasant fare but a key ingredient in Eastern Mediterranean cuisines, with twice the protein of wheat, and among the first fresh spring vegetables on the plot. Most garden varieties are tall, with very fragrant black and white blooms ('**Crimson Flowered**' is a colourful

**Young broad bean pods ready to pick for cooking whole.**

exception) and fat pods of large white, green or buff seeds, about 8 in longpod types such as '**Express**' (first from a spring sowing), '**Aquadulce**' (hardiest for autumn sowing) and Victorian '**Bunyard's Exhibition**', or 4 in the tastier but less hardy '**Windsor**' varieties. '**The Sutton**' is a fast and prolific dwarf that may be sown up to midsummer. Field beans, grown in Europe for agricultural feed and green manures, have small, almost round, brown seeds and are used in North Africa (where they are called ful medames) as the basis of fuul and falafel.

**KEY TIMES**

**SOW INDOORS** late winter **TRANSPLANT** early spring
**SOW IN SITU** early to late spring and again late autumn to early winter **HARVEST** late spring to late summer

## FRENCH BEANS

Also grown and loved under the guises of kidney, string, snap and common bean, French beans are cultivated for their slender, tender pods or the beans inside (or both) and can take the form of a dwarf bush or twining climber ('pole beans') up to 3m (10ft) high. Pods are slim and cylindrical or flat – green, yellow, maroon or a combination of those colours, sometimes speckled with black – and contain kidney-shaped seeds in a spectrum of colours, ranging from white to black (fresh seeds are known as flageolets, as haricots when dried). All are frost-sensitive, with fragile foliage, so grow in a warm, sunny and sheltered position; allow 8–12 weeks to harvest, and freeze any surplus. Most varieties available today are commercial introductions selected for yield ('**Cupidon**' has masses of baby filet pods), performance (many are resistant to some common diseases) or habit – '**Opera**' and '**Maxi**', for example, are 'tepee' types, with pods held clear above the foliage – and differ little in eating quality. Older kinds are worth exploring for their distinctive flavours or uses: '**Marie Louise**' is a mealy pulse for stews, while '**Brown Dutch**' makes the tastiest Boston baked beans, red kidney beans are turned into chilli con carne, speckled pinto and borlotti beans complement rice dishes, and black (turtle) beans are used in refried beans.

**KEY TIMES**

**SOW INDOORS** mid-spring **TRANSPLANT** late spring under cloches **SOW IN SITU** late spring to late summer **HARVEST** midsummer to early autumn

French beans 'Cobra'

**ADZUKI BEANS** A small Asian bean, red with a white stripe and a delicious sweet flavour, on weak bushy plants that are easily grown under glass if sown early.

**CHICK PEAS** Another tender branching annual for growing under glass, with feathery foliage and short blunt pods of 1–2 large seeds (*see picture, below left*), which are blander and less nutritious than lentils. Used to make flour and hummus.

**GRAM BEANS** There are two types, both for growing under glass: black gram is a drought-resistant bushy annual with long pods of tiny seeds used for making dhal and producing bean sprouts, while green gram (mung bean) has up to 15 seeds per pod and is used in similar ways.

**GROUNDNUTS** Also known as peanuts and goober peas, these legumes are only economical under glass because plants require at least Mediterranean conditions to crop well. After pollination, the yellow flowers of these bushy annuals elongate to push the young pods under the soil, where they develop rapidly. Plants are lifted complete and hung in a dry airy place to ripen the pods – discard any that go mouldy, as eating or handling them can be dangerous. Use your crop to make the best-flavoured peanut butter ever.

**LABLABS** Also called hyacinth beans. This is an ancient and decorative indoor crop produced on twining climbers with 3–6 seeds per pod. The beans are dried, but whole immature pods, young green seeds and young leaves are all edible.

**LENTILS** An easy and pretty dwarf annual, grown like French beans, and an essential ingredient of dhal, but with only 2 seeds per pod you need to grow a lot. Green Puy lentils have a supreme flavour.

**LIMA BEANS** A very tender twining bean, best grown under glass in cooler districts. Young pods are edible, but the dried shelled 'butter beans' are the main crop.

**PEA BEANS** A form of common bean, easily grown outdoors, with round startlingly bicoloured seeds, which are dried for cassoulet and similar haricot bean dishes.

**SOY BEANS** An upright bushy annual (*see picture, below right*) for warm gardens and long growing seasons ('**Envy**' is earliest on cool sites), producing masses of short pods, each with 2–3 oily seeds, eaten in Japan as edamame beans.

**YARD-LONG BEANS** Very long and slim-podded beans for growing under glass, where they are rampant and productive late in the season. The black-eye bean is a bushy relative.

## PEAS

Popular and irresistible when freshly harvested and either lightly cooked or eaten raw in salads. Shelling peas are grown for their seeds, from large marrowfat varieties like '**Lincoln**' (harvested ripe and starchy for drying, or sweet and immature for freezing and fresh use) to diminutive petit pois types like '**Waverex**'. Flat mangetout kinds such as '**Carouby de Mausanne**' and the fatter snap pod (snow or sugar pea) varieties like '**Sugar Snap**' are eaten in their entirety, pods and all.

Hardy round-seeded peas ('**Meteor**', '**Pilot**') are best for autumn and early spring sowing, while sweeter, wrinkled-seeded kinds ('**Greenshaft**', '**Kelvedon Wonder**') are sown from spring until late summer. Dwarf varieties, 45–75cm (18–30in) tall, need twiggy sticks for support, although semi-leafless kinds like '**Markana**' are almost self-supporting. Tall varieties ('**Alderman**', '**Telephone**') are more prolific and can reach 1.5m (5ft) or more on strong supports. Approximate time to maturity varies between 60 and 100 days.

> **KEY TIMES**
> SOW INDOORS late winter TRANSPLANT spring SOW IN SITU early spring to late summer and again late autumn HARVEST early summer to late autumn

## RUNNER BEANS

The essential summer crop, this is a perennial usually grown as a tender annual for its immature green pods, although the ripe nutritious seeds can be dried for winter stews and soups. Most varieties are tall, up to 4–5m (13–16ft) if not pinched out, and make a handsome red, white or bicoloured flowering screen; dwarf kinds, like '**Hestia**', are bushy and mature a little earlier. Harvest pods before they are dull, rough and stringy – regular picking prolongs the harvest – and always check under leaves for overlooked pods. Older varieties, like '**Scarlet Emperor**' and '**Streamline**', have superior flavour; '**Kelvedon Marvel**' and '**Red Flame**' mature early; white-flowered '**Czar**' and '**White Emergo**' often set well in dry weather.

> **KEY TIMES**
> SOW INDOORS early spring TRANSPLANT late spring SOW IN SITU late spring to early summer HARVEST late summer to early autumn

Mangetout 'Oregon Sugarpod'

**SOUP PEAS** Most varieties can be left on the vines until fully mature, to shell and dry for use in pea soups and purées (up until the 18th century, peas were grown exclusively for this purpose). Alternatively, you can grow various kinds of field pea, which are rather bland when shelled and eaten fresh but large and mealy as dried peas, to soak overnight (simply pre-boil if you are impatient) before use. '**Lincoln**' is a traditional kind, or you could try '**Carlin**' peas (also known as grey, maple, parched or badger peas), a North of England heirloom-type of medieval mushy pea, which is traditionally made into pease pudding or pea fritters, or fried for eating on Carlin Sunday (the fifth Sunday after Lent). The plant grows 1.8m (6ft) high and has purple and white flowers.

## BRASSICAS

A huge family of mainly leafy vegetables and herbs, formerly called *Cruciferae* and now *Brassicaceae* because their distinctive flowers have four petals arranged in the shape of a cross. They are cool-season crops, best grown in moist, rich firm soil in an open position. As they all share a preference for alkaline conditions (pH7.0 or higher) and a susceptibility to the same pests and diseases, they are usually grown and rotated together. They are a rich source of dietary fibre and tend to be high in minerals, vitamin C (although half this is destroyed by cooking) and sulphur compounds, which produce the typical 'cabbagey' smell during cooking. The greener the leaves, the higher the content of carotenes, a source of vitamin A.

### BRUSSELS SPROUTS

A favourite hardy winter crop that can be harvested as early as midsummer from a precocious variety like 'Oliver' or 'Maximus', sown at the start of the year. Modern F1 hybrids yield top-quality sprouts on sturdy stems that can be cut complete for picking later indoors, but older kinds are still cherished for their flavour or colour (red 'Rubine', large size 'Fillbasket') or other special qualities – compact 'Early Half Tall' is ideal for windy gardens, for example. Cultivars are bred to mature at different times: earlies from late summer to mid-autumn, maincrop or mid-season kinds from mid-autumn to early winter, and lates from midwinter to early spring. The leafy heads can be cooked as 'greens'.

**KEY TIMES**

SOW OUTDOORS early to late spring TRANSPLANT early summer HARVEST late summer to early spring

### CABBAGES

A hugely varied race of heading and leafy vegetables, all derived from a weedy wild form. By choosing appropriate varieties and sowing times, it is possible to have cabbages for harvesting all year round. Long slow cooking or steaming preserves their sweet and distinctive flavours.

Fast-growing summer cabbages like 'Greyhound' and 'Hispi' are mild and juicy, while winter cabbages, available from autumn onwards, are more robust in

Brussels sprout 'Red Delicious'

Like all brassicas, cabbages should be netted.

flavour and slow-growing. The best kinds are '**Christmas Drumhead**', '**Winnigstadt**' and '**January King**'. Savoy cabbages such as '**Clarissa**', '**Celtic**' and '**Best of All**' are mild, a rich green, and nutritious, and make the best coleslaw. Spring cabbages (collards) like '**Flower of Spring**' and '**Wintergreen**' are loose leafy varieties, although some ('**Durham Early**', '**Pixie**') eventually develop firm hearts. '**Duncan**' may be sown repeatedly for greens all year. Red cabbages have a unique flavour and are a rich magenta colour (add vinegar when cooking to retain the colouring). White or Dutch varieties are pale and store well, and are the kind to ferment as *sauerkraut*.

## CALABRESE

Sometimes called 'broccoli spears', this popular summer crop is grown for its large central heads of fused, or 'fasciated', green flower stems. One of the most nutritious and succulent brassicas, it needs fast growth (ideally without transplanting, so start in pots or in situ) and careful attention to keep the tight curds free from aphids and other intruders. Never overcook calabrese, which tastes best when still slightly crisp. Most varieties are F1 hybrids of similar quality and performance, usually distinguished by their speed to maturity, sometimes as fast as 10 weeks from sowing ('**Mercedes**'). Sow an early kind in late summer to overwinter in a frame for spring use. '**De Cicco**' and '**Green Sprouting**' yield a prolific crop of small tasty spears until the first frosts.

**OTHER BRASSICAS**

Several vegetables are true brassica relatives, although seldom recognized as such (swedes, turnips and radishes are also brassicas but usually regarded as root crops, *see pages 182–5*). Where appropriate, the brassicas listed here can be grown in the same group for rotation purposes (*see page 20*).

**GARDEN CRESS** A tiny delicate annual with crisped leaves that is widely grown as an indoor seedling crop with white mustard or rape.

**HORSERADISH** A persistent perennial herb with long green or cheerfully variegated leaves and thong-like roots, which valiant cooks grate to make a fierce sauce. Invasive unless dug up and replanted every autumn as an annual crop.

**LAND CRESS** Similar to watercress but a less thirsty crop, and valuable for its very early harvest (*see picture*).

**ROCKET** A pungent annual salad leaf, seedling crop and accompaniment for grilled meat and fish. Salad rocket has a rich spicy flavour, whereas wild rocket is a peppery perennial.

**SEAKALE** A handsome, sprawling perennial with cabbage-like leaves and enormous flower- and seedheads to dry for decoration. Force and blanch the shoots under straw or pots for cutting each spring.

**WATERCRESS** Although usually grown in running water, watercress is often successful in an old sink or bath of very moist compost. May be grown from seed or rooted stalks from bought supplies.

crop focus: brassicas

Oriental brassicas are a range of usually mild leaf crops, many of which are sown after midsummer to prevent bolting, although up-to-date varieties are more tolerant of heat and long days. Pak choi and Chinese cabbage are particularly popular.

**CHINESE CABBAGE** Also called pe-tsai, this can form loose-leaved rosettes (for example, '**Maruba Santoh**' and chihli varieties) or have compact cylindrical heads, as with '**Green Rocket**', '**Wong Bok**' and '**Nagaoka**'. Delicately flavoured and tender, these brassicas are best steamed, stir-fried or lightly crisped in a very hot pan.

**PAK CHOI** A non-hearting cabbage or 'celery mustard', with spoon-shaped leaves arranged in a spiral, and pronounced stems and midribs that can be used as a separate vegetable. The leaves are used in soups and stir-fry dishes, but rarely eaten raw. '**Joy Choi**' is outstanding.

**OTHER ORIENTAL BRASSICAS** These include komatsuna (mustard spinach), a mild and freshly flavoured leaf or seedling crop; mizuna (Japanese salad), for eating raw and stir-frying; Chinese kale, similar to a mild green sprouting broccoli; and choi-sum, with serrated leaves, purple ribs and numerous tender flowering shoots.

**p.140** *see* Stir-fried mixed vegetables

## CAULIFLOWERS

One of the hardest crops to grow well, needing rich, moist and very firm ground to produce large, solid heads. Summer-heading varieties ('**Snowball**', '**Snowcrown**', '**Wallaby**') will crop until late autumn, followed by winter kinds, such as '**Janus**', '**Valentine**' and '**May Star**'. Purple ('**Purple Cape**', '**Violetta Italia**'), golden ('**Marmalade**') and green-encrusted forms ('**Romanesco**') are available. In a hot summer, break some leaves over the developing heads to maintain colour and quality. Heads may be boiled, steamed, stir-fried or added raw to salads.

Where the soil is less than ideal, transplant seedlings 15cm (6in) apart each way to produce 'mini-caulis' about 8cm (3in) across after 3–4 months' growth; sow every 3–4 weeks from mid-spring to midsummer for a sequence of heads.

> **KEY TIMES**
> **SUMMER CAULIS** SOW INDOORS early spring
> TRANSPLANT late spring HARVEST late summer to late autumn
> **WINTER CAULIS** SOW OUTDOORS early summer
> TRANSPLANT late summer HARVEST early winter to late spring

Kohlrabi 'White Delicacy' (syn. 'Green Vienna')

## KALE

There are several kinds of kale, from the coarse and plain-leaved cattle crop '**Thousand-head**' and decorative red-tinted '**Ragged Jack**' or '**Red Russian**' to the ever-popular and delicately crimped varieties like '**Dwarf Green Curled**'. All are hardy winter and spring vegetables, easily grown and very dependable: pick young leaves from autumn onwards, then wait until the young sideshoots appear in spring for a second harvest.

> **KEY TIMES**
> SOW OUTDOORS late spring TRANSPLANT early summer HARVEST late autumn to late spring

## KOHLRABI

A neglected oddity that forms green, white or purple bulbous stems studded with leaves (which can be cooked like turnip tops, *see page 43*). Although dating back to medieval times in Europe, it is now more popular in the Far East. The crop is best sown in situ and grown very fast for harvest while the turnip-like stems are still smaller than tennis balls. Remove the tough skin with a kitchen knife and then boil until tender.

> **KEY TIMES**
> SOW IN SITU early spring to late summer HARVEST early summer to late autumn

## SPROUTING BROCCOLI

This bulky and hardy crop is one of the easiest brassicas to grow well and gives a prolific yield over a long period if the delicate leafy sideshoots are cut regularly before their flower buds open. Early and late purple or white forms are available to spread the harvest, or you can buy a mixture for random picking all season. Modern varieties like '**Red Arrow**' are very early and consistent, while '**Perennial Nine Star**' is a large white form that will persist for several years. Purple sprouting broccoli is especially popular in Italy, where it is often baked or fried with anchovies or garlic. It must be young, tender and freshly harvested – excellent reasons to grow your own.

> **KEY TIMES**
> SOW OUTDOORS late spring TRANSPLANT early summer HARVEST late winter to late spring

**THE BLACK CABBAGE OF TUSCANY** Also known as nero di Toscana, cavolo nero and black kale. This fashionable leaf vegetable, midway between a cabbage and a kale, is an old Italian heirloom brassica, with dark, narrow, heavily puckered leaves. It is easy to grow and produces masses of small tender pickings from the centre (and, later, the sideshoots) for use as 'greens', in soups or fried with chillis. It survives a mild winter to give edible flowering shoots like sprouting broccoli.

# ONION FAMILY

Universal favourites and possibly the most versatile and indispensable cookery ingredient, onions and their related crops have been grown since ancient times for culinary and medicinal purposes. All of them are distinguished by a volatile high-sulphur content responsible for the family taste and smell, which varies from delicate to tearfully pungent. They grow readily on most soils, and by teaming various kinds – bulbing onions with leeks and salad onions, for example – their distinctive flavours can be constantly available to redeem the most austere dish. Flavour is their main dietary value, although they also supply variable amounts of minerals and vitamins.

## BULBING ONIONS

A varied maincrop producing flat, globe- or torpedo-shaped bulbs with brown, livid red or silvery white skins. Bulbing onions grow from seeds or sets (immature bulbs), with most varieties started in spring for autumn harvest, although a few such as '**Buffalo**', '**Reliance**', '**Radar**' and '**Senshyu**' will overwinter to mature early the following summer. Golden globe types like '**Giant Zittau**' are considered the most pungent; pale kinds such as '**Ailsa Craig**', '**Walla Walla**' and various large Spanish varieties are the mildest. Red onions have a mild sweet fruitiness, torpedo varieties ('**Long Red Florence**', '**Owa**') slice conveniently, while champion

Bulbing onions 'Sturon'

kinds like '**The Kelsae**' make huge bulbs and perfect onion rings. The best bulbs are grown over a long season on very firm ground.

> **KEY TIMES**
>
> **SUMMER VARIETIES** SOW IN SITU late winter to late spring
> **PLANT** early to late spring **HARVEST/DRY** early autumn
> **FOR OVERWINTERING** SOW IN SITU late summer
> **PLANT** early autumn **HARVEST/DRY** early summer

## CHIVES

A tussocky herb that grows into dense clumps of slender bulbs and thin hollow leaves with a fresh refined flavour shared by their handsome pinkish-mauve flowers that can seduce bees from far away. Easily raised from seed or division in early spring, chives make a pretty edging or carpet under fruit, and occupy little space. Resow or split every three years to retain vigour and flavour. Chives may be frozen but do not dry successfully. For winter use, pot up divisions after flowering to bring in before the frosts; the variety '**Grolau**' thrives at low light levels under glass or on a windowsill, and may be cut all year round. Garlic (Chinese) chives are more robust, with flattened garlic-flavoured foliage and a bonus crop of unopened flower heads to use as a fried vegetable.

Chives in flower.

> **KEY TIMES**
>
> **SOW/PLANT** late spring **HARVEST** early summer to late autumn

# GARLIC

Of all the onion flavours, garlic is the most pungent, and it is an important ingredient of warm-climate cuisines worldwide, from the Mediterranean to India and China. Growing best on well-drained soil in full sun (under glass where summers are cool or wet), a single clove multiplies into a papery-skinned bulb of numerous segments. Avoid planting imported garlic sold for consumption, as this may harbour virus disease, and choose instead stock raised for growing in local conditions: varieties like '**Early Wight**', '**Solent Wight**', '**Thermidrome**' and '**Printanor**' (spring planting only), for example, are better adapted to the UK climate than French or Italian kinds. Grow plenty: garlic has valuable medicinal and insecticidal properties in addition to its varied roles in the kitchen, both as flavouring and as a vegetable in dishes like the classic Provençal 40-clove Chicken.

**KEY TIMES**

PLANT late autumn or early spring HARVEST/DRY early to late summer

**Garlic 'Early Wight'**

Various minor onion crops all have their uses and devotees and seeds and sets are readily available:

**ELEPHANT GARLIC** Also known as great-headed or jumbo garlic, this is actually a true leek, with enormous bulbs up to 450g (1lb) in weight and buried bulbils for propagation. Its variant Babington's leek is a UK native with numerous small tasty bulbs.

**KURRAT** A Near-Eastern version of leeks, but slimmer and with fatter bulbs.

**RAKKYO** Similar to chives in habit, popular in Chinese and Japanese cuisines, and often exported pickled. Usually sold as plants or bulbs, rarely seeds.

**TREE ONIONS** Sometimes called Egyptian or walking onions, these develop a characteristic cluster of small bulbs on a stem instead of flowers. Plant these and harvest the main bulb, which has a pungent garlic/shallot flavour.

**WELSH ONIONS** The best known of the green perennial onions, these can be grown from seed and fatten gradually into dense evergreen clumps that benefit from division every 3–4 years (*see picture*). Use single leaves and whole plants for seasoning or as salad onions. Everlasting (ever-ready), potato and Japanese bunching onions are similar.

crop focus: onion family

195

A number of ornamental garlics, leeks and onions can be grown in a wild flower corner for their attractive flowers (many edible), irresistible appeal to bees and butterflies, especially tortoiseshells, and for emergency kitchen use.

**GRAPE HYACINTHS** These are close onion relatives with colourful flowers and an invasive habit that might be tamed by harvesting the small bulbs (*see picture*). In Italy and Greece, these are boiled in water and a little vinegar to remove their bitterness before being used in antipasto or relishes.

**RAMSONS** A cheerful spreader under hedges and trees, with starry white flowers and broad leaves with a mild garlic flavour when cooked.

**ROSE LEEKS** Pinkish-white flowers, often mixed with bulbils that can be planted and grown on. Use the whole plant like a salad onion.

**SAND LEEKS (ROCAMBOLE)** Both bulbs and stems of this slender species from sandy and rocky places can be used like garlic.

**WILD (FIELD) GARLIC** A spreading species that is happy naturalized in grass, with garlic-flavoured leaves and heads of mixed flowers and bulbils that can be added to soups and stews. Crow garlic is very similar to wild garlic.

## LEEKS

Leeks do not share the bulbing tendency of other alliums, and even when well developed, the rounded base to the edible blanched shank is not a true bulb. There is a host of good varieties – from traditional kinds, like '**Musselburgh**' and '**The Lyon**', which benefit from blanching under soil, to modern '**Pancho**' (early), '**Porbella**' (mid-season) and '**Poristo**' (late) for sowing and growing on the surface. There's also a whole race of leeks, like '**Blue Solaise**' and '**Monstruoso de Carentan**', from France, where they are a major and much-appreciated crop. Always check a variety's season of use, as winter hardiness varies widely. Earth up every 3–4 weeks for extra-long shanks; exhibition 'pot leeks' are fat rather than long, but as tasty as other kinds. Prepare leeks for the kitchen as you harvest them: chop off most of the green 'flag' and the disc-like root plate, then slit lengthways and peel off the soiled fibrous outer layer.

**KEY TIMES**
**SOW INDOORS** early spring **TRANSPLANT** early summer
**SOW IN SITU** late spring **TRANSPLANT** late summer
**HARVEST** early autumn to late spring

Leek 'Swiss Giant'

Salad onions 'Purplette'

Shallots 'Longor'

## SALAD & PICKLING ONIONS

This crop is a sprinter, often ready only 8–10 weeks after sowing, and produces a succession of slim stems like miniature leeks, although a few varieties ('**White Lisbon**', '**Purplette**') eventually produce small bulbs, which can be pickled. Red varieties like '**Crimson Forest**' and '**Deep Purple**' add extra colour to salads; '**Ramrod**', '**Guardsman**' and '**White Lisbon Winter Hardy**' can be sown in autumn for cold weather harvest. Fast and undemanding, they make the perfect catch crop to sow between other vegetables. True pickling onions are left to grow until the foliage turns yellow. '**Paris Silverskin**' makes round crisp bulbs that can be eaten whole, cooked or raw.

**KEY TIMES**

**SOW IN SITU** late winter to late summer **HARVEST** early spring to early autumn

## SHALLOTS

These grow from a single bulb and divide to form a loose cluster of 5–6 or more pear-shaped bulbs. Different kinds are distinguished by their skin colour (red, gold or brown) and shape – '**Hative de Niord**' is large, handsome and almost symmetrical, while French kinds, like '**Longor**', are slim and elongated. Very easy to grow and perpetuate from saved bulbs, standard varieties like '**Topper**' and '**Golden Gourmet**' can be planted around the shortest day, but French varieties and modern hybrids such as '**Red Sun**' are best kept back until mid-spring. Use shallots with respect, as they have a light, sweet flavour of their own that's quite different from (and some say it's superior to) that of onions.

**KEY TIMES**

**PLANT** early winter to early spring **HARVEST/DRY** late summer

crop focus: onion family

197

# PUMPKIN FAMILY

Even expert taxonomists admit that the cucurbits, as family members of the pumpkin family are known, are a mess, with terms like 'squash' and 'pumpkin' applied casually to different species. Nevertheless, all share frost-tenderness, and so must be started or grown under glass in the UK, and prefer very rich moisture-retentive soil, regular watering and efficient drainage. They also all have a characteristic fleshy fruit called a 'pepo', made up mainly of water and useful amounts of vitamin C, and large seeds, some kinds edible and popular raw, toasted or deep-fried as snacks, rich in oil and protein.

In practical terms, summer squashes comprise all soft-skinned cucurbits, harvested while still immature. They are listed in various ways in catalogues, usually under the headings marrows, courgettes and squash (summer). The stems and leaves of winter squashes are not as prickly as those of summer squashes, while the fruits have softer, less angular stalks. Their flesh is firmer, with a more pronounced, sometimes nutty, flavour that improves with long, slow growing.

Cucumbers and melons are refreshing when eaten raw, cooked summer squashes suit low-calorie diets, while baked winter squashes are a good source of carbohydrate. The male and female blooms of courgettes, marrows and other large-flowered squashes are sometimes picked and eaten stuffed, deep-fried in batter or chopped up in risottos. The leaves and shoots of many cucurbits are also eaten.

## COURGETTES

Originally these were simply baby marrows and other summer squashes (*courgette* is the diminutive of *courge*, French for gourd), while zucchini was a distinct dark green Italian summer squash, slim and up to 30cm (12in) long. Modern courgettes are special varieties bred for compact growth and prolific yields. If left to ripen, fruits turn into marrows, but their flavour and texture are inferior to true vegetable marrows. Fruits may be cylindrical ('**Ambassador**'), round ('**Rondo di Nizza**') or bent ('**Trombolino**'), in various shades of green (pale '**Genovese**', dark shiny '**Patriot**') or bright yellow (round '**Floridor**', long '**Goldie**'). Water regularly and pick often.

> **KEY TIMES**
> **SOW INDOORS** early spring to late spring **TRANSPLANT** late spring to early summer **SOW IN SITU** early summer **HARVEST** early summer to early autumn

**Courgette 'Parador'**

**Cucumber 'Carmen'**

## CUCUMBERS

One of the best reasons for gardening organically is that cucumbers grown without chemicals and excessive water have superb flavour. Fruits are always eaten while immature – when ripe they are bitter and need peeling, salting and draining to be palatable.

Although their food value is low, apart from useful amounts of vitamin C plus carotenes in the skin, they are essential summer salad vegetables with a host of other uses: add them to yoghurt to produce raita for tempering fiery curry, mix them with chives and paprika as they do in Hungary, or blend with mint to make a refreshing soup.

**GREENHOUSE CUCUMBERS** are long and slim, and develop unfertilized (hence no seeds), which is why traditional varieties like '**Telegraph**' and '**Conqueror**' must be inspected for male flowers that need removal (pollinated fruits are misshapen and bitter). All-female hybrids like '**Flamingo**' and miniature '**Passandra**' produce male flowers only under stress. Otherwise, they are trouble-free and often highly disease-resistant.

**RIDGE (FIELD) CUCUMBERS** such as '**Marketmore**', '**La Diva**' and pale-skinned '**Long White Paris**' have smaller, fatter fruits approximately 12–15cm (5–6in) long, and crop prolifically outdoors in the open or under cloches. All outdoor cucumbers, except all-female cultivars, need pollination by insects or by hand (*see page 201*) to set fruit. Plants trail on the ground or over straw, but Japanese strains and longer-fruited hybrids like '**Muncher**' and '**Bono**' are best trained on trellis for shapely produce. Apple cucumbers like '**Crystal Lemon**' are ridge varieties with thick-skinned globular fruits.

**GHERKINS** grown in Europe are small-fruited ridge cucumbers that are very productive and used for making pickles and sauces: '**Venlo Pickling**' and '**Vert Petit de Paris**' are traditional slightly prickly kinds, '**Adam**' is a prolific smooth-skinned hybrid. The West Indian gherkin is a prickly species borne on particularly ornamental vines.

---

**KEY TIMES**

**GREENHOUSE SOW** late winter to early spring **TRANSPLANT** early to late spring **HARVEST** midsummer to late autumn

**RIDGE SOW INDOORS** early spring **TRANSPLANT** late spring **HARVEST** late summer to early autumn

---

**BALSAM PEAR** A 4m (13ft) climber with vine-like leaves (both shoots and leaves are edible) and vanilla-scented bright yellow blooms, followed by oval, ribbed orange fruits with a scarlet lining. Soak to remove bitterness and use to make Indian or Cantonese pickles and curries.

**CHAYOTE** A sprawling perennial climber, with edible young shoots and tuberous roots, and furrowed pear-shaped fruits seasoned or sweetened for soups, salads and desserts. Dry the slender fibrous vines to weave as rope.

**CHILACAYOTE** The fig-leaf or Malabar gourd is a vigorous tender perennial (grow as a half-hardy annual), with edible leaves, shoots and enormous handsome yellow flowers. The large green or white fruits are eaten young like cucumbers or ripened for candying or fermenting.

**HORNED CUCUMBER** Also known as kiwano or jelly melon (*see picture*), this annual climber is fast, rampant and trained on nets under glass, when it produces spiny 10cm (4in) orange fruits with smooth green flesh tasting of bananas and limes.

**LOOFAH** Another vigorous greenhouse or polytunnel vine, with large yellow flowers and cylindrical fruits used in Chinese cuisine while young and fresh, or dried when mature to produce skeletal bath loofahs.

**SNAKE GOURD** Rampant in a warm greenhouse, this tender perennial has long flower spikes and twisted orange 'cucumbers' up to 90cm (3ft) long, used in India for curries. Ki-karasu-uri is a Japanese relative with yellow egg-shaped fruits and starchy tuberous roots used to make thin crackers.

**p.171**   *see* Bitter gourd curry

## MARROWS

Whether sprawling vines ('**Long Green Trailing**') or bushy plants ('**Green Bush**', '**Minipak**'), marrows bear cylindrical green, cream or striped fruits to harvest when about 30cm (12in) long for eating fresh, or they can be left to grow larger to store for up to two months. Fresh marrows are steamed or stuffed with ingredients such as meat, onions and tomatoes to season the rather bland flesh. Mature marrows make excellent jams with ginger or richly flavoured fruit like damsons, but allotment tradition reserves the largest for exhibition, wine and marrow 'rum'. Like all summer squashes, they need lashings of organic food at the roots (a bucketful of manure each is the minimum) and water in dry weather, up to 11 litres (2 gallons) per plant per week.

> **KEY TIMES**
> **SOW INDOORS** late spring to early summer **TRANSPLANT** early to late summer **HARVEST** early to late autumn

## MELONS

Melons grow on softly hairy vines for training on nets under glass or over straw in a cold frame. Where summers are usually long and warm, some varieties can be cropped outdoors under plastic tunnels or on trellis against a sunny fence or shed wall. Like squashes, melons are grouped according to fruit type, although hybrids between them blur the distinction. Varieties with pink or orange flesh have a higher vitamin content than other kinds and are usually more aromatic – the scent of these as they ripen under glass is unforgettable and worth all their necessary care. Use in fruit salads, sorbet or ice creams, or avoid dressing them up (ground ginger is a redundant cliché) and celebrate success with generous slices lightly dusted with sugar.

**WATERMELONS** are rampant, branching tropical climbers, bearing large smooth fruits up to 75cm (30in) long. These are filled with crisp refreshing red flesh and variable quantities of seeds (with more food value than the flesh, these are eaten dried or roasted). They are only worth growing under glass on most allotments, in a light fertile greenhouse bed with frequent watering. Sow in early spring, grow on at 21°C (70°F) and plant 4–6 weeks later. Limit each plant to 2–4 fruits, and prune excess greenery to focus energy on cropping.

Support melons in nets for uniform ripening.

**ASIAN** Ribbed elongated fruits like cucumbers, 90cm (3ft) or more long and used as vegetables or for desserts.
**CANTALOUPE** Typically thick, warty or scaly skin and rich orange flesh; includes Charentais melons.
**MUSK, NETTED OR NUTMEG** Skins netted with a tracery of white lines; flesh green or salmon pink and very aromatic.
**OGEN** Derived from cantaloupes; small fruits, yellow or orange with green ribs, and sweet green aromatic flesh.
**WINTER** Fairly smooth skins, very thick and green, and green flesh, which is not strongly scented; includes honeydew and Spanish melons.

> **KEY TIMES**
> **SOW INDOORS** late spring to early summer **TRANSPLANT** early to late summer **HARVEST** early to late autumn

## SUMMER SQUASHES

In addition to courgettes and marrows, there are many other kinds of non-keeping summer squashes, some that look spectacular when sporting their extravagant fruits. Distinct types include the **custard marrows** or **patty-pans**, such as '**Custard White**' and '**Scallopini**', with white or yellow scalloped fruits; small pumpkins like '**Jack Be Little**' and '**Tom Fox**'; assorted **butternut** and **crookneck varieties**; and the unique '**Vegetable Spaghetti**', or '**Spaghetti Marrow**', a fat, blocky yellow fruit to bake whole (prick the skin first), when its flesh is transformed into long sweet strands.

**KEY TIMES**

**SOW INDOORS** early spring to late spring **TRANSPLANT** late spring to early summer **SOW IN SITU** early summer **HARVEST** early summer to early autumn

## WINTER SQUASHES

These hard-skinned cucurbits can be stored for several months after picking, especially if they are well tempered in the sun. Train trailing kinds on trellis to ventilate fruits well for perfect durable skins. There are several groups:
**BANANA** Delicate yellow flesh and pink skins when mature. Try '**Nice Long**'.
**BUTTERNUT** Elongated fruits with a bulbous end and mild, melting flesh. Try '**Waltham**'.
**HALLOWEEN PUMPKINS** With their fearsome faces and toothy grins, these are traditionally made from huge exhibition varieties, hollowed out to house a candle or night-light. Try '**Atlantic Giant**' or, for gate-posts and table-tops, miniature '**Jack-O-Lantern**' types.
**HUBBARD** Slightly pear-shaped, very thick skins and top table quality. Try '**Blue Kuri**'.
**TURBAN (BUTTERCUP)** Shaped like an acorn in its cup, very ornamental and tasty. Try '**Turk's Turban**'.

Connoisseurs distinguish many more types of winter squash (cushaw, kabocha, delicata) plus thousands of individual varieties, making up an extravagant autumn festival of colours and flavours to explore (despite their reputation, pumpkin pies do not all taste alike). Outstanding favourites include '**Bon Bon**', flattened boxes on upright bushes, with awards for flavour; glowing orange '**Uchiki Kuri**', sweet, nutty and ornamental; spicy, aromatic '**Sucrine du Berry**', a French classic; and pebbled '**Marina di Chioggia**', a long-keeping warty globe packed with rich flavour.

Include decorative (inedible) gourds in your plans: these amphorae, calabash bottles and bizarre biotic shapes can be dried, varnished or hollowed-out to make durable goblets, vases and curios.

**KEY TIMES**

**SOW INDOORS** early spring to late spring **TRANSPLANT** late spring to early summer **SOW IN SITU** early summer **HARVEST/DRY** early to late autumn

**Store squashes for the winter in a cool place.**

**POLLINATING CUCURBITS** The beautiful blooms of cucurbits are either male or female, and you need to distinguish between them when pollinating melons and (occasionally) other cucurbits. Male blossoms have simple straight stems, whereas a female flower sits on top of a tiny immature fruit. To fertilize a female flower, pick a fully opened male in the morning, remove the petals and brush its pollen-laden anthers all over the central stigma of the female flower (pollination is more certain if several males are used for each female).

# LEAVES & SALADS

The ingredients of a salad are many and various, from dandelion leaves and chickweed stems to nasturtium flowers and pine nuts – all potential candidates for growing on the plot. A few leafy vegetables are staples, however, and form the basis of most salads while young or, in many cases, can be left to mature as green vegetables for cooking. Although normally thought of as vegetable crops, some brassica relatives are notable salad ingredients, including landcress, garden cress, watercress and rocket. These are discussed on *page 191*.

## CHICORY

A mixed group of leaf crops, sometimes confusing in their diversity (French varieties even more so, since forcing chicory is called *endive* and curly endive is *chicorée*).

**WILD CHICORY** is a tap-rooted perennial with appealing clear blue flowers that attract wildlife and earn space in a natural corner. Large-rooted kinds like '**Magdeburg**' are grown for drying and grinding as a coffee substitute or additive.

**WITLOOF** (Belgian or Brussels) chicory has broad, coarse leaves and fat roots, which are blanched outdoors or lifted in autumn and forced in warm darkness for a winter crop of crisp, tightly furled buds called *chicons*. '**Zoom**' is naturally self-blanching and needs no soil cover when forcing.

**BROAD-LEAVED CHICORIES** form leafy, lettuce-like heads. '**Sugar Loaf**' ('**Pan di Zucchero**') forms dense conical heads of crisp leaves when mature or it can be cut young as a loose-leaf lettuce. '**Grumolo**' is typical of a group of hardy varieties that form dark green leaf rosettes and edible flowers.

**RADICCHIO** (Italian name for all chicories) is a red-leaved or variegated kind with prominent white midribs. Best known are '**Red Treviso**' with long pointed leaves (may be forced), '**Red Verona**', which has loose round heads like a small cabbage, and '**Castelfranco**', a tight head of decorative crisped leaves (also good for forcing).

**ENDIVE** is very similar to chicory, but with smooth hairless leaves and larger heads. Curled or frizzled varieties like '**Pancalieri**' and '**Fine Maraichere**' have attractive, deeply toothed foliage, while the hardier Batavian, or escarole, types ('**Blonde Full Heart**' and '**Cornet de Bordeaux**') have broad bitter leaves that benefit from blanching before use in winter salads with walnuts and crispy bacon.

> **KEY TIMES**
> **SOW IN SITU** late spring to early autumn **HARVEST** early spring to early winter

## LETTUCE

For many, lettuce is the key salad leaf crop. Available in an infinity of guises and varieties, all lettuces are derived from an unknown early Egyptian ancestor. There are two main groups: cabbage (round) lettuce, which is made up of butterheads, icebergs and looseheads, and cos (romaine).

Use all lettuces soon after harvesting, before they wilt and lose their fresh crispness. Whole lettuce will keep for a day or two with its stem in a little water in a covered saucepan, or wrapped in a plastic bag in the fridge. If a lettuce flags, plunge it in cold water, shake dry and wrap lightly in a damp teatowel until it revives.

**CABBAGE (ROUND) LETTUCE** Butterhead lettuces in this group have soft, floppy leaves that are generally green but may have varying red tinges ('**Sierra**', '**Marvel of Four Seasons**'). They are considered by some to be

Radicchio 'Grumolo Rossa'

the least interesting and flavoursome, although classic varieties like '**Buttercrunch**' and dwarf '**Tom Thumb**' are tastier than others.

Icebergs (crispheads) have paler leaves and tight hearts that are juicy and crunchy, especially in a hot summer. They are not notably well flavoured, except for older kinds, such as '**Webb's Wonderful**', and Batavian varieties, like decorative red-edged '**Babylon**'.

Looseheads (loose-leaf) have no heart but masses of tightly packed leaves that can form large ornamental clumps, such as green '**Frillice**', red-tinged '**Oakleaf**' and dark '**Red Fire**'. This type supplies the fastest and most prolonged pickings, especially early and late in the season when other kinds are sometimes reluctant to heart up.

**COS (ROMAINE) LETTUCE** These lettuces are tall and usually large, although '**Little Gem**' and '**Pinokkio**' are popular miniatures, offering dense, nutty hearts wrapped in vigorous, sweet and full-flavoured outer leaves. '**Counter**' combines the flavour of '**Little Gem**' with the typical romaine build, and succeeds even in wet summers. '**Lobjoits Green Cos**' and '**Winter Density**' are very hardy for autumn sowing and spring use. If left unthinned in rows or trays, this kind can be cut repeatedly as salad leaves, and combines well with loose-leaf varieties for an instant cut-and-come-again salad bowl.

**KEY TIMES**

**SOW IN SITU** early spring to mid-autumn **HARVEST** late spring to early winter

## PERPETUAL SPINACH & CHARD

These succulent-leaved forms of beetroot and sugar beet are grown as easy-care and long-lasting substitutes for true spinach (*see right*), which they closely resemble in flavour. Perpetual spinach (spinach beet) and most chards (seakale beet) can be harvested all year – in summer and autumn from a spring sowing, and winter and spring from a late summer batch. Chard has broad, fleshy white leaf stalks often eaten as a separate vegetable. Coloured forms such as red-stemmed **ruby (rhubarb) chard**, '**Canary Yellow**' and '**Oriole Orange**' add glamour to the plot, and are often combined in mixtures such as '**Rainbow Chard**'.

**KEY TIMES**

**SOW IN SITU** early spring to late summer **HARVEST** all year

**Red-stemmed ruby chard**

## SPINACH

A host of succulent leafy vegetables are grown and cooked 'as a spinach', from the common weed fat hen to deep red orache, a tall ancient annual sometimes called mountain spinach. However, true spinach is a nutritious annual that grows quickly and also bolts fast in hot weather. Varieties are divided into two main types: summer or round-seeded spinach, and winter or prickly-seeded spinach, which is larger and hardier. Neither kind crops for long, so repeated sowing is essential, or you could grow a more weather-resistant kind such as New Zealand spinach for summer use (*see page 92*) or perpetual spinach (*see left*) for crops all year.

'**Matador**', '**Medania**' and several up-to-date F1 hybrid varieties like '**Lazio**' and '**Tornado**' have good resistance to bolting in a hot, dry summer. Older kinds like '**Giant American**' often crop for longer; '**Giant Winter**' is still the best for cold weather use; '**Monnopa**' contains less oxalic acid than others and is not so bitter. Pick generously, at least 225g (8oz) per person, because all spinach shrinks alarmingly when cooked.

**KEY TIMES**

**SOW IN SITU** early spring to early summer (summer spinach); early autumn (winter spinach) **HARVEST** early summer to late autumn (summer spinach); early winter to late spring (winter spinach)

## STEM & PERENNIAL VEGETABLES

This is a miscellaneous group of crops, some of them perennial and therefore grown in the same place year after year. All benefit from fast growth to ensure juicy, stringless stems, so keep fertility levels high with annual helpings of compost or manure, and water consistently in dry weather.

The perennial vegetables are often given a bed to themselves because they do not fit into standard crop rotation schemes, but they thrive equally happily tucked into odd spare corners or in large containers provided they don't go short of water.

### ASPARAGUS

No longer the luxury crop of former years, this perennial fern can be grown in beds, single rows or in deep boxes of sandy compost (good drainage is vital). Plants are raised from seed or introduced as 1- or 2-year-old crowns: wait two years after planting before cutting freely and then enjoy annually for a whole generation. The season is short, about 8 weeks, after which cutting must stop to let plants rebuild their strength for subsequent years, but the harvest is an annual highlight. The young shoots or 'spears', cut when about 15–20cm (6–8in) tall, are generally green or purple; the white continental version is simply earthed up to 30cm (12in) deep to exclude light. Feed annually in early spring and later summer. All-male hybrids like '**Grolim**' and '**Jersey Knight**' produce the fattest spears and no competing seedlings; traditional kinds ('**Connover's Colossal**', '**Martha Washingto**n') are more variable. Wild asparagus ('**Amarus**') has slender, intensely flavoured spears, or 'sprue', for soup and eating cold.

> **KEY TIMES**
>
> **SOW IN SITU/PLANT** late spring **HARVEST** early spring to midsummer

### CARDOONS

A close relative of the globe artichoke (*see page 208*) and looking very similar, the cardoon has silvery-grey, deeply cut leaves that could earn it a place in the wild or flower garden. The whole plant is blanched by wrapping brown paper or straw round the gathered foliage in late summer to early autumn; tie in place with raffia and then mound up soil all round. After 6–8 weeks, the whole plant can be harvested like a head of celery: the leaf ribs are the part

**The soft tips of asparagus peeping through in spring.**

**Self-blanching celery 'Victoria'**

eaten, peeled and then boiled or fried, or served raw with a traditional anchovy, garlic and oil sauce.

Plants are tender perennials and may be left with winter protection to produce small, spiky 'artichokes'. Harvesting plants for their stems is final, of course, so fresh crops are usually raised annually from seed. '**Gigante di Romagna**' is a superior variety.

**KEY TIMES**

SOW IN SITU late spring HARVEST mid-autumn to early winter

## CELERY

A strongly flavoured vegetable, crunchy and stimulating eaten raw in salads, and an indispensable flavouring in soups, stews and casseroles. There are two main kinds: trench celery, which is earthed up as it grows to blanch and tenderize the stems, and self-blanching, which is naturally pale but benefits from some protection from light – try packing plants 20–23cm (8–9in) apart each way within an empty solid-sided cold frame. For greater pungency, choose a green-stemmed variety like '**Utah**' or the leaves of nearly wild leaf celery (smallage) or Chinese celery for cooking.

**KEY TIMES**

SOW INDOORS late winter to early spring TRANSPLANT early summer HARVEST early autumn until the frosts, although hardier trench celery tastes best after frost

## FLORENCE FENNEL

This stem vegetable, a cousin of the herb fennel but quite different, forms fat, crisp white 'bulbs' the size of large apples, which are eaten raw, braised or baked. Harvest bulbs just before they are needed, and use the aniseed-flavoured leaves any time for fish dishes. Top fennel varieties include '**Romanesco**' (sweet and pleasant), '**Amigo**', '**Zeva Fino**', and bolt-resistant '**Colossal**' for early sowing; older varieties tend to bolt into flower if sown before midsummer and produce sweeter bulbs when earthed up to exclude light.

**KEY TIMES**

SOW IN SITU early spring to late summer HARVEST 70–80 days later

**Wrap a collar around the fennel bulb to blanch it.**

## GLOBE ARTICHOKES

These perennials resemble small cardoons (*see page 206*), with greener leaves but larger flower heads. Grow them in full sun with protection from hard frost, especially younger plants and choice varieties. They can be grown from seeds sown outdoors in mid-spring or from *offsets* taken from the best plants in late winter and early spring. Green varieties such as '**Green Globe**' have larger heads, purple kinds ('**Globe Romanesco**', '**Violetta di Chioggia**') are smaller but superior in quality when grown on hot dry sites. (Despite their apparent family tie, the three artichokes featured here are quite unrelated and used in different ways.)

### KEY TIMES

**SOW IN SITU/PLANT** early to late spring **HARVEST** early summer

**Jerusalem artichokes**

## JERUSALEM ARTICHOKES

These sunflower relatives are grown for their large, sweetish and delicately flavoured tubers that are cooked and used like potatoes. See page 42 for growing information and recommended varieties.

### KEY TIMES

**PLANT** late winter to early spring **HARVEST** mid-autumn to early spring

**Globe artichoke 'Purple Globe'**

Pull rhubarb stems firmly from the base when harvesting.

## RHUBARB

A traditional and robust allotment staple, dependable even when left to its own devices and usually grown to supply the earliest fresh fruit, with later pickings when nothing else is available. Its dramatic ornamental appearance is often overlooked, as are its varied culinary possibilities, both when forced to produce brilliant tender sticks of delicate flavour and even more so when mature. All available kinds of rhubarb are good for growing from crowns (*see page 132* for planting and renewing rhubarb).

Rhubarb is traditionally forced from late autumn (*see page 133*), but carries on cropping until midsummer, when rest is beneficial. Bright red kinds for forcing include '**Reed's Early Superb**', '**Stockbridge Arrow**', '**Stockbridge Harbinger**' and '**Timperley Early**'.

> **KEY TIMES**
> **PLANT** late autumn or late winter **HARVEST** early spring to midsummer

> **CHINESE ARTICHOKES** are a gourmet vegetable, popular in France and China. The hardy, greyish ornamental plants, which grow to about 45cm (18in) tall, produce trailing underground stems tipped with small tapering tubers. Plant tubers in a large pot of compost and grow outdoors in full sun until stems die down in autumn. Then, empty out the pot and gather all the nutty tubers for eating hot or cold after blanching. Use soon after harvest, as they dry out quickly, but replant a few immediately in fresh compost.

Forest gardening enthusiasts grow a range of perennials together to create a stable and self-sustaining community of edible plants that supply a steady if not spectacular harvest. These are a few crops you could include.

**ANGELICA** is a multi-purpose biennial but it can survive for several years if flowering is prevented (simply cut back flower stems by half when buds appear). Although best-known for its vivid green candied leaf-stalks, its leaves are used in fish dishes, the young stems add sweet liquorice hints to acid fruit, the roots are used in gin distillation and the seeds in vermouth and chartreuse. Plants are usually raised from seeds sown outdoors in autumn for frost to stimulate germination. Wild angelica, a UK native, is slighter and less aromatic, but otherwise similar in appearance and use. Always grow your own wild angelica from seed rather than harvest it from the wild, as there are a number of poisonous look-alikes.

**DAY LILIES** are widely grown in the Far East, where the flowers and buds are dried for thickening soups and very young shoots boiled as a vegetable. Tubers of some varieties are eaten or used medicinally. A hardy, prolific and colourful asset once established.

**GOOD KING HENRY**, also known as mercury or poor man's asparagus, is an East Anglian native with edible leaves and shoots (*see page 56*).

**LOVAGE** is a vigorous, celery-flavoured perennial, with edible leaves, stems (if blanched), seeds and roots. Bees and hoverflies find the flowers irresistible. Sow or plant in moist rich soil.

**PERENNIAL BROCCOLI** is a bulky plant, 1.2m (4ft) tall and wide, bearing a single small central 'cauliflower' in spring, followed by up to a dozen more on sideshoots. Renew from seed or cuttings after 3-4 years and feed well. Watch out for brassica pests and diseases carrying over from one year to the next.

**ROCK SAMPHIRE** has salty, fleshy cylindrical leaves, which are traditionally pickled as a savoury salad ingredient or cooked as a fashionable accompaniment to fish. Grow in sandy or stony soil from seed or bought plants.

**TURKISH ROCKET** is tall, early and indestructible. Pick young leaves to eat in salads while they are mild-flavoured; eat older ones raw for their spicy heat or cooked like spinach. Easy to grow from seed.

## SUMMER-FRUITING CROPS

A few important cold-sensitive vegetables feature in almost everyone's cropping plans. In a good year – hot and sunny outdoors, mild and bright under glass – they can give rewarding, even overwhelming yields.

### AUBERGINES

Also known as eggplants, aubergines bear incredibly beautiful fruits – purple, rose or white, round or long and slim – which can have a slightly acrid flavour (sweat in salt before cooking to remove bitterness) and are key ingredients of ratatouille, moussaka, caponata and numerous Middle Eastern dishes. Harvest when plump and shiny; long varieties ('**Little Finger**', '**Long Purple**') are drier and best for frying.

**Sweet peppers are ready when shiny and fully coloured.**

### PEPPERS

Peppers as a pungent spice are the tiny fruits (peppercorns) of a climbing vine (*Piper nigrum*), which are dried or shelled and then ground to a powder. To most allotment gardeners, however, peppers are bushy plants of the *Capsicum* genus that produce large, mild hollow fruits (sweet or bell peppers) or smaller round, tapering or elongated berries with varying heat and pungency (chillis and hot peppers).

Fruits come in a range of colours (from green to festive red) and shapes: blocky, elongated or top-, banana- or cherry-shaped. Most green fruits turn yellow or red if left to mature, although picking while green and mild prolongs cropping. There are hundreds of varieties of sweet bell peppers ('**Golden Bell**', '**Jumbo**' and long, curved '**Corno di Toro Rosso**'), pungently fruity paprikas like '**Hungarian Yellow Wax**', chillis ('**Red Peter**'), peperoncinis ('**Robustini**'), jalapenos ('**Mucho Nacho**'), serranos ('**Serrano del Sol**'), habaneros ('**Caribbean Red**') and bird chillies ('**Tabasco**') in ascending intensity.

Peppers take a little longer than tomatoes to ripen, and all but the earliest varieties to mature should be grown under glass.

**KEY TIMES**

**SOW INDOORS** late spring **TRANSPLANT** early summer **HARVEST** late summer to early autumn

### SWEETCORN

This type of maize contains a high proportion of sugar instead of starch, and is harvested while immature, its grains still moist and milky rather than ripe and dry. Varieties of this warm-climate crop can take up to 140 days to mature, although early 80-day kinds have been bred for cool climates. Most modern varieties are F1 hybrids with concentrated sugar levels ('supersweet', 'sugar-enhanced' and 'tender-sweet' varieties) that must be grown well away, preferably up-wind from ordinary kinds to avoid diluting flavour by cross-pollination. Eat or freeze very soon after harvest – at best, cobs maintain their quality for only 2–3 days in plastic bags in the fridge.

For good results, always start early under glass by sowing in pots (plants resent root disturbance) and planting out after the last frosts; wait for temperatures above 10°C (50°F), below which plants refuse to grow.

The following are just some of the many tomato relatives, and all require similar growing conditions. They are members of the Solanaceae family, which also includes potatoes and deadly nightshade!

**CAPE GOOSEBERRIES** The golden yellow berries, individually wrapped in a lantern-shaped husk on a bushy plant resembling a nightshade, have a stimulating acid flavour. The berries are used fresh or dried, and can be made into jams and jellies or coated with fondant icing as petits fours.

**GROUND CHERRIES** Similar to Cape gooseberries, but a little sweeter, and used in the same ways or for making a purée for tarts.

**TOMATILLO** Perennial in warm climates, these fruits are very similar in appearance to the tomato. They have a sharp apple flavour, and are a popular ingredient of Mexican sauces, stews and salsa.

'**Kelvedon Glory**' is a long-established extra-early variety for first pickings, '**Swift**' has awards for flavour and tenderness, '**Landmark**' is exceptionally cold-tolerant, and '**Extra Early Sweet**' is compact and wind-resistant. '**Minipop**' is a sugar-enhanced baby corn variety; '**Red Strawberry**' has compact cobs used whole for microwave popcorn.

> **KEY TIMES**
>
> SOW INDOORS early spring to late spring TRANSPLANT late spring to early summer SOW IN SITU early summer HARVEST late summer to late autumn

## TOMATOES

Many generations elapsed after the tomato's European debut in the 16th century before its status changed from poisonous to popular. Now there are dozens of new F1 hybrids every year, while enthusiasts treasure heritage collections of thousands more.

Their diversity is startling: colours include white, lime green, lemon yellow, gold, orange, peach and purple, some striped, as well as the standard rich red. Shapes and sizes range from ancestral currants and grapes, through cherries, to fleshy plums (best for bottling, cooking, drying and purée) and massive ugly 'beefsteak' types weighing up to 450g (1lb) each.

From a practical point of view, the most important difference between varieties is growth habit, which affects the way plants are trained. Most are tall and trained as cordons, while bush varieties are sprawling with bushy side branches and no prominent main shoot. Most varieties are equally happy under glass or in the open air. In wet areas, choose disease-resistant kinds such as '**Alicante**' against mildew or '**Ferline**' where blight is common.

Flavour is controversial and subjective, dependent as much on the growing regime (plenty of sun, controlled watering almost to the point of stress, and not too much nitrogen) as choice of variety. Each kind has its individual acid/sugar composition that results in its typical flavour, although sweetness is often thought paramount in modern varieties such as '**Sungold**'. Connoisseurs consider 'potato-leaved' kinds ('**Matina**' and most '**Brandywine**' variants) to have the most intense tomato flavour.

> **KEY TIMES**
>
> **OUTDOOR** SOW INDOORS early to late spring TRANSPLANT late spring to early summer HARVEST late summer to late autumn
>
> **INDOOR** SOW late winter to early spring TRANSPLANT early to late spring HARVEST early summer to late autumn

# HERBS

The range of herbs that might be grown is huge, especially if you define a herb in its broadest sense as any plant useful to humanity. Often whole plots have been devoted to specialist collections: dye plants such as woad, madder, bloodroot and heather, for example, herbs for healing (lavender, rosemary, agrimony and orris root) or for flavouring home-made wines and liqueurs (elecampane, hyssop, juniper, pinks, lovage, clary sage and angelica).

On most plots, the emphasis will be culinary, whether focused on salad herbs such as chives, nasturtiums, fennel and lemon balm, or the more savoury kinds for seasoning: horseradish, dill, fenugreek, sage, thyme, coriander and garlic. A personal selection of favourites can be gathered in a special bed or corner, or dispersed as individual perennial plants with odd rows of annuals tucked among the vegetables.

## CULINARY CLASSICS

A select group of herbs is regarded as indispensable by almost every cook. Herbs make easy and dependable outdoor plants in most allotment soils.

**BASIL** (*see box, opposite*)

**BAY** Just one kind is normally grown, the evergreen tree *Laurus nobilis* with firm waxy leaves to dry or use fresh all year for stocks, soups and bouquet garni.

**CHIVES** (*see page 194*)

**CORIANDER** The pungent plain species (often listed as '**Cilantro**') is best for leaf production, while '**Morocco**' has heavy crops of orange-scented seeds. Sow several times because this tender annual has a short season.

**DILL** Sow repeatedly for its fragrant leaves and sharply aromatic seeds that spice up lamb, fish and rice dishes; grow apart from fennel because cross-pollination confuses the flavours.

## HERB FAMILIES

Many popular herbs are closely related, which can be helpful when you are deciding where to grow them because they often share the same preferences.

**UMBELLIFERS** The seed-bearing members of the carrot family like moist but well-drained soils and full sun. They are all strongly aromatic herbs, and include caraway, coriander, cumin, dill and fennel. Leafy umbellifers like parsley, chervil, lovage and angelica, on the other hand, prefer heavier soils, steady moisture and even a little summer shade for best crops.

**MINT FAMILY** The labiates (*Lamiaceae*) are Mediterranean plants rich in warm flavours and aromatic oils, all with a taste for sun and dry light soils. Peppermint, spearmint, oregano, marjoram, thyme, basil, savory, lemon balm, lavender and rosemary belong in this group.

**COMPOSITES** The daisy or sunflower family (*Asteraceae*) includes tansy, chamomile, costmary, calendula, curry plant, plus all the artemisias, such as tarragon and southernwood. Their concentrated and volatile aromatic oils need hot sun and calm surroundings for maximum potency.

**FENNEL** Green and bronze forms of fennel are equally valuable hardy perennials for leaf and seed production, making large clumps that need plenty of space, well away from dill (*see opposite*).

**LEMON BALM** This persistent hardy perennial in all its forms – green, gold and variegated – can add delicious lemon flavour to fish and mushroom dishes, desserts, and tonic teas to relieve flatulence and melancholia.

**MINT** A family of varieties with peppermint, pineapple, lemon, orange and other flavours. Almost all forms are hardy, potentially invasive perennials, so restrain your collection in sunken or surface containers.

**OREGANO** Explore all the Mediterranean marjorams for their diverse warm flavours: sweet marjoram is best for cooking, whereas true oregano is only full-bodied in a hot summer.

**PARSLEY** Curly forms are decorative, but for intense flavour, whether in cooking or wine, most cooks prefer flat-leaved French or Italian forms; always add just before cooking finishes.

**ROSEMARY** A hardy evergreen shrub from Mediterranean hillsides, with early blue flowers that bees love, and aromatic foliage to add to lamb, bread, rice and fish recipes or burn on a stove to perfume the room.

**SAGE** Common sage is the best for culinary use, packed with flavour in a hot dry position and evergreen for picking all year.

**SAVORY** Grow both kinds, summer savory (a tender annual) and its perennial semi-evergreen winter cousin for a year-round source of peppery warmth, but use these strong herbs cautiously in the kitchen.

**TARRAGON** The superior French form enjoys a sheltered warm dry position and regular division or renewal every 3–4 years to keep its refined flavour fresh and lively.

**THYME** A host of forms for collectors and alchemists, but just one, common thyme, is sufficient for general kitchen use. Hardy, evergreen, decorative and warmly aromatic, it has everything.

# THE BASILS

Some herbs exist only as a simple species, whereas others (like thyme or parsley) offer a choice of varieties. Basil has perhaps the largest range of cultivars and species, all subtly or dramatically different in appearance and flavour. They come from hot climates and possess an aromatic warmth redolent of sunny summers. All require rich, well-drained positions sheltered from wind and exposed to maximum sunshine. Clay pots of basil outside a sunny door are traditional for easy picking and to repel flies.

**SWEET BASIL** The most popular kind of basil and parent of countless others is an Italian native and a natural companion for garlic, pasta and tomatoes.

**BUSH (POT) BASIL** This has smaller leaves than sweet basil and a noticeably sweeter flavour; Greek basil is even more petite and easy in pots, with tiny leaves to use whole.

**PURPLE (OPAL) BASIL** A rich colour that goes well with rice dishes. It has a strong perfume but a more muted flavour.

**LEMON BASIL** A paler basil than other kinds, with a pronounced citrus flavour. A temperamental variant, it needs plenty of sun and warmth.

**THAI (ANISE) BASIL** Greenish crimson leaves and purple stems, mauve flowers and a richly pungent scent like aniseed.

**CINNAMON BASIL** This Mexican variant has brownish green leaves and pink flowers. It contributes spicy flavour to Latin salad dressings and main dishes.

**p.138**   *see* Basil pesto
**p.138**   *see* Pasta, green beans, potatoes & pesto

crop focus: herbs

# FRUIT

Unless you intend turning your plot into a mini-orchard (in which case check your conditions of tenancy, as many allotment associations forbid the planting of large trees), fruit will inevitably be accessory crops to fit in and around vegetables. This is not too difficult if you choose compact varieties or train plants in restricted shapes that occupy less ground space. Almost all the popular kinds are perennial to some degree, from large-fruited strawberries, which remain for 3–4 years in the same place, to apples and plums that could easily outlive you. This means that choice, siting and planting all need some forethought. The majority are easy to tend and in most years will produce a crop, sometimes a glut, of fruit that is fresher and tastier when picked at its peak and still warm from the sun.

Whether you inherit stocks from a previous tenant or intend to introduce new plants, your shortlist is likely to concentrate on a familiar range of fruits that have earned popularity by their easy care, tolerance of our climate and value as food crops.

When choosing fruit, make sure that the varieties suit your soil, local climate and exposure. Match vigour, size and shape of variety and rootstock to the available space, and if room is precious, choose fruits that are versatile, reliable and rarely sold in shops. Buy only named varieties and rootstocks, certified disease-free, from reputable suppliers, and also check pollination requirements, as some varieties need two different partners. Selecting a mix of early, mid-season and late varieties will mean that supply is spread through the year.

## APPLES

These are the easiest of fruits to grow almost anywhere, except in very wet or hot districts, where pests or diseases are troublesome. There are four main kinds – dessert, culinary, ornamental crab (good pollinators) and cider varieties (prolific but specialist) – and a range of rootstocks to limit height and spread from 1.8–6m (6–20ft). Hundreds of classic flavour varieties, rare in shops but all worth growing, range from the earliest '**Irish Peach**' or '**George Cave**' to Easter-ripening '**D'Arcy Spice**' and '**Orleans Reinette**'.

Maximize productivity by selecting varieties that are equally good for dessert and culinary use, rather than needing to be eaten quickly. Early dessert apples, for example, do not keep and one tree might satisfy appetites, whereas '**Blenheim Orange**' is a dual-purpose that keeps for 3 months, and even '**Bramley's Seedling**' ripens to dessert quality after long storage. Cooking varieties are often expensive in shops or unobtainable, and offer more options for use. Other multi-purpose fruits to consider include '**Annie Elizabeth**' and '**Lane's Prince Albert**'.

> **KEY TIMES**
>
> **PLANT** autumn or spring (container-grown any time)
> **HARVEST** late summer to late autumn

## BLACKCURRANTS

Rarely sold as fresh fruit (over 90 per cent of commercial crops go for juicing). A greedy crop, fruiting heavily if annually well dressed with manure and pruned to remove one-third of the oldest stems. Difficult to train, so modern space-saving bushes like '**Ben Sarek**' have replaced older sprawling kinds like '**Laxton's Giant**'.

> **KEY TIMES**
>
> **PLANT** autumn or spring (container-grown spring to autumn **HARVEST** midsummer to early autumn

## BLUEBERRIES

Happiest on acid soils, blueberries fruit prolifically. Grow a tall variety like '**Earliblue**' and underplant with dwarf fruits like lowbush blueberries, lingonberries or cranberries. In the autumn, blueberry bushes ignite the autumn plot with their fiery red leaf tints.

> **KEY TIMES**
>
> **PLANT** autumn or spring (container-grown any time)
> **HARVEST** harvest midsummer to early autumn

## CHERRIES

For firmness and rich flavour, grow your own red '**Stella**', yellow '**Merton Glory**' or black '**Early Rivers**', but make sure a pollen partner grows nearby ('**Stella**', '**Sunburst**', and acid '**Morello**' and '**Nabella**' are self-fertile). Defend dessert kinds from birds – choosing a dwarfing rootstock and pruning to a compact shape makes for easy netting.

> **KEY TIMES**
>
> **PLANT** autumn or spring (container-grown any time)
> **HARVEST** mid- to late summer

## GOOSEBERRIES

The most dependable of all bush fruits, often prolific and supplying two crops: the early thinnings for cooking and mature berries for dessert. Old bushes could be classic varieties such as '**Broom Girl**', '**Early Sulphur**' or '**Langley Gage**'. Prune bushes to an open structure to reduce mildew or train them as cordons, fans and standards.

**KEY TIMES**

**PLANT** autumn or spring (container-grown spring any time)
**HARVEST** early summer (thinnings); late summer (dessert)

## GRAPES

Often the first choice for growing in a greenhouse, although many kinds ('**Siegerrebe**', '**Précoce de Malingre**', '**Chasselas d'Or**') succeed outdoors, especially wine-making varieties. The finest indoor grapes need extra heat at ripening time, but '**Buckland Sweetwater**' and '**Foster's Seedling**' perform well in a cool greenhouse. Careful pruning/training controls size, enhances yields and ensures efficient greenhouse shading as a bonus.

**KEY TIMES**

**PLANT** autumn or spring (container-grown any time)
**HARVEST OUTDOOR** late summer to mid-autumn,
**HARVEST UNDER GLASS** early autumn to
early winter

## PEARS

Harder than apples to grow well, except where seasons are long and hot; avoid areas of high rainfall, cool summers and late frosts (pears bloom 2–4 weeks earlier than apples). For best results, train as fans or espaliers on a warm wall, fence or shed. Cross-pollination is essential with a specific partner (some are incompatible), although '**Conference**' and '**Seckle**' are partially self-fertile. Varieties that are equally good for dessert and culinary use are '**Conference**' and '**Williams' Bon Chrétien**' ('**Bartlett**').

**KEY TIMES**

**PLANT** autumn or spring (container-grown any time)
**HARVEST** late summer to mid-autumn

**Grapes 'Black Hamburgh'**

**Tolerant and prolific 'Conference' is the allotment favourite.**

# OTHER FRUIT WORTH TRYING

*the living larder*

Many other kinds of fruit have proved successful on allotments and could merit trial if you can supply space and the required growing conditions.

**ALPINE STRAWBERRIES** Non-running, everbearing, untouched by birds and packed with concentrated flavour, these are the perfect edging plants, easily renewed by division or seed. All varieties, including yellow kinds, are good.

**APRICOTS** Treat like peaches, and grow a vitamin-rich variety like '**Moorpark**' or genetic dwarf '**Aprigold**'. With their firm flesh and rich succulence, they are good cooked, in tarts and dumplings, or dried.

**FIGS** A handsome leafy tree to train on a wall or over a shed, but protect from hard frost. '**Brown Turkey**' is hardy, '**White Marseilles**' the tastiest. Expect one annual crop outdoors or two under glass.

**GARDEN HUCKLEBERRIES** An annual tomato relative with loose clusters of purple-black berries for pies, jellies and jams. Prolific in a warm summer.

**HAZELNUTS** Even a young bush will yield nuts in a squirrel-free area, while its annual pruning supplies plenty of strong twiggy stems for supporting dwarf peas. Ideal for a wildflower corner or hedge.

**LOQUATS** A heat-loving evergreen tree, producing yellow or orange fruits in early summer (*see picture, top right*). Slightly insipid raw, it is best in jellies, jams and sauces with some of the almond-flavoured seeds.

**OLIVES** A sun-loving and slow-growing evergreen for warm sheltered sites where frost is rarely serious, so a good candidate for urban plots and climate change. Keep in a container while young to protect in winter. Labour-intensive and often biennial.

**PEACHES** Plant in warmth and shelter outdoors or train as a fan under glass. Plants are self-fertile, so try one to start, like the natural dwarf '**Bonanza**'. Grow nectarines such as dwarf '**Nectarella**' in the same way.

**POMEGRANATES** This large shrub, deciduous in our climate, is best grown in a warm spot sheltered from frost and cold wind to ripen the fruits. There are a number of cultivars, with beautiful white or red flowers.

**QUINCES** An easy, ornamental tree for growing on moist, warm soils. The fragrant fruits (*see picture, right*) ripen in store for cooking in pies and jams. Look for '**Vranja**' or '**Portugal**'.

**p.141** *see* Moroccan tagine of chicken & quinces

Damsons are often found growing wild on allotments.

## PLUMS

Very common on allotments – often as a single specimen of '**Victoria**', the most popular variety – especially on heavy moist soils with shelter from cold winds at flowering time. Thinning is important to ensure good size and to prevent breakage of heavily laden branches. Difficult to restrict in size, although festooning provides effective growth control. Varieties that are equally good for dessert and culinary use are '**Victoria**', '**Cambridge Gage**' and '**Yellow Pershore**'. Gages are superior quality varieties for warm sites and wall-training, while damsons are hardiest on cold or windy sites, where they act as windbreaks.

> **KEY TIMES**
>
> **PLANT** autumn or spring (container-grown any time)
> **HARVEST** midsummer to early autumn

## RASPBERRIES

A popular summer fruit, although autumn-bearing kinds like '**Autumn Bliss**' and '**Heritage**' extend picking until the frosts; yellow ('**Golden Everest**', '**Fallgold**'), purple ('**Glencoe**') and black ('**Starlight**') varieties vary the flavours. The flexible canes need strong supports to keep them tidy, and suckers can stray into nearby crops unless ruthlessly chopped out.

> **KEY TIMES**
>
> **PLANT** autumn or spring **HARVEST** mid- to late summer (summer kinds), late summer to mid-autumn (autumn kinds)

Whitecurrant 'White Grape', unmatched for flavour.

## REDCURRANTS & WHITECURRANTS

Redcurrants are a tasty and visually exciting fruit that crop well in sun or shade, and hang for a long time without loss. Birds love them. Try classic '**Fay's Prolific**' or modern '**Rovada**'. Whitecurrants are similar but taste pleasantly different.

> **KEY TIMES**
>
> **PLANT** autumn or spring (container-grown any time)
> **HARVEST** mid- to late summer

## STRAWBERRIES

The other top summer soft fruit, especially older flavour varieties such as '**Royal Sovereign**' or '**Cambridge Late Pine**' that are too soft and juicy for commercial handling. Spread the season by growing early and late maincrop varieties, plus a perpetual (everbearing) kind such as '**Aromel**' to extend pickings up to the frosts. Plants are easy to force for extra-early harvest.

> **KEY TIMES**
>
> **PLANT** late summer to early spring **HARVEST** (summer) late spring to late summer, (perpetual) early summer to mid-autumn, (alpine) midsummer to late autumn

# glossary

**annual** any plant completing its normal life cycle within a maximum period of 12 months, after which it dies (*see also biennial, perennial*)

**biennial** a plant that lives for two seasons, flowering and seeding in its second year after a winter rest (*see also annual, perennial*)

**big bud (disease)** unusually fat winter buds on blackcurrants, home to a mite that spreads a virus called reversion

**biodynamic gardening** an eco-friendly organic approach that emphasizes soil vitality and lunar influences

**blanching** making plants (such as chicory) pale, tender and less bitter; self-blanching varieties do this even in light

**broadcast sowing** scattering seeds all over the surface rather than in rows

**canker** various diseases causing decay on crops such as fruit trees, tomatoes and parsnips

**catch crop** a rapidly grown vegetable fitted between the finish of one main crop and the start of the next

**chitting potatoes** stimulating potato tubers to produce shoots before planting

**cloche** a handlight or continuous glass or plastic crop-cover for warming and protecting plants

**companion planting** growing two or more types of plant close together for mutual benefit

**copper sulphate** a fungicide, one of few acceptable to organic gardeners

**cordon** a plant such as tomatoes, sweet peas and many fruits trained with one, two or three stems

**dibble in** to plant by pushing rather than scooping a hole in the soil when sowing, pricking out or transplanting

**double-digging** an onerous but often effective way to cultivate soil to the depth of two spades (*see also spit*)

**dwarfing rootstock** the bottom part of a grafted (joined) fruit tree that limits its size and growth rate

**espalier** a trained fruit form with a single upright mainstem and one or more pairs of horizontal branches

**F1 hybrid** a variety formed by crossing two different parent plants to combine their unique qualities in a single strain

**fan** a trained fruit form, with several branches all radiating like spokes from a short trunk or 'leg'

**forcing** hurrying plants to grow or start growth faster by artificial means

**forest gardening** an increasingly popular growing style that groups edible plants together according to different heights and needs, like the layers of natural woodland

**graft** the artificial union of two different plants or plant parts to grow as one

**green manure** a special crop of plants grown for digging in to decay and improve the soil

**hydroponic** growing plants in water and a dilute solution of nutrients without soil

**John Innes compost** a soil-based mix made to standard formulae in various grades such as JI No. 1, No. 2 and No. 3

**leafmould** the partially rotted material from stored tree leaves, with some nutrients and immense value as a soil conditioner and peat substitute

**monoculture** growing one crop or variety exclusively over a large area

**mulch** a layer of natural or inorganic material spread to protect the soil surface; a sheet mulch is used to clear and reclaim weedy ground

**nematode** tiny worm-like parasites found in the soil; some can spoil crops like potatoes, others can control pests

**no-dig methods** various cultivation techniques that reduce or eliminate routine digging

**offset** a young plant that develops naturally alongside its parent

**organic gardening** a system that aims to grow plants using nothing that does not occur naturally

**perennial** a plant that lives for at least three seasons and usually much longer, but not forever (*see also annual, biennial*)

**permaculture** a design approach that adapts no-dig and organic methods to match site, locality, natural resources and ambitions in a sustainable way

**pH** the scale used to measure levels of acidity or alkalinity (an abbreviation of percentage Hydrogen)

**pioneer crop** a first sowing or planting intended to break in or reclaim ground rather than produce a heavy yield

**propagate** to increase or multiply plants by an appropriate method such as taking cuttings or sowing seeds

**rotavate** to cultivate with a powered rotary machine

**soil pH meter** an electronic device with a probe inserted in the soil to measure its acidity or alkalinity (*see also pH*)

**soil testing kit** a complete set of materials for measuring acidity by adding soil to a chemical solution

**spit** a spade's depth

**successional sowing** a sequence of repeated sowings made at intervals to prolong continuous harvest

**thinning** reducing overcrowding, usually of seedlings or fruits, to ensure those remaining develop properly

**tilth** a finely broken, crumbly soil texture produced by good cultivation and usually suitable for sowing seeds

**top-dressing** an application of materials such as manure, lime or fertilizer spread on the soil surface

**topgrowth** the portion of a plant above ground, as distinct from its root mass

**topsoil** the upper layer of soil, more fertile and usually darker than the subsoil below and the level at which most feeding roots grow

**truss** a compact cluster of flowers or fruits, such as those of tomatoes

# resources

**SEED SUPPLIERS**

**Abundant Life Seed Foundation**
www.abundantlifeseeds.com
US organic source of heritage and
gourmet varieties

**Anioleka Vegetable Seeds**
www.vegetableseed.net

**J W Boyce**
Tel: 01638 721158
Long-established growers' list, with
seeds in a range of quantities

**D T Brown and Co**
Tel: 0845 166 2275
www.dtbrownseeds.co.uk
Another plot-holders' favourite, blending
new and heritage varieties

**Chiltern Seeds**
Tel: 01229 581137
www.chilternseeds.co.uk
Botanical paradise, offering thousands of
species including unexpected edibles

**Dobies Seeds**
Tel: 0870 112 3625
www.dobies.co.uk/default.aspx
Mainstream seed supplier

**Mr Fothergill's Seeds Ltd**
Tel: 01638 751161
www.fothergills.co.uk
Nicely balanced list, plus large tempting
potato, tomato and squash selections

**Garden Organic (Henry Doubleday
Research Association)**
www.gardenorganic.org.uk
Heritage seedbank for members;
*see also Organizations*

**S E Marshalls & Co**
Tel: 01480 443390
www.marshalls-seeds.co.uk
Classic fruit and vegetable catalogue,
with special rates for allotment societies.
Also do fruit bushes and plug plants

**The Organic Gardening Catalogue**
Tel: 0845 130 1304
www.organiccatalog.com
Comprehensive organic list, plus green
manures and approved pest treatments

**The Real Seed Collection Ltd**
www.realseeds.co.uk
An exciting not-for-profit company with
a range of choice and heirloom varieties

**Robinsons Seeds**
www.mammothonion.co.uk
Heirloom and exhibition (but still edible)
varieties

**Roguelands Seeds (USA)**
www.seedfest.co.uk
Old, rare and unusual varieties

**Seeds-by-Size**
Tel: 01442 251458
www.seeds-by-size.co.uk
Over 12,000 vegetable, herb, flower and
grass cultivars

**Seeds of Italy**
Tel: 020 8427 5020
www.seedsofitaly.co.uk
Mouth-watering Mediterranean and Slow
Food ingredients

**Simpson's Seeds**
Tel: 01985 845004
www.simpsonsseeds.co.uk
Specialized seeds and vegetable plug
plants, especially tomatoes and peppers

**Suffolk Herbs**
Tel: 01376 572456
www.suffolkherbs.com
The widest range of vegetable, herb and
wildflower seeds in a single list

**Suttons Seeds**
Tel: 0800 783 8074
www.suttons.co.uk
Mainstream seed supplier

**Tamar Organics**
Tel: 01822 834 887
www.tamarorganics.co.uk
Seed and garden supplies

**Terre de Semences**
www.terredesemences.com
Supplier of organic seeds

**Thompson & Morgan Ltd**
Tel: 01473 688821
www.thompson-morgan.com
Many new, unusual or exclusive varieties
of seeds and plug plants

**Unwins Seeds**
Tel: 01945 588522
www.unwins-seeds.co.uk
Mainstream seed supplier

**Vida Verde Seed Collection**
Tel: 01239 821107
www.vidaverde.co.uk
Heirloom and rare vegetable seeds

**PLANT SUPPLIERS**

**The Fruit & Vegetable Company**
Tel: 0870 9505911
Tree and soft fruit, potatoes, onions,
seeds and plants

**Horti-Halcyon**
Tel: 01483 232095
www.hortihalcyon-organic.co.uk
Organic vegtable grower and supplier of
vegatable boxes

**Jekka's Herb Farm**
Tel: 01454 418878
www.jekkasherbfarm.com
Range of organic herb plants and seeds

**Keepers Nursery**
Tel: 01622 726465
www.fruittree.co.uk
Far-ranging tree fruit list; will propagate
other varieties to order

**Ken Muir Ltd**
Tel: 01255 830181
www.kenmuir.co.uk
Reliable source of soft fruit (plus some
others) and sound cultural information

**National Fruit Collection**
Tel: 01795 535286
www.brogdale.org
Thousands of fruit varieties, some
centuries old, and a graft-to-order service

**Reads Nursery**
Tel: 01508 548395
www.readsnursery.co.uk
Large, discriminating collection of grape,
peach, citrus varieties, amongst others

**Rocket Gardens**
Tel: 01209 831468
www.rocketgardens.co.uk
UK's only organic supplier of vegetable
and herb plants, plus instant gardens

## ORGANIZATIONS

**Agroforestry Research Trust**
46 Hunters Moon, Dartington,
Totnes, Devon TQ9 6JT
Tel: 01803 840776
www.agroforestry.co.uk
Masses of information on edible and
useful trees, plus forest gardening

**Allotments Regeneration Initiative**
The Greenhouse, Hereford Street,
Bedminster, Bristol BS3 4NA
Tel: 0117 923 1800
www.farmgarden.org.uk
Lively campaign partnership, with a range
of events and essential newsletters

**Federation of City Farms and
Community Gardens**
The Greenhouse, Hereford Street,
Bedminster, Bristol BS3 4NA
Tel: 0117 923 1800
www.farmgarden.org.uk
Provides information and advice on
a wide range of community projects
throughout the UK

**Garden Organic (Henry Doubleday
Research Association)**
Ryton Organic Gardens, Coventry,
Warwickshire CV8 3LG
Tel: 024 7630 3517
www.gardenorganic.org.uk
The chief UK society for organic gardeners;
*see also Seed suppliers*

**National Society of Allotment &
Leisure Gardeners**
O'Dell House, Hunters Road, Corby,
Northants NN17 5JE
Tel: 01536 266576
www.nsalg.org.uk
Umbrella organization; good source of
info about finding and starting a plot

**National Vegetable Society**
5 Whitelow Road, Heaton Moor,
Stockport SK4 4BY
www.nvsuk.org.uk
Advice and information on growing
and showing produce

**Royal Horticultural Society**
80 Vincent Square, London SW1P 2PE
Tel: 0845 260 5000
www.rhs.org.uk
Huge databases to explore online, superb
journal and numerous useful events

**Soil Association**
South Plaza, Marlborough Street,
Bristol BS1 3NX
Tel: 0117 314 5000
www.soilassociation.org.uk
Organization at the heart of the campaign
for organic food and farming

**Thrive**
The Geoffrey Udall Centre, Beech Hill,
Reading, Berks RG7 2AT
Tel: 0118 988 5688
www.thrive.org.uk
Unrivalled advice, support and tuition for
disabled and disadvantaged gardeners

## REFERENCE LIBRARY

**The Allotment**
DVD set produced by Wild Fire
Productions, based on TV series,
from Permanent Publications
Tel: 01730 823311
Email: info@permaculture.co.uk

**The Allotment Book**
Andi Clevely; Collins 2006

**The Allotment Handbook: A Guide to
Protecting and Promoting your Site**
Sophie Andrews; Eco-Logic Books, 2001

**The Allotment: Its Landscape and
Culture**
David Crouch & Colin Ward; Five Leaves,
2003

**Collins Kitchen Garden**
Andi Clevely; Collins, 1999

**Collins Practical Gardener:
Kitchen Garden**
Lucy Peel; Collins, 2003

**The Complete Book of Vegetables,
Herbs and Fruit**
Matthew Biggs, Jekka McVicar and Bob
Flowerdew; Kyle Cathie, 2004

**Digging for Victory**
C H Middleton; George, Allen & Unwin,
1942

**Early Garden Crops (Wisley Handbook
30)**
F W Shepherd; RHS, 1981

**Growing Fruit**
Harry Baker; RHS/Mitchell Beazley, 1999

**Grow Vegetables**
Alan Buckingham; Dorling Kindersley 2007

**The Integrated Garden**
Andi Clevely; Barrie & Jenkins, 1988 (in
the USA entitled *The Total Garden*; Sterling,
1989)

**Jekka McVicar New Book of Herbs**
Dorling Kindersley, 2004

**Jekka's Complete Herb Book**
Jekka McVicar; Kyle Cathie, 1997

**The Kitchen Garden**
Andi Clevely; RHS/Conran Octopus, 1995

**The Kitchen Garden Month-by-Month**
Andi Clevely; David & Charles, 1996

**Plants for a Future**
Ken Fern; Permanent Publications, 1997

**RHS Simple Steps: Vegetables in a
Small Garden**
Jo Whittingham; Dorling Kindersley, 2007

**Seeds: The Ultimate Guide to
Growing Successfully from Seed**
Jekka McVicar; Kyle Cathie, 2001

**Seed to Seed: Seed-saving Techniques
for the Vegetable Gardener**
Suzanne Ashworth; Seed Saver
Publications/Chelsea Green, 1991

**The Vegetable Garden Displayed**
Joy Larkcom; RHS, 1992

**The Vegetable Grower's Handbook**
Arthur J Simons; Penguin, 1948

## WEBSITES TO EXPLORE

**www.allotments-uk.com**
UK's largest online allotment community
(including seed and plant links)

**www.allotments4all.co.uk**
Lively information site and active forum

**www.allotment.org.uk**
Helpful info, diary, recipes, poultry pages
and busy forum

**www.allotmentforestry.com**
Allotment forestry

**q.webring.com/hub?ring=
allotmentring**
Allotment & Vegetable Gardening Ring

**www.communitygarden.org**
American Community Garden Association

**www.bbc.co.uk/gardening**
The BBC's gardening website

**www.biodynamic.org.uk**
Biodynamic Agricultural Association

**www.cityfarmer.org**
Canadian City Farmer

**www.uk.gardenweb.com**
Gardenweb

**www.permaculture.org.uk**
Permaculture Association

**www.btinternet.com/~richard.
wiltshire/potshed1.htm**
QED virtual potting shed

# index

index

# acknowledgments

**THE AUTHOR'S** Any practical book of this scope distils experience and information from a host of sources. I want to thank all my past gardening mentors, tutors and colleagues who shared with me the subtle craft of self-reliance, often in great detail – every gardener knows best, and will usually tell you so unprompted.

Since I wrote *The Allotment Book*, the community in my tiny mid-Wales home town has taken on the vital challenge of preparing for life after oil and in a changing climate. Transition to this new and uncertain world will depend on reviving local food supplies and 'grow-your-own' skills. My respect to those involved in this far-sighted process, and thanks for all the ideas, support and endless good coffee (not an allotment crop, sadly): if only governments would set growing and supplying food at the top of national priorities.

My family, as always, are constant mates and supporters, and infinite love and thanks are due to my wife Meg and our children Tim, Ruth and Sarah, gardeners and excellent cooks one and all.

But first and last, a huge thank you and boundless admiration to Airedale Publishing, who create outstanding books from raw pix and paras like a gardener growing prize-winning plants from seed: my love and thanks to you all – you're tops!

**FOR AIREDALE PUBLISHING** A big thank you from Ruth to Andi, as ever, for his marvellous copy that is always inspirational. To the in-house team: Helen, who never misses anything editorial; Murdo, who never misses anything pictorial. To David, Mike and Sarah for their superlative photos and for going out in all weathers! To Pany, John and Geoff at Chiswick Horticultural Society for all their help. To Henry, Sarah, Jon, James and Raj for sharing their allotment experiences. To Halcyon at Horti-Halcyon for her cake recipe. To Linda for recipes and brilliant cooking for the shoots. To Meg C. for recipes. To Claire for the props. To Kate for beautiful food pictures. To Norma and Alison for recipe checking. To Ione at HarperCollins for her endless help.

We would also like to thank the following: Rowena Hall at Thompson & Morgan for seeds and plants; Paolo Arrigi at Seeds of Italy for seeds; Matthew Simpson at Simpsons Seeds for seeds; Indra Starnes at The Organic Gardening Catalogue for seeds; and Mike Kitchen at Rocket Gardens for vegetable and herb plants.

**PICTURE CREDITS** Cover flap picture of Andi by David Murphy © Airedale. All pictures in the book by David Murphy, Sarah Cuttle, Mike Newton © Airedale, except for **27** bl, **29** cl © Murdo Culver; **26** br, **43** tl © Dorling Kindersley; **44** tr, **209** t © Dorling Kindersley: Peter Anderson; **56** bc © Dorling Kindersley: Dave King; **47, 61, 75, 79, 83, 97, 105, 107, 119, 139, 143, 145, 156, 161, 173, 177** Kate Whitaker

index/acknowledgmerts